contemporary church architecture

contemporary church architecture

Reinhard Gieselmann

Thames and Hudson · London

First published in Great Britain in 1972 by
Thames and Hudson Ltd, London

Printed in West Germany

ISBN 0 500 34055 2

Contents

Inhalt

I wish to express my thanks to my wife, Maria Verena, for reading the manuscript and to Messrs. Friedrich Lehman and Gerhard Karner for redrawing the plans.

R. G.

Ich danke meiner Frau Maria Verena für Korrekturen sowie Friedrich Lehmann und Gerhard Karner für das Umzeichnen der Pläne.

R. G.

"The building of a church awakens a world full of contradictions" – this has been the experience of one of the progressive church architects represented in this book.[1] The same may well apply to writing about church architecture.

With the formulation of a "Theology after the death of God"[2], the discussion about the future of the Christian religions has now reached a climax also within theological circles. As will also be apparent from our architectural synopsis, the centre of gravity of these argumentations lies in Western Europe: it is here that Christendom became a world-wide force, and it is here that it still has its centre. At the same time, however, it is in Western Europe that the modern industrial society has been created which turns its back to the aged churches. It is obvious that the future of the churches will be decided in their struggle for recognition within this society.

Vienna, August 1970   Reinhard Gieselmann

»Das Bauen einer Kirche ist das Wachrufen einer Welt voller Widersprüche« – diese Erkenntnis stammt von einem der in diesem Buch vertretenen, progressiven Kirchenarchitekten.[1] Das gleiche mag für das Schreiben über Kirchenbau gelten.

Mit dem Entwurf einer »Theologie nach dem Tode Gottes«[2] hat die Diskussion um die Zukunft der christlichen Religionen nun auch im eigenen Kreis einen Höhepunkt erreicht. Der Schwerpunkt der Auseinandersetzung liegt, wie auch unsere bauliche Übersicht zeigt, im westeuropäischen Raum: Hier wuchs das Christentum zur weltbestimmenden Kraft, hier ist auch heute noch sein Zentrum – in Westeuropa entfaltete sich aber zugleich die moderne Industriegesellschaft, die den gealterten Kirchen den Rücken kehrt. Es ist offensichtlich, daß sich die Zukunft der Kirchen im Bemühen um diese Gesellschaft entscheiden wird.

Wien, August 1970   Reinhard Gieselmann

The church in our society

A discussion of church architecture must involve a discussion of religion. Yet the church is not only the home of a religious congregation but, more than that, a building belonging to society at large. Hence the second thesis: A discussion of religion must, especially today, also involve a discussion about society at large. The concept of religion is interpreted as a "re-association with God"; but it also signifies a re-association with society.

Our society is primarily manifest in our cities which have been described by a contemporary prophet as "inhospitable"[3]. It is in them that the dramatic play between society and technology takes place. Yet the industrially most advanced societies also have the cities with the worst environment. In our play with technology, the first round has been lost.

The seductive strength of technology is so great that its inherent laws are also imparted to our social environment: standardisation and packaging – two aspects of great importance to any technical process – are also applied to housing construction. To many people, the difference between other technical and human functions has also become blurred. For instance, the technicians of space research regard Man as representing a faulty design. It is not Man that has become the universal criterion but the applicability of technical laws. This means the omission of what is (seemingly) unnecessary, and a restriction to that which can be justified and shown to be necessary.

It is this line which the majority of (established) society has followed. It is the line of the middle-aged generation – often enough a cause for protest on the part of the younger.

We have modified our historic townscapes to suit financially speculative building activities without being able to generate a new and valid environment. We have accorded priority to motor traffic and relegated the pedestrian above or below ground.

In natural science, and especially in the applied disciplines, the opinion prevails that technology is the only factor which has generated, and will be generating, real progress. Technology is indeed a means of creating faith in progress. With the growth of technology, the need for religion has diminished. (In Austria, no more than about 20 per cent of the Roman Catholics are now reckoned to be practising, in Switzerland no more than 12 per cent of the Protestants). More than any other factor in the history of mankind, technology has widened our awareness and significantly contributed to the autonomy of Man. At the same time, it holds the promise of a better future. It is perhaps especially the latter aspect which has caused technology to be regarded by many as an aequivalent for religion.

The question is whether technology is able to promote religion, whether certain aspects or consequences of technology can be compensated by religion and, mainly, whether religion is necessary in the life of the technocratic society.

With the growing influence of technology on human society, the religions too, were forced to adapt themselves although, being concerned with continuity and eternal values, they were obviously unable to change at the same rapid rate as the technical process. If the technical process has been going on for about a hundred years and has accelerated in the past twenty-five years, an acceleration of religious changes can only be discerned during the last five years or so. Even today, certain journals exclusively concerned with church architecture are only partly facing the problem; to a large part, their basic attitude seems to ignore the existence of even a single factor disturbing the continuity of church architecture since the time of the Gothic. The numerous anthologies dealing with modern architecture are only sparsely, almost bashfully, concerned with churches – and one of the architects represented in this book even told the author that he was not going to build any more churches since the theme was no longer keeping with our time.

To theologians such as Dietrich Bonhoeffer, God is no longer a person ("A God who exists, does not exist"[4]) but is interpreted as a social happening which may be a good deed, an act of solidarity with fellow men, the experience of society.

At a time when everything must be arranged, regulated, insured, there are also other things which may indicate traces of religiosity: all that is superfluous and yet human, the doing of something that is unnecessary, the changing of conditions, meditation, faith, mourning, happiness (Ill. 1–4). And the architect would add: "God is in detail" (Mies van der Rohe). Religion is reflected in the unmeasurable, in the redundant. In this way, how-

1

ever, religion can also become complementary to technology.

In contemporary housing construction, the application of the law of packaging has created an environment which Le Bon would have included among the mass-forming factors. Identical elements are indiscriminately superimposed on the originally heterogeneous population. Here, the religions are able to provide a compensation: They satisfy a basic urge, that for community. In contrast to the mass media, the Church may be a medium capable of forming a community – a community representing a structured form of life of our society.

One practical consequence is that the Church has become a leisure-time institution in a society where, because of the technical progress, leisure-time is no longer merely a time for pleasure or entertainment but is also increasingly becoming a task and a problem. The Church would be able to provide a counter-magnet to other leisure-time institutions (sport, television).

In this way, the religious communities may be able to make new, positive contributions to modern society. Other ideas, previously regarded as essential, tend to

2

Kirche in unserer Gesellschaft

Wer über Kirchenbau redet, muß über Religion reden – die Kirche ist aber nicht nur das Haus einer religiösen Gemeinschaft, sondern darüber hinaus ein Bau der Gesellschaft. Deshalb die zweite These: Wer über Religion redet, muß gerade heute auch über die Gesellschaft reden. Der Begriff Religion wird gedeutet als »Rückverbindung zu Gott«, er bedeutet in gleichem Maß Rückverbindung zur Gesellschaft.

Unsere Gesellschaft äußert sich in erster Linie in unseren Städten, die von einem der Propheten unserer Zeit als »unwirtlich«[3] bezeichnet werden. In ihnen findet das dramatische Spiel zwischen Gesellschaft und Technik statt. Die industriell am weitesten fortgeschrittenen Gesellschaften haben aber zugleich die Städte mit dem übelsten Environment. Im Spiel mit der Technik wurde die erste Runde verloren.

Die Verführung der Technik ist so groß, daß ihre Eigengesetze auch auf die Umwelt unserer Gesellschaft projiziert werden: Standardisierung und Packbarkeit, zwei für jeden technischen Prozeß wesentliche Momente,

3

4

1, 2, 3, 4. Religious traces – Prayer, Protest, Mourning, Happiness.

1, 2, 3, 4. Religiöse Spuren – Gebet, Protest, Trauer, Glück.

werden auf den Wohnbau übertragen. Vielen verwischte sich der Unterschied auch zwischen anderen technischen und menschlichen Funktionen. Beispielsweise bezeichnen die Techniker der Weltraum-Forschung den Menschen als Fehlkonstruktion. Zum Maß aller Dinge wurde keineswegs der Mensch, sondern die Anwendbarkeit technischer Gesetze. Das bedeutet Weglassen des (scheinbar) Unnötigen, Beschränkung auf das Begründbare und Notwendige.

Auf diese Linie ist der größte Teil der (etablierten) Gesellschaft eingeschwenkt. Es ist die Linie der mittleren Generation – oft genug Anlaß zum Protest der nachfolgenden.

Wir haben unsere alten Stadtbilder zugunsten finanzspekulativen Bauens verändert, ohne daß wir ein neues, gültiges Environment zu erzeugen in der Lage waren. Wir haben dem Motorverkehr den Vorrang gegeben und den Fußgänger in die zweite Ebene verbannt.

Bei den Naturwissenschaftlern, vor allem in den angewandten Disziplinen, herrscht die Meinung vor, daß die Technik der einzige Faktor sei, der wirklich Fortschritt erzeugt hat und erzeugen wird. Technologie ist in der

Tat ein Anlaß zum Glauben an den Fortschritt. Mit dem Anwachsen der technischen Welt ist das Bedürfnis nach Religion gefallen (in Österreich praktizieren heute 20% aller Katholiken, in der Schweiz 12% aller Protestanten ihren Glauben). Technologie hat das Bewußtsein erweitert wie kein anderer Faktor in der Geschichte der Menschheit und zur Autonomie des Menschen wesentlich beigetragen. Gleichzeitig verheißt sie Hoffnung auf eine bessere Zukunft. Vielleicht ist es gerade dieses Moment, das sie für viele zum Religions-Äquivalent werden läßt.

Die Frage ist, ob Technik Religion provozieren kann, ob Aspekte oder Folgen der Technik durch Religion kompensiert werden können, und vor allem, ob Religion im Leben der technisierten Gesellschaft eine Notwendigkeit darstellt.

Mit dem Wachsen des Einflusses der Technik auf die Gesellschaft mußten auch die Religionen mutieren – der Schnelligkeit des technischen Prozesses entsprach dieser Mutationsvorgang bei den auf Beständigkeit und Ewigkeitswerten angelegten Religionen naturgemäß nicht. Wenn der technische Prozeß seit rund 100 Jahren in Gang ist und seit 25 Jahren Beschleunigung gewonnen hat, so kann man eine Akzeleration der religiösen Mutation erst seit etwa fünf Jahren feststellen. Auch heute noch greifen Zeitschriften, die ausschließlich das Thema Kirchenbau behandeln, nur teilweise die Problematik auf; zum großen Teil sind sie so konzipiert, als wenn es keinen einzigen Faktor gäbe, der die Kontinuität des Kirchenbaues seit der Gotik gestört hätte. In den zahlreichen Anthologien über moderne Architektur wird der Kirchenbau nur spärlich, beinahe verschämt, behandelt – und einer der in diesem Buch vertretenen Architekten erklärte dem Verfasser gar, er wolle keine Kirchen mehr bauen, weil das Thema nicht mehr unserer Zeit entspräche.

Gott wird von Theologen wie Dietrich Bonhoeffer nicht mehr als Person geglaubt (»Einen Gott, den es gibt, gibt es nicht«[4]); Gott sei ein soziales Geschehen, wie beispielsweise die gute Tat, die Solidarisierung mit dem Mitmenschen, das Erlebnis der Gemeinschaft.

In einer Zeit, in der alles geordnet, geregelt, versichert ist, können noch andere Dinge auf religiöse Spuren weisen: Alles, was überflüssig ist und dennoch menschlich, das Tun von Unnötigem, die Änderung von Zuständen, das Meditieren, das Glauben, die Trauer, das Glück (Abb. 1–4). Und der Architekt fügt hinzu: »Gott ist im Detail« (Mies van der Rohe). Religion ist im Unmeßbaren, Überflüssigen. Damit aber kann sie zum Komplement der Technik werden.

Die Anwendung des Gesetzes der Packbarkeit hat im Wohnbau unserer Gesellschaft eine Umwelt geschaffen, die Le Bon zu den massebildenden Faktoren gezählt haben würde. Die gleichartigen Elemente werden unterschiedslos den ursprünglich ungleichen Bewohnern übergestülpt. Die Religionen können hierzu den Ausgleich schaffen: Sie befriedigen ein Urbedürfnis, das nach Gemeinschaft. Gegenüber den Massenmedien kann Kirche ein gemeinschaftsbildendes Medium sein; sie kann Gemeinschaft als strukturierte Lebensform unserer Gesellschaft bilden.

Eine praktische Folgerung ist Kirche als Freizeit-Institution in einer Gesellschaft, in der durch den technischen Fortschritt Freizeit nicht nur Genuß und Unterhaltung, sondern zunehmend auch Aufgabe und Problem geworden ist. Kirche könnte gegenüber anderen Freizeit-Institutionen (Sport, Fernsehen) einen Gegenpol bilden.

Dies können neue positive Beiträge der Religionsgemeinschaften zur modernen Gesellschaft sein. Andere, bisher als essentiell angenommene Ideen treten in den

fade into the background. If, for example, the Christian religions have hitherto seen their primary task as the pursuit of the transcendental, this task is nowadays more and more replaced by a religiosity more clearly orientated towards earthly matters. But this does not mean that dogmas and moral standards have come into the fore – on the contrary: Hubertus Halbfas, one of the progressive German Roman Catholic theologians, insists that, in the church of the future, formal worship and dogmatic systems will no longer be of vital relevance; what matters now is "the supremacy of the human element which applies to all formal, dogmatic and legalistic orders"[5].

An entirely new and important aspect of religious development must be seen in the fact that the religious communities are now beginning to respect each other. Religious convictions are no longer regarded as divisive influences. Struggles of the kind now going on between Roman Catholics and Protestants in Ireland are, throughout the world, regarded as anachronistic exceptions. Tolerance nowadays goes so far that religious believers are prepared to acknowledge religious feelings even in an agnostic. It is again Dietrich Bonhoeffer who was the first to abandon this hitherto unquestionable monopoly of the church.

In the Christian religious communities, the spirit of mutual tolerance and respect has given rise to the "ecumenical movement". Its long-term objective is the merger of all the Christian denominations in a single church; its short-term aim is to create theological harmony. There is already inquiry about the first indications of a "Super-Religion"[6]: On the other hand, there are still many vital Christian splinter groups, and the sects are flourishing. This may lead to the conclusion that a Super-Religion could not be created by an initiative from below and that, even in future, the breakaway of splinter groups from the established religion is likely to take place; it may also be concluded that the search for religious truth is still a fervent human quest. Finally, such vitality may be taken as a reflection of the fact that religion is associated with a strongly opinionated society.

Church Architecture Since the Turn of the Century

The times when the religious communities tried to emphasise their sacral buildings through monumentality and symbolism appear to be over. And yet, it is necessary to be mindful of those times if one wants to understand the present situation. Neo-Gothic was undoubtedly inspired by an endeavour to bring about the – impossible – regeneration of mediaeval faith. The "heaven-aspiring" symbol of the tower, the mystical twilight of the nave, the occult remoteness of the altar in the brightly lit choir, the chancel floating high above the crowd, the painted cross-vaulting, the sacrament house – to the believer, all these attributes were symbols of the right faith, quite apart from all the individual symbols with which the churches were adorned (Ill. 5). It can be stated that none of these symbols has survived, and that Man's quest for symbolism is altogether receding. Compared with those years, it seems as if contemporary church architecture is beginning from scratch.

This is how the Christian faith was envisaged around the 1900s: transcendental, all-comprehensive, of child-like humility yet self-conscious – the believing man in an enlightened age was to be an example, a pillar and a rock on which Christ could build His church. In keeping with this vision, the church was to be a vigorous, solid building amidst the urban throng, a dominant feature, God's own keep, a step on the way to heaven, an organ to praise the Lord, a symbol of the city on a high pedestal, with a spire to break and turn upwards the worldly skyline of the long street like a raised forefinger expressing the warning: Lo, the true goal is there above! (Ill. 6).

The revival of mediaeval forms of architecture was accompanied by a striving to rekindle a mediaeval intensity of faith. But there is no rekindling of former spiritual currents. At that time, the churches did not recognise the new forces, neither the beginnings of socialism nor those of technology. It would seem that they were fully preoccupied with the greatest church building programme of all times. This applied especially to the Roman Catholic Church in Germany which had successfully survived the struggle between the Prussian government and the Vatican. The special preference for Gothic designs was due first of all to the eclectic predilection for this style which, at that time, was even applied to "Gothic" factories, described as "churches of labour"; in addition, the Gothic style was regarded, at the time, as the architectural discipline representing the very embodiment of church design. The semantic standard set by the Gothic church will have to be discussed later. It therefore seems quite logical that even the first church erected in concrete, built by Anatole de Baudot in Paris (Ill. 7, 8), showed Gothic features[7]. Admittedly, the Gothic style has here undergone formal and structural modifications through the use of large shells and through changes in ornamental patterns, e. g. in the balustrades. For a long time, Saint-Jean-de-Montmartre remained the only church built in concrete, while a "perfected" Gothic style remained the most popular style although, occasionally, other historic styles – Neo-Romanesque and Neo-Baroque – were also dusted up. Antoni Gaudí's Sagrada Familia church in Barcelona (Ill. 9, 10), which was started somewhat later, is structurally less interesting than Saint-Jean-de-Montmartre. Gaudí regarded himself as a kind of executor of the Gothic style; today, we see the significance of his church mainly in the way in which a mediaeval concept is paraphrased and diluted. From Baudot's church in Paris (1894) to Pietilä's cathedral in Tampere (1966),

6

5

5. Votivkirche, Vienna, 1856–1879; Architect: H. von Ferstel.
6. St. Bernhardus, Karlsruhe, 1895–1901; Architect: Max Meckel.
7, 8. Saint-Jean-de-Montmartre, Paris, 1894; Architect: Anatole de Baudot.
9, 10. Sagrada Familia, Barcelona, since 1882; Architect: Antoni Gaudí.

5. Votivkirche, Wien, 1856–1879; Architekt: H. von Ferstel.
6. St. Bernhardus, Karlsruhe, 1895–1901; Architekt: Max Meckel.
7, 8. Saint-Jean-de-Montmartre, Paris, 1894; Architekt: Anatole de Baudot.
9, 10. Sagrada Familia, Barcelona, seit 1882; Architekt: Antoni Gaudí.

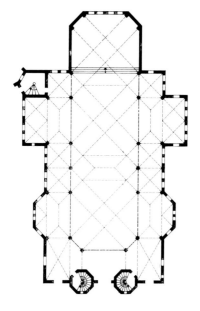

7

8

Hintergrund. Wenn die christlichen Religionen zum Beispiel bisher ihre vornehmste Aufgabe in der Vermittlung des Übersinnlichen sahen, so wird diese heute zugunsten einer mehr diesseitig orientierten Religiosität zurückgedrängt. Das heißt aber nicht, daß Dogmen und moralische Normierungen in den Vordergrund träten, im Gegenteil: Hubertus Halbfas, einer der progressiven katholischen Theologen, fordert, daß für die Kirche in Zukunft Kult und Dogmensysteme nicht mehr normierende Relevanz haben, er fordert den »Primat des Menschlichen, der gegenüber allen kultischen, dogmatischen und gesetzlichen Ordnungen gilt«[5].

Ein ganz neues und wichtiges Moment in der religiösen Entwicklung ist die Tatsache, daß sich die Religionsgemeinschaften nun gegenseitig zu achten beginnen. Es gibt keine Scheidung mehr durch Religionen in Klassen. Auseinandersetzungen, wie zwischen Katholiken und Protestanten in Irland, werden in der ganzen Welt als anachronistische Ausnahmen empfunden. Die Toleranz geht so weit, daß der Religionsgläubige auch dem »Ungläubigen« Religiosität zuerkennt. Es war wieder Dietrich Bonhoeffer, der dieses bisher unbezweifelbare kirchliche Privileg der Religiosität aufgab.

Aus der gegenseitigen Toleranz und Achtung ist in den christlichen Religionsgemeinschaften die »Ökumenische Bewegung« entstanden. Ihr Fernziel ist der Zusammenschluß der Konfessionen zu einer einheitlichen Kirche; ihr Nahziel ist theologische Übereinstimmung. Schon wird die Frage nach Anzeichen für einen »Superglauben«[6] gestellt. Andererseits gibt es viele vitale christliche Splitter-Religionen, und Sekten haben Zulauf. Hieraus kann man schließen, daß ein Superglauben nicht von der Initiative von unten ausgehen würde, daß vielmehr auch in Zukunft Ausbrüche aus der etablierten Religion wahrscheinlich sein werden, und außerdem, daß Suche nach religiöser Wahrheit eine immer noch virulente menschliche Eigenschaft ist. Weiter ist es ein Anzeichen dafür, daß Religion Sache einer dezidierten Gemeinschaft ist.

Kirchenbau seit der Jahrhundertwende

Die Zeiten, in denen die Religionsgemeinschaften ihre Kultbauten mit Monumentalität und Symbolik stärkten, scheinen heute vorbei zu sein. Und doch ist es notwendig, sich ihrer zu erinnern, um die jetzige Situation verstehen zu können. Zweifellos war die Neugotik von dem Streben nach der – unmöglichen – Regeneration des mittelalterlichen Glaubens beseelt. Das »Himmelstrebende« des Turmes, der mystische Dämmer des Schiffes, die geheimnisvolle Ferne des Altars im lichtdurchfluteten Chorraum, die hoch über der Menge schwebende Kanzel, das bemalte Kreuzgewölbe, das Sakramentshäuschen – diese Attribute verkörperten den Gläubigen den rechten Glauben, abgesehen von all den Einzelsymbolen, mit denen die Kirchen geschmückt waren (Abb.5). Man kann feststellen, daß von allen kein einziges übriggeblieben ist, daß der menschliche Bedarf an Symbolik überhaupt zurückgeht. Verglichen mit jenen Jahren ist es, als ob der heutige Kirchenbau beim Nullpunkt anfängt.

So stellte man sich um 1900 den christlichen Glauben vor: jenseitsgerichtet, allumfassend, kindlich-demütig und doch selbstbewußt – der gläubige Mensch in einer aufgeklärten Zeit sollte Vorbild, Säule und Fels sein, auf den Christus seine Kirche bauen konnte. Die Kirche entsprechend ein markiger, festgefügter Bau im Getriebe der Stadt, eine Dominante, eine Burg Gottes, eine Treppe zum Himmel, eine Orgel zum Lobe des Herrn, ein Wahrzeichen der Stadt auf hohem Podest, mit einem Turm, der die weltliche Horizontale der langen Straße zu stoppen und hochzuklappen scheint, wie ein erhobener Zeigefinger mit der Mahnung: Seht, dort oben ist das wahre Ziel! (Abb. 6).

Mit dem Wiederaufgreifen mittelalterlicher Architekturformen erstrebte man eine Wiedererweckung mittelalterlicher Glaubens-Intensität. Nur gibt es keine Wiedererweckung einer früheren geistigen Strömung. Die Kirchen erkannten damals die neuen Kräfte nicht, nicht die Anfänge des Sozialismus und nicht die der Technik. Es scheint, daß sie vollauf damit beschäftigt waren – die katholische Kirche besonders nach dem glücklich überstandenen Kulturkampf –, das größte Kirchenbauprogramm aller Zeiten durchzuführen. Daß gotische Formen für den Kirchenbau besonders bevorzugt wurden, hat seine Ursache einmal in der eklektizistischen Vorliebe für diesen Stil – es gibt aus jener Zeit auch »gotische« Fabriken, die mit »Kirche der Arbeit« bezeichnet wurden – Gotik erschien den Zeitgenossen aber vor allem als die Baukunst, die Kirche schlechthin verkörperte. Von der semantischen Norm der gotischen Kirche wird noch zu reden sein. So ist es ganz selbstverständlich, daß auch die erste Betonkirche, gebaut von Anatole de Baudot in Paris (Abb. 7, 8), gotische Formelemente zeigt.[7] Die Gotik erfuhr hier allerdings durch flächige Schalen eine formale und konstruktive Abwandlung; auch das Ornament, zum Beispiel der Balustraden, wird entsprechend variiert. Saint-Jean-de-Montmartre blieb lange Zeit die einzige Betonkirche, perfektionierte Gotik der meistverwendete Stil, wenn auch zuweilen andere historische Stile – Neuromanik und Neubarock – durchexerziert wurden. Antoni Gaudís etwas später begonnene Kirche Sagrada Familia in Barcelona (Abb. 9, 10) ist konstruktiv weniger interessant als Saint-Jean-de-Montmartre. Gaudí fühlte sich als Vollstrecker gotischen Bauwillens, und wir sehen die Bedeutung seiner Kirche heute vor allem in der Paraphrasierung und Verfremdung eines mittelalterlichen Konzeptes.

Von Baudots Kirche in Paris (1894) bis zu Pietiläs Dom in Tampere (1966) ist Gotik in verschiedenster Weise

9

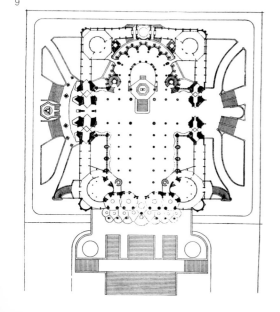

10

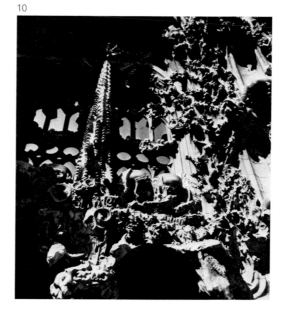

Gothic traces are recognisable in the most variegated ways. To overcome the Gothic style means overcoming a mediaevally formalised faith. An attempt to achieve this aim was made outside the Church by the anthroposophical movement which seeks "to develop by means of intellectual training the psychic force inherent in every human being"[8]. The centre of this *Geisteswissenschaft* (Ill. 11) planned by Rudolf Steiner in 1925 is a mighty dome far removed from the Gothic style which, in its autonomous mega-shape, dominates the Jura slopes near Aesch from a long distance. But the Goetheanum had no direct influence on church architecture.

In contrast, Auguste Perret's church of Notre-Dame in Le Raincy, built in 1922, still shows clear traces of the struggle with the Gothic style. Daylight enters through a diaphanous wall of glass-concrete panels – a motif which came to be frequently used later (Kaiser-Wilhelm-Gedächtniskirche, Berlin) and which, in this case, has made an important contribution to the shaping of the space. Nor are Gothic features entirely absent from the Antoniuskirche in Basle (Ill. 12), designed by Karl Moser and consecrated in 1927. The vehement polemics against

12

11

this church by contemporary architects may have something to do with the fact that Moser had been expected to continue the tradition of his Neo-Gothic churches. Today, this protest is difficult to understand. That church is a landmark in the history of 20-Century church architecture. Whilst all other churches of that time were conceived as isolated monuments, this church was inserted in a row tenement houses, exhibiting, for the first time, a social relevance. Admittedly, however, the entrance is still monumental in character, thus showing a "Gothic" emphasis; the nave, too, though a modern exposed concrete structure with simple cubical details, has "Gothic" loftiness, with vaults and stained-glass windows.

Even the Roman Catholic architects who, during the heyday of the *Wandervogel* movement after the First World War, debated under Romano Guardini[9] at Rotenfels Castle on the Main within the "Liturgical Movement"[10] (which had originated in Belgium in 1909) the originality of the liturgic functions and the "pure" form of the new church – even they had, in the innermost corner of their hearts, remained faithful to Gothic

ideals. Just as Claude Nicolas Ledoux (1736–1806) – leading the architectural revolution against the Baroque – had adopted for his church a classicist and therefore again a historising design, Gothic features are still occasionally recognisable in the Catholic churches built by Dominikus Böhm and Rudolf Schwarz, and in the Protestant churches designed by Otto Bartning. Even the Fronleichnamskirche in Aachen (Ill. 13), which was the first church built by Schwarz together with Hans Schwippert in 1928–1930, can be regarded as a cubical Gothic hall. Gothic details such as rose-windows can still be found, albeit in modified form, in some of these churches. Gothic associations are created for example, by the cruciform beams above a kind of central cupola in the church of Maria König in Saarbrücken built by Schwarz, or by certain details of Böhm's churches at Neu-Ulm (1926) and Mainz-Bischofsheim (1926) or of Bartning's Gustav-Adolf-Kirche in Berlin (1934).

Yet the merits of these architects in bringing about a fruitful confrontation with the ideas of the 1920s should not be overlooked. They consistently pursued the new liturgical ideas and combined them with modern functionalism. Greater simplicity, cubic shapes and intelligibility of the structure – these architectural postulates of the time after the first World War – were introduced into church architecture by them. In particular, Otto Bartning's steel church at Essen (1928) provided a good example for a design logically based on the construction method.

Rudolf Schwarz was less concerned with the intelligibility of the structure[11]. His space concepts are often based on poetic metaphors and symbolic signs. Here is a kinship with Pater Desiderius Lenz, the architectural and artistic aesthete of the Benedictine Order. Certain explanations such as "God's marching column" for the interior of the Corpus-Christi-Kirche, or the "holy gorge" for the interior of the Michaelskirche appear to exaggerate the semantic associations of his church. The church should appear to be a church without any need for explanation, merely by virtue of its non-literal form – this has been, and still is, the modern attitude for fifty years. But even the last church designed by Schwarz, St.-Bonifaz in Aachen (1959–1964), which is so attractive through its brightness, its simplicity and its liberal use of space, has been burdened with an attribute ("mountain of light"). The spatial concept preferred by Schwarz

11. Goetheanum, Dornach, 1925–1928; Architect: Rudolf Steiner.
12. Antoniuskirche, Basle, 1926; Architect: Karl Moser.
13. Fronleichnamskirche, Aachen, 1928–1930; Architect: Rudolf Schwarz (collaborator: Hans Schwippert).
14. Sternkirche, 1919, Project; Architect: Otto Bartning.
15. Christozentrische Idealkirche, 1922, Project; Architect: Dominikus Böhm.
16. Protestant church in Planegg near Munich, 1926; Architect: Theodor Fischer.

14

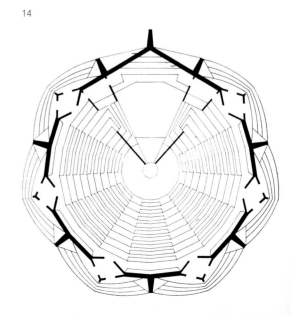

13

spürbar. Überwindung der Gotik bedeutet Überwindung mittelalterlich formalisierten Glaubens. Ein außerkirchlicher Versuch hierzu wurde mit der Anthroposophie gemacht, die »die in jedem Menschen schlummernde Seelenkraft durch geistige Schulung«[8] zu entwickeln sucht. Das 1925 von Rudolf Steiner geplante Zentrum dieser »Geisteswissenschaft« (Abb. 11) ist ein mächtiger Kuppelbau, der von Gotik weit entfernt ist und mit seiner autonomen Großform den Jura-Hang bei Aesch weithin beherrscht. Das Goetheanum hatte jedoch auf den Kirchenbau keinen direkten Einfluß.

In Auguste Perrets 1922 erbauter Kirche Notre-Dame in Le Raincy dagegen ist die Auseinandersetzung mit der Gotik noch deutlich spürbar. Als Belichtung wird eine aus verglasten Beton-Elementen konstruierte diaphane Füllwand eingeführt, die häufig wiederaufgegriffen werden sollte (Kaiser-Wilhelm-Gedächtniskirche in Berlin), und die hier wesentlich zur Raumbildung beigetragen hat. Auch die Antoniuskirche in Basel (Abb. 12) von Karl Moser, die 1927 geweiht wurde, ist nicht ganz frei von gotischen Zügen. Daß von den Zeitgenossen so heftig

gegen sie polemisiert wurde, hängt vielleicht damit zusammen, daß man von Moser eine Fortsetzung seiner neugotischen Kirchen erwartet hatte. Heute ist dieser Protest kaum noch verständlich. Die Kirche bedeutet einen Markstein in der Kirchenbaugeschichte des 20. Jahrhunderts. Gegenüber den anderen Kirchen dieser Zeit, die durchweg als frei stehende Monumente aufgefaßt waren, zeigt dieser Bau durch Einreihung in die Wohnhauszeile erstmalig eine soziale Relevanz. Der Eingang freilich ist noch monumental und damit »gotisch« betont, der Langraum – zwar in seinen Einzelheiten einfache, moderne Sichtbeton-Konstruktion – hat wiederum »gotische« Höhen, Gewölbe und farbige Fenster.

Selbst die katholischen Architekten, die in den Wandervogeljahren nach dem Ersten Weltkrieg mit Romano Guardini[9] auf Burg Rotenfels am Main in der 1909 in Belgien entstandenen »Liturgischen Bewegung«[10] um die Ursprünglichkeit der liturgischen Handlung und um die »reine« Form der neuen Kirche rangen – selbst sie sind im verborgensten Winkel ihres Herzens heimlich Gotiker geblieben. Ähnlich wie Claude Nicolas Ledoux (1736–1806), der Architektur-Revolutionär gegen den Barock, seiner Kirche eine klassizistische, also auch wieder historisierende Gestalt gab, finden sich in den katholischen Kirchen von Dominikus Böhm und Rudolf Schwarz, aber auch in den protestantischen von Otto Bartning gotische Reminiszenzen. Schon die Fronleichnamskirche in Aachen (Abb. 13), die erste Kirche von Schwarz, die er 1928–1930 zusammen mit Hans Schwippert baute, kann man als eine kubisierte gotische Halle bezeichnen. Auch gotische Details, wie die Fensterrose, finden sich in übersetzter Form in manchen dieser Kirchen. So stellten die gekreuzten Unterzüge über einer Art Vierung der Kirche Maria König in Saarbrücken von Schwarz Assoziationen zur Gotik her, wie auch Einzelheiten der Kirchen von Böhm in Neu-Ulm (1926) und Mainz-Bischofsheim (1926) und der Gustav-Adolf-Kirche in Berlin von Bartning (1934).

Man sollte jedoch die Verdienste dieser Architekten um eine fruchtbare Auseinandersetzung mit den Ideen der zwanziger Jahre nicht verschweigen. Mit Konsequenz verfolgten sie die neuen liturgischen Ideen und vereinigten sie mit der Neuen Sachlichkeit. Reduzierung des Aufwandes, kubische Formgebung und Ablesbarkeit der Konstruktion – diese Architekturmaximen der Zeit nach dem Ersten Weltkrieg fanden durch sie Eingang in den Kirchenbau. Gerade Otto Bartning hat mit seiner Stahlkirche in Essen (1928) die räumlichen Konsequenzen aus der Konstruktion gezogen.

Rudolf Schwarz verfolgte weniger die Ablesbarkeit der Konstruktion.[11] Seinen Raumkonzepten liegen vielfach poetische Metaphern und symbolische Zeichen zugrunde. Hier besteht eine Verbindung zu Pater Desiderius Lenz, dem Bau- und Kunstästheten des Benediktinerordens. Manche Erklärungen, wie »Marschkolonne Gottes« für den Raum der Corpus-Christi-Kirche, wie »Heilige Schlucht« für den Raum der Michaelskirche, scheinen die Gestalten seiner Kirche semantisch zu überfordern. Ohne Erläuterung, nur durch ihre unliterarische Gestalt, sollte die Kirche Kirche sein – das war und ist die Auffassung der Moderne schon seit fünfzig Jahren. Aber selbst die letzte Kirche von Schwarz, St. Bonifaz in Aachen (1959–1964), die durch ihre Helligkeit, Einfachheit und räumliche Freiheit so anziehend wirkt, ist mit einem Attribut (»Berg des Lichtes«) befrachtet. Die Raumkonzeption von Schwarz basiert auf der Vorstellung von einem auf »heiliger Fahrt« befindlichen Gottesvolk, das dem Ziel in der Unendlichkeit zustrebt, dem Altar – der »die ferne Faltung der Erde« ist. Es ist

11. Goetheanum, Dornach, 1925–1928; Architekt: Rudolf Steiner.
12. Antoniuskirche, Basel, 1926; Architekt: Karl Moser.
13. Fronleichnamskirche, Aachen, 1928–1930; Architekt: Rudolf Schwarz (Mitarbeiter: Hans Schwippert).
14. Sternkirche, 1919, Projekt; Architekt: Otto Bartning.
15. Christozentrische Idealkirche, 1922, Projekt; Architekt: Dominikus Böhm.
16. Protestantische Kirche in Planegg bei München, 1926; Architekt: Theodor Fischer.

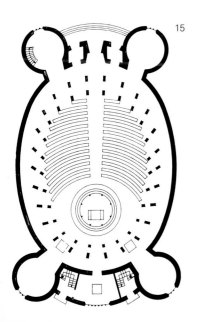

15

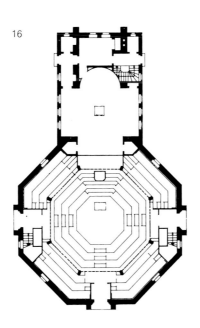

16

17   18

is based on the notion of God's people engaged in a "holy pilgrimage" tending towards infinity, with the altar representing the "remote folding up of Earth". This description is applied to the nave which, despite all efforts at democratisation, remains the basic theme preferred by Schwarz.

In contrast, the idea of a centrically or elliptically orientated church interior was pursued by the older architect, Dominikus Böhm. As early as 1922, he designed the "Christozentrische Idealkirche" for South America. Here the intention was to intensify the relationship between the devout congregation and the altar. But, whilst in the Roman Catholic Church, interiors with consistently centric orientation did not at first find favour, the soil for such a development was better prepared in the Protestant church. Ever since the time of secularisation, the long nave had come to be regarded as not very suitable for divine worship. In many secularised Gothic churches, the pews are placed at right angles to the longitudinal axis – an architecturally unsatisfactory solution which does, however, greatly facilitate the participation of the community in the service. Similarly, the much practised installation of transverse and longitudinal galleries in long naves, though certainly not producing any architectural marvels, contributed to the creation of concentrated spaces. As early as 1926, Theodor Fischer was able to build his church at Planegg as an octagon with pews on seven sides, placed on steps descending towards the centre. In 1919, Otto Bartning conceived the ideal expressionistic design of the "Sternkirche". This building, too, with its seven shed-type roofs of pointed arches, has amphitheatrically arranged pews. The twelve entrances show expressionistic features with Gothic leanings.

The spatial concepts of Roman Catholics and Protestants began to approach each other. Whether the space should be conceived from the centre – "Christocentric" – or from the congregation orientated towards the "happening in the centre", may well be worth a theological discussion; architecturally, however, it leads to the same results (Ill. 14–16). Admittedly, the initial effect of these ideas was not very widespread; church architecture was affected by too many other factors, and there was too little response from "God's people". At this time, the term *circumstantes* – those flocking around the altar – came into fashion. This means, first of all, a form of celebration shared by everybody, i.e. a reduction in

private participation and a kind of de-mystification. Functional considerations, distrusted at first, play a part: the simple facts of improved audibility and visibility. Although some architects and a few theologians recognised and realised this social aspect of church architecture, the churches themselves had not yet progressed so far, and even the influential Rudolf Schwarz followed other ideals. It is here that the great diversification in church architecture began.

Church construction in Germany had almost entirely come to a standstill during the Nazi period. In other countries, the development showed a trend towards regional design tendencies (Netherlands, Switzerland, Denmark, Finland). From the Scandinavian countries, two important examples should be mentioned: the cemetery chapel near Turku by Erik Bryggman (1941) and Grundtvigs Church, Copenhagen (Ill. 17), built by Peter Vilhelm Jensen Klint (1920–40). Whilst, in the cemetery chapel, the pure white merges with bare rubble masonry into a sensitive, asymmetric room, Grundtvigs church has the appearance of a mighty monument to defiant brick Gothic. Dating back to the same years is the Reformed church in Zurich-Altstetten by Werner M. Moser. With its nave covered by an asymmetric pent roof and with its associated parish premises, this church has become the prototype of Swiss church centres. With his early, functionally simple churches, Hermann Baur, too, made a considerable contribution to developments in Switzerland, like Pius Parsch and Robert Kramreiter in Austria (Ill. 18).

An important contribution towards a church designed with structural considerations in mind was made in Basle with the construction of the Protestant Johanneskirche by architects Karl Egender and Ernst F. Burckhardt (1936) (Ill. 19). In this two-storey steel structure, the church at ground floor level occupies just as much space as the parish premises in the lower floor. In its simple austerity, this is one of the first churches which should be measured by social rather than aesthetic criteria.

The inspiration to church architecture derived from the Second World War was not as profound as after the First World War. On the contrary: Despite all the good will to create something new, despite all the idealistic notions of a new church and a new society, no lasting idea emerged, at least in German church architecture. Restorative forces were quite powerful, and the significance of the revived socialism – for instance in the form

17. Grundtvigs Church, Copenhagen, 1920–1940; Architect: Peter Vilhelm Jensen Klint.

18. Church in Pernitz, Austria, 1936; Architect: Robert Kramreiter.

19. Johanneskirche, Basle, 1936; Architects: Karl Egender, Ernst F. Burckhardt.

20. Friedenskirche, Karlsruhe-Weierfeld, 1948; Architect: Otto Bartning.

21. Unitarian church in Madison, Wisconsin, 1950; Architect: Frank Lloyd Wright.

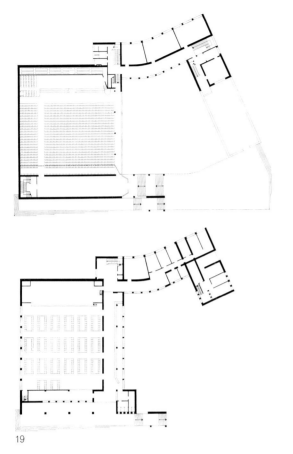

19

17. Grundtvigskirche, Kopenhagen, 1920–1940; Architekt: Peter Vilhelm Jensen Klint.

18. Kirche in Pernitz, Österreich, 1936; Architekt: Robert Kramreiter.

19. Johanneskirche, Basel, 1936; Architekten: Karl Egender, Ernst F. Burckhardt.

20. Friedenskirche, Karlsruhe-Weierfeld, 1948; Architekt: Otto Bartning.

21. Unitarierkirche in Madison, Wisconsin, 1950; Architekt: Frank Lloyd Wright.

21

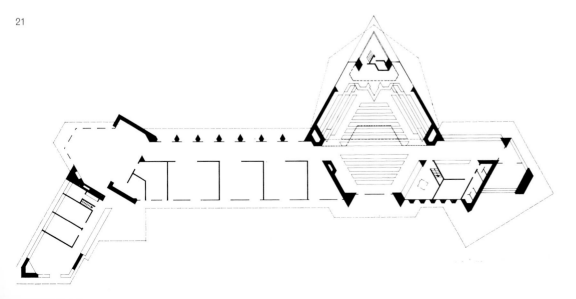

der Langraum, der hier umschrieben wird, der allen Demokratisierungsbestrebungen zum Trotz das Raumthema von Schwarz blieb.

Der zentrisch oder elliptisch orientierte Kirchenraum wurde dagegen von dem älteren Dominikus Böhm verfolgt. Bereits 1922 entwarf er die »Christozentrische Idealkirche« für Südamerika. Die Intensivierung der Beziehung der Gläubigen zum Altar ist hier angestrebt. Während sich aber in der katholischen Kirche konsequent zentrisch orientierte Räume zunächst nicht durchsetzen konnten, war der Boden hierfür in der protestantischen Kirche besser vorbereitet. Der Langraum war schon seit der Säkularisation für die Funktionen des Gottesdienstes als nicht sehr geeignet erkannt worden. In vielen säkularisierten gotischen Kirchen stehen die Bänke quer zur räumlichen Längsrichtung – architektonisch eine unbefriedigende Lösung, die aber den Mitvollzug des Gottesdienstes erheblich erleichtert. Auch der vielgeübte Einbau von Quer- und Längsemporen in Langräume trug nicht gerade zu architektonischen Wunderwerken, aber zur Vorbereitung konzentrierterer Räume bei. Schon 1926 konnte Theodor Fischer seine Kirche in Planegg als Oktogon mit siebenseitig umlaufenden, zur Mitte hin abgestuften Bänken bauen. Otto Bartning konzipierte 1919 den expressionistischen Idealentwurf der »Sternkirche«. Auch dieser Bau mit den sieben spitzbogigen Schuppen-Sheds hat zur Mitte abgetreppte Stufenbänke. Die zwölf Eingänge zeigen gotisierend-expressionistisches Maßwerk.

Die räumlichen Ideen der Katholiken und Protestanten begannen sich zu nähern. Ob der Raum von der Mitte aus, »christozentrisch«, konzipiert ist oder von der Gemeinde her mit Richtung auf das »Geschehen in der Mitte«, das mag einer theologischen Diskussion wert sein, architektonisch führt es zu gleichen Ergebnissen (Abb. 14–16). Diese Ideen hatten allerdings zunächst keine große Breitenwirkung, zu viele andere Momente wirkten auf den Kirchenbau ein, und zu wenig Echo fanden sie beim »Gottesvolk«. In dieser Zeit wird der Ausdruck »Circumstantes« – um den Altar Geschart – gebraucht. Es bedeutet vor allem gemeinschaftliches Feiern, also Verminderung der privaten Teilnahme und dazu Entmystifizierung. Zunächst mit Mißtrauen begegnete funktionalistische Überlegungen spielen eine Rolle: die einfachen Erkenntnisse des besseren Hörens und Sehens. Wenn auch einige Architekten und wenige Theologen diese soziale Seite des Kirchenbaus erkann-

20

ten und realisierten, so waren doch die Kirchen selbst noch nicht so weit, und auch der einflußreiche Rudolf Schwarz verfolgte andere Vorstellungen. Hier begann die große Diversifikation im Kirchenbau.

Im Deutschland der Hitler-Zeit wurde der Kirchenbau fast ganz eingestellt. In den anderen Ländern ging die Entwicklung im Sinne einer regionalen Ausformung weiter (Holland, Schweiz, Dänemark, Finnland). Aus den skandinavischen Ländern sollen zwei wichtige Beispiele erwähnt werden: die Friedhofskapelle bei Turku von Erik Bryggman (1941) und die Grundtvigskirche in Kopenhagen (Abb. 17) von Peter Vilhelm Jensen Klint (1920–40). Während in der Friedhofskapelle das reine Weiß mit unverputztem Bruchstein-Mauerwerk zu einem sensiblen, asymmetrischen Raum zusammengeht, erscheint die Grundtvigskirche wie ein machtvolles Monument wehrhafter Backsteingotik. In den gleichen Jahren entsteht die reformierte Kirche in Zürich-Altstetten von Werner M. Moser. Sie ist mit ihrem von einem asymmetrischen Pultdach überdeckten Langraum und den zugeordneten Gemeindebauten zum Prototyp schweizerischer Kirchenzentren geworden. Auch Hermann Baur hatte mit seinen frühen, funktionalistisch einfachen Kirchen wesentlichen Anteil an der Entwicklung in der Schweiz, wie Pius Parsch und Robert Kramreiter in Österreich (Abb. 18).

Ein wesentlicher Beitrag zu einer von der Konstruktion her konzipierten Kirche wurde 1936 in Basel durch den Bau der protestantischen Johanneskirche (Abb. 19) von den Architekten Karl Egender und Ernst F. Burckhardt geleistet. In dieser zweigeschossigen Stahlkirche nimmt der Kirchenraum im Erdgeschoß soviel Fläche ein wie die Gemeinderäume im Untergeschoß. Diese Kirche ist in ihrer schlichten Kargheit eine der ersten, die mehr mit sozialem als mit ästhetischem Maßstab gemessen werden müssen.

Das Ende des Zweiten Weltkrieges brachte für den Kirchenbau keine so tiefgehenden Impulse wie das Ende des vorausgegangenen Krieges. Im Gegenteil: Bei allem guten Willen zu etwas Neuem, bei idealistischen Vorstellungen von einer neuen Kirche und einer neuen Gesellschaft war – wenigstens in Deutschland – keine tragfähige Idee da. Restaurative Elemente waren durchaus mächtig, und der neu belebte Sozialismus (etwa in der Form der Arbeiterpriester) wurde von den Kirchen in seiner Bedeutung nicht immer gewürdigt. Heimatstil – eine national-romantische Abart der regionalistischen Tendenzen der neuen Architektur, die von den Nationalsozialisten gefördert worden war – steht neben dem hier und da wieder aufgelebten International Style, Repräsentationsbedürfnis der Kirchen neben der Überzeugung vom Vorrang ökonomischer Bedingungen. Es ent-

of worker priests – was not always fully appreciated by the churches. A deliberately fostered local style – a national-romantic variant of the regionalistic tendencies of the new architecture promoted by National Socialism – stands side by side with the occasionally revived, international style; the desire of the churches to possess representative buildings conflicts with the conviction that economic considerations deserved prior consideration. There arose the *Notkirchen* (make-shift churches) of the Protestants (Ill. 20), of a design entrusted to Otto Bartning, and at the same time the anti-functional churches of "supreme purposelessness".

In the United States, Frank Lloyd Wright built one of the few significant churches of those years, the Unitarian Church in Madison in 1950 (Ill. 21). The rising roof appears to grow out of the slope and shows a dynamically intensified movement up to the steeply converging culmination point. This church is a typical example for Wright's notion of organic architecture. At the same time, he uses it as a demonstration for the parallelism of Christianity and democracy. In connection with the latest trend, this church is important because the social

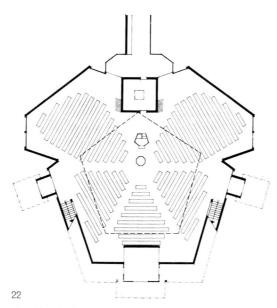

22

22. Thomaskirche, Gellertsiedlung, Basle, 1951, Project; Architect: Otto H. Senn.
23. St. Johannes Baptist, Karlsruhe-Durlach, 1962–1965; Architect: Rainer Disse.
24, 25. Matthäuskirche, Pforzheim, 1953; Architects: Egon Eiermann, Robert Hilgers.
26, 27. St. Johann von Capristan, Munich, 1960; Architect: Sep Ruf.
28, 29. Santa Maria Miraculosa, Mexico, D.F., 1954; Architect: Felix Candela.

23

premises are integrated with it. For instance, the space on the entrance side which can be separated from the church proper and is distinguished by a fireplace of heavy rubble masonry, can also serve as a vestibule for the Sunday School classes and other premises.

There are only a few churches built during the 1950s where this arrangement of the social premises has been recognised as a means of relating the church to adjacent secular buildings, anticipating a future trend. One of the few who pursued this idea was the Swiss architect Otto H. Senn. In his Gellertkirche (Ill. 22) designed in 1951, he created a pentagonal space which permitted a direct link with the parish premises. In post-war Germany, the notion of the church as an isolated monument, representing a "totally different space" (so termed by the present author), proved to be more virulent at first. Moreover, the church construction programme was, in several respects, regarded as forming a contrast to the extensive housing programmes of the 1950s[12]. The idea prevailed that the church should be set apart from the humdrum activities of everyday life as a special place, building, space. This demand seemed to be inherent in the situation: The architectural misery of social housing con-

struction during the early post-war years cried out for counter-weights, for singular buildings distinguished from their monotonous surroundings. Even today, it is still often possible to observe a polarity between housing construction and church building, as in Rainer Disse's church at Karlsruhe-Durlach (Ill. 23). The formal results from those years show a pluralistic variety. That is why the architects of the 1950s are often reproached for indulging in "private symbolics" or "self-affirmation". The more serious reproach applies to the client who "induces the architect to undertake the design work without guidance, standard rules or firm specifications[13]. In the few cases where guidance was given, it was hardly ever an inspiration to new experiments. (For instance, up to the time of the Second Vatican Council, the specifications of the Freiburg Archdiocese still insisted on the central aisle).

The churches designed during this time demonstrate the first tentative steps along new paths, toward a new orientation of faith, away from tradition – often based on the initiative of a single individual and wrested from traditionally inclined bishops and congregations.

And it was just during this period of spiritual instability that the whole world had to cope with a very extensive church building programme: Everywhere, the population was on the increase, and everywhere, the churches had the necessary means available. In the plan, rectangular (Ill. 24, 25) churches predominate, but hexagonal and octagonal plans are not rare; oval and circular shapes are being tried out; saddle and pent roofs (Ill. 28, 29), domes and flat roofs cope with the third dimension. The altar space is often designed as a stage or – less frequently – more directly related to the space occupied by the congregation.

One specific solution which gave rise to a considerable impulse was the Pilgrim's Church of Notre-Dame-du-Haut near Ronchamp, built in 1954. On a site which had been used for sacral purposes even in pre-Christian times, Le Corbusier reverted in his individual language to archaic expressions. With partly convex and partly concave shells, a cave-like space was created. It can hardly be regarded as a demonstration of the feeling of freedom which Man has acquired in the age of technology; it rather suggests a protection against the forces of nature, a means of defending a safely anchored faith and, at the same time, a child-like belief in the miracle-dispensing figure, a trust in symbols and signs and their

24

25

22. Thomaskirche, Gellertsiedlung, Basel, 1951, Projekt; Architekt: Otto H. Senn.

23. St. Johannes Baptist, Karlsruhe-Durlach, 1962–1965; Architekt: Rainer Disse.

24. 25. Matthäuskirche, Pforzheim, 1953; Architekten: Egon Eiermann, Robert Hilgers.

26. 27. St. Johann von Capristan, München, 1960; Architekt: Sep Ruf.

28. 29. Santa Maria Miraculosa, Mexico, D.F., 1954; Architekt: Felix Candela.

26

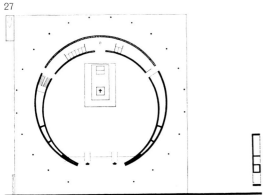

27

stehen die Notkirchen der Protestanten (Abb. 20), deren Bau Otto Bartning anvertraut wird, und gleichzeitig antifunktionalistische Kirchen von »hoher Zwecklosigkeit«.

In den USA baut Frank Lloyd Wright 1950 eine der wenigen bedeutenden Kirchen dieser Jahre, die Unitarierkirche in Madison (Abb. 21). Das ansteigende Dach scheint aus dem Hang herauszuwachsen und erfährt eine dynamisch gesteigerte Bewegung bis zum spitz zulaufenden Kulminationspunkt. Die Kirche ist ein typisches Beispiel für Wrights Auffassung von organischer Architektur. Gleichzeitig demonstriert er mit ihr die Parallelität von Christentum und Demokratie. Für die neueste Entwicklung ist diese Kirche wichtig, weil hier die Sozialräume in die Anlage integriert sind. So kann der vom Kirchenraum abtrennbare, eingangsseitige Raumteil mit seinem schweren Bruchsteinkamin als Foyer dienen, an das auch die Klassen der Sonntagsschule und andere Räume angeschlossen sind.

Bei wenigen Kirchen der fünfziger Jahre ist dieser Einbau der Sozialräume als Möglichkeit der Bezugnahme zu der anschließenden »profanen« Bebauung und damit als Perspektive für die Zukunft erkannt. Einer der wenigen Architekten, die diese Idee weiterverarbeiteten, war der Schweizer Otto H. Senn. In seiner 1951 konzipierten Gellertkirche (Abb. 22) entwarf er einen fünfeckigen Raum, in den die Gemeinderäume nahtlos einbezogen werden können.

Die Vorstellung von Kirche als frei stehendem Monument und als der »gänzlich andere Raum« (Verf.) erwies sich im Nachkriegsdeutschland zunächst als virulenter. Hierzu kam, daß die Kirche in mehrfacher Hinsicht ein Kontrastprogramm zu den umfangreichen Wohnbau-Aufgaben der fünfziger Jahre wurde.[12] Es herrschte die Idee vor, die Kirche vom Alltag als einen besonderen Ort, Bau, Raum abzusetzen. Die Situation schien dies zu erfordern: Das architektonische Elend des sozialen Wohnbaues der Nachkriegsjahre verlangte geradezu Gegengewichte, singuläre Gebäude, die sich von der monotonen Umgebung abhoben. So ist vielfach noch heute eine Polarität zwischen Wohnbau und Kirchenbau zu beobachten – etwa bei der Kirche in Karlsruhe-Durlach von Rainer Disse (Abb. 23). Das formale Ergebnis dieser Jahre ist von pluralistischer Vielfalt. Deshalb wird den Architekten der fünfziger Jahre gern »Privatsymbolik« und »Selbstbestätigung« vorgeworfen. Der ernstere Vorwurf trifft den Bauherrn, der den Architekten »ohne Wegleitung, Normen und verbindliche Unterlagen in die Projektierung schickt«[13]. Wenn es einmal solche Wegleitungen gab, dann waren sie fast nie anregend für neue Versuche. (Beispielsweise verlangte die Erzdiözese Freiburg in ihren Anordnungen zum Kirchenbau bis zum Konzil zwingend den Mittelgang.)

Die Kirchen dieser Zeit demonstrieren erste tastende Schritte auf neuen Wegen, zu einer neuen Orientierung des Glaubens, weg von der Tradition – oft auf der Initiative eines Einzelnen basierend und traditionell eingestellten Bischöfen und Gemeinden abgetrotzt.

Ausgerechnet in dieser geistig unsicheren Zeit mußte auf der ganzen Welt ein sehr großes Kirchenbauprogramm bewältigt werden: Überall nahm die Bevölkerung zu, überall standen den Kirchen die notwendigen Mittel zur Verfügung. Im Grundriß rechteckige (Abb. 24, 25) Kirchen dominieren, sechs- und achteckige sind nicht selten, das Oval und der Kreis (Abb. 26, 27) werden als Grundrißform versucht, mit Sattel- und Faltdächern (Abb. 28, 29) Kuppeln und Flachdächern wird die dritte Dimension bewältigt. Der Altarraum wird oft als Bühne gebaut oder auch – in selteneren Fällen – in direktere Beziehung zum räumlichen Bereich der Gläubigen gesetzt.

28

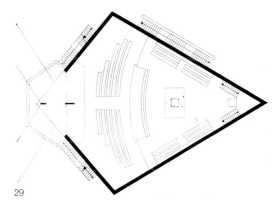

29

Eine Einzellösung, die einen erheblichen Anstoß verursachte, war die 1954 entstandene Wallfahrtskirche Notre-Dame-du-Haut bei Ronchamp (Abb. 30–32). Le Corbusier griff – an einem schon in vorchristlicher Zeit sakralen Ort – in individueller Sprache auf archaischen Ausdruck zurück. Mit teils nach innen, teils nach außen gewölbten Schalen wurde ein höhlenartiger Raum gebildet. Er ist kaum eine Demonstration des Gefühls der Freiheit, die sich der Mensch des technischen Zeitalters erstritten hat; er ist ein Ausdruck des Schutzes vor den Naturkräften, der Möglichkeit der Verteidigung eines festen Glaubens-Fundamentes und zugleich des Kinderglaubens an das wundertätige Gnadenbild, des Vertrauens auf Symbole und Zeichen und ihre geheimnisvolle Bedeutung. Hier entstand etwas absolut Neues, eine Kirche, die ohne theologische und architektonische Skrupel gebaut ist. Man glaubte zunächst, Ronchamp könne keinen neuen Stil begründen, höchstens Epigonen zeugen; mit dieser Kirche wurde jedoch sehr wohl ein Anfang für eine neue Entwicklung gesetzt. Sie bedeutet für den Raum: Verwendung einfacher, unverfälschter Mittel und Unterwerfung der Konstruktion unter die Bedingungen des Gefühls, des Sinnlichen; damit wird auch der Gebrauch freier, ungeometrischer Kurven und plastischer Formen initiiert. Gleichzeitig wird die Auffassung von der Kirche als Solitärbau dokumentiert: Ronchamp ist das Heiligtum auf den Hügeln, eins mit den »Schwingungen der Landschaft«. Von ihr abgesetzt und tiefer gelegt sind das Pfarrhaus und die Pilger-

30

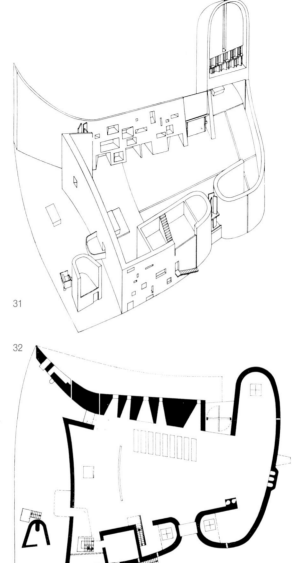

31

32

mysterious significance. Here, something absolutely new has been created, a church built without any theological or architectural scruples. Initially, it was thought that Ronchamp would not be able to initiate a new style but merely create epigones; in the event, however, this church did mark the beginning of a new development. As far as the treatment of the space is concerned, it signifies the use of simple undiluted means and the subjection of the structural design to sentiment, to the reaction of the senses; in this way, it also initiates the use of informal, non-geometrical curves and plastic shapes. At the same time, it also provides a documentation for the notion of the church as a solitary building: Ronchamp is the sanctuary on the hills, at one with the "swingings of the landscape". Detached from it and placed at a lower level are the rectory and the pilgrim's hostel. Ronchamp signifies the final victory over the Gothic style, and architectural form of the highest innovative value. Since Ronchamp, church architecture has known plastically shaped interiors with sentimental overtones – i.e., three-dimensional concepts where a clear distinction between plan and elevation is no longer attempted. There are lighting effects where bright interiors are contrasted with darker parts of the room, occult twilight with radiant brightness. Le Corbusier's architectural ideas contained so much original force that his influence has been lasting and is, indirectly, still affecting us today. The churches designed by Mutschler (Ill. 33), Gieselmann (Ill. 34), Gisel (Ill. 35) and Striffler (Ill. 36) can still, despite all the differences, be regarded as genuine descendants.

A different heritage has been left by Mies van der Rohe with his IIT Chapel, Chicago (Ill. 37, 38), built in 1952. This church cube is a simple, nobly designed hall structure which, as the architect said, was not meant to be a "show piece" but, with its beautiful proportions and with its consistent use of the technical aids, to achieve genuine monumentality. Brick, steel and glass are the subtly used materials. The concept of an idealised technology and an abstraction of functional conditions was able to give rise to a new school with a world-wide following.

The Unitarian Church, Ronchamp and the IIT Chapel can be regarded as the prototypes of church architecture in the 1950s. They are so different from each other that they can well be taken to characterise the diversification of church architecture. Le Corbusier's second great church, that of the monastery of Sainte-Marie-de-la-

Tourette in Eveux-sur-l'Arbresle, was no longer able to provide the same kind of impulse as did Ronchamp. The high nave is revived – with the historic proportions of the sacred. The altar is a monument placed on a high pedestal, with the nave slightly rising towards it so that the mystical remoteness of the sacrificial action is further intensified. A surprising feature is the historic association of the church, its kinship to the Cistercian churches in Burgundy. Alvar Aalto's Vuoksenniska Church in Imatra (Ill. 39), was built at the same time (1958). This church has a free-form interior with a roof rising along the longitudinal axis. To serve congregations of different size at divine services and parish celebrations, the church can be divided by concrete sliding walls into three parts, each with its own entrance. The building can thus be used as a great church, as a small chapel with parish premises, and in other ways.

Aalto's church is plastered white, although the material preferred for church buildings in the late 1950s and early 1960s was concrete. This is no longer the material strictly confined to its necessary dimensions by structural and aesthetic considerations but rather a plastic material

30, 31, 32. Notre-Dame-du-Haut, Ronchamp, France, 1950–1954; Architect: Le Corbusier.

33. Pfingstbergkirche, Mannheim, 1958–1963; Architect: Carlfried Mutschler.

34. St. Jacobus, Sinsheim, Germany, 1964–1966; Architect: Reinhard Gieselmann.

35. Protestant parish centre, Stuttgart-Sonnenberg, 1963–1966; Architect: Ernst Gisel.

36. Evangelische Versöhnungskirche in the former KZ, Dachau, Germany, 1965–1967; Architect: Helmut Striffler.

30, 31, 32. Notre-Dame-du-Haut, Ronchamp, Frankreich, 1950–1954; Architekt: Le Corbusier.

33. Pfingstbergkirche, Mannheim, 1958–1963; Architekt: Carlfried Mutschler.

34. St. Jakobus, Sinsheim, Baden-Württemberg, 1964 bis 1966; Architekt: Reinhard Gieselmann.

35. Evangelisches Gemeindezentrum in Stuttgart-Sonnenberg, 1963–1966; Architekt: Ernst Gisel.

36. Evangelische Versöhnungskirche im ehemaligen KZ Dachau, 1965–1967; Architekt: Helmut Striffler.

herberge. Ronchamp ist die definitive Überwindung der Gotik, eine Architekturform von höchstem Innovationswert. Seit Ronchamp gibt es im Kirchenbau raumplastische, gefühlhafte Räume, also dreidimensionale Konzeptionen, in denen die »saubere« Trennung von Grund- und Aufriß nicht mehr angestrebt ist. Es gibt Lichtführungen, in denen hellere gegen dunklere Raumteile ausgespielt sind, mystisches Dämmer gegen strahlende Helle. Le Corbusiers architektonische Ideen hatten soviel ursprüngliche Kraft, daß sein Einfluß nachhaltig und indirekt bis heute anhält. Kirchen von Mutschler (Abb. 33), Gieselmann (Abb. 34), Gisel (Abb. 35) und Striffler (Abb. 36) sind bei aller Verschiedenheit echte Nachkommen.

Ein anderes Erbe hat Mies van der Rohe mit seiner 1952 erbauten IIT-Kapelle in Chicago (Abb. 37, 38) hinterlassen. Dieser Kirchenkubus ist ein einfacher, edel geformter Saalbau, der kein »Schaustück« sein sollte, wie der Architekt dazu bemerkt, sondern der mit seinen schönen Proportionen, mit der konsequenten Anwendung der technischen Mittel echte Monumentalität erreichen sollte. Backstein, Stahl und Glas sind die subtil angewendeten Baustoffe. Das Konzept der Idealisierung der Technologie und der Abstraktion funktioneller Bedin-

Jeder Teil hat seinen eigenen Eingang. Es entstand ein Raumgebilde, das als große Kirche, als kleine Kapelle mit Gemeindesälen und anders nutzbar ist.

Die Kirche von Aalto ist weiß verputzt. Bevorzugtes Material des Kirchenbaues der ausgehenden fünfziger und der frühen sechziger Jahre ist jedoch der Beton. Es ist nicht mehr der konstruktivistisch-ästhetisch auf seine notwendigen Dimensionen festgelegte Baustoff, sondern er wird nun als gerade, geknickte, gekrümmte, raumbegrenzende, reliefierte Wand, als dicke, durchhängende Schale und als mächtiger Pfeiler verwendet (Abb. 40). Gerade im Kirchenbau dieser Zeit werden seine Gestaltqualitäten ans Licht geholt. – Daneben gibt es den vom Brutalismus wiederentdeckten Backstein, der manchmal mit Beton kombiniert und ebenso frei wie der Beton gehandhabt wird. Die technologische Perfektion der Mies-Architektur hat auch auf freiere Architekten ihren Eindruck nicht verfehlt, so daß in dieser Zeit der Prosperität Kirchenbauten von hoher technischer Qualität und konstruktivem Raffinement entstehen.

Im Zweiten Vatikanischen Konzil wurden 1963 und 1964 durch Ausführungen zur neuen Liturgie[14] die Wege für einen neuen katholischen Kirchenbau auf der Grundlage einer zeitgemäßen Theologie geebnet. Ob das Konzil

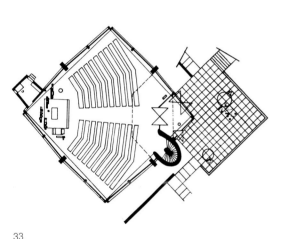

33

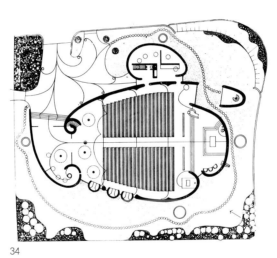

34

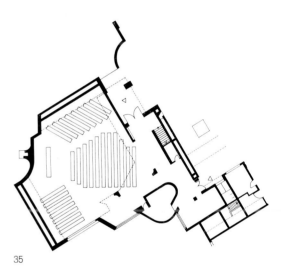

35

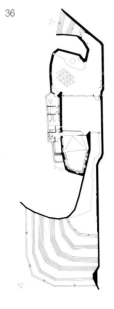

36

gungen war in der Lage, eine weltweite Schule zu begründen.

Die Unitarierkirche, Ronchamp und die IIT-Kapelle waren die Prototypen des Kirchenbaues der fünfziger Jahre. Sie sind untereinander so verschieden, daß sie gut die Diversifikation des Kirchenbaues charakterisieren. Die zweite große Kirche von Le Corbusier, die des Klosters Sainte-Marie-de-la-Tourette in Eveux-sur-l'Arbresle konnte nicht mehr ein solcher Anstoß sein wie Ronchamp. Der hohe Langraum lebte wieder auf – mit den historischen Proportionen der Sakralität. Der Altar ist ein auf hohem Podest stehendes Mal, das Kirchenschiff steigt leicht zu ihm an – die mystische Ferne der Opferhandlung ist so noch verstärkt. Überraschend ist die Historizität des Raumes, die Verwandtschaft mit den Kirchen der Zisterzienser in Burgund. Zur gleichen Zeit entstand die Vuoksenniska-Kirche in Imatra (Abb. 39) von Alvar Aalto (1958). Sie hat einen freigeformten Hauptraum mit einem über die Längsachse ansteigenden Dach. Er ist, um den verschiedenen Frequenzen der Gottesdienste und Gemeindefeiern gerecht zu werden, durch Schiebewände aus Beton dreifach unterteilbar.

einen Einschnitt in den Kirchenbau unserer Zeit bedeutet, kann wegen der kurzen zeitlichen Distanz noch nicht beurteilt werden. Schon heute kann man aber sagen, daß im katholischen Kirchenbau ein nicht mehr aufzuhaltender Demokratisierungsprozeß in Gang gesetzt wurde – der im protestantischen Bereich im Grunde bereits mit der Reformation begann.

Für beide Konfessionen gilt heute in erster Linie, die ungehinderte und aktive Teilnahme aller am Kultgeschehen zu ermöglichen. Die funktionale Grundlage ist gleichmäßig optimale Sichtbarkeit und Hörsamkeit. Diese Forderungen sind von zwei Faktoren abhängig: von der Menge der Gläubigen und von der Orientierung der Plätze auf die liturgischen Orte.

Die von den kirchlichen Instanzen als optimal angesehene Größe liegt bei 200–450 Plätzen. Unabhängig von statistisch-ökonomischen Bedingungen spielen hier folgende Überlegungen eine Rolle: Reduziert man diese Zahl, wird die Teilnahme aktiviert, dagegen geht das Gefühl einer größeren Gemeinschaft verloren. Vergrößert man die Zahl, gibt es akustische und visuelle Schwierigkeiten – eine akustische Verstärkung wird not-

used as a straight angular, curved, room-enclosing, relief-treated wall, as a thick suspended shell, and as a mighty column (Ill. 40). It was just during that period of church architecture that the plastic qualities of concrete were deliberately exploited. – In addition, there is the traditional brick, rediscovered by modern Brutalism, sometimes combined with concrete and treated just as informally. The technological perfection of Mies van der Rohe's architecture has not failed to make an impression also on more informally orientated architects so that, in this age of prosperity, church buildings of high technical standard and structural refinement are being created.

During the Second Vatican Council in 1963–1964, commentaries on the new liturgy[14] paved the way for a new Roman Catholic church design based on contemporary theology. Because of the short time which has since elapsed, it is not yet possible to say whether the Council has made a vital impact on contemporary church architecture. But even now, it can be stated that, in Roman Catholic church architecture, a democratisation process has been triggered off which can no longer be arrested –

more to the centre of the congregation. For the Roman Catholic Church, in which the other liturgical places and the sequence of the service are also being reorganized, this means a revolutionary reshaping of the worship: The mystery is dissolved, the priest's body no longer conceals the liturgical actions from the congregation – – *versus populum* – standing behind the altar. For the sake of this new form of liturgy, even ancient churches have been completely remodelled. In the Gothic cathedral in Münster, for instance, in anticipation of the new liturgical concepts, the altar was removed from the high choir and placed into the brightly lit intersection of the nave (Emil Steffan, 1955).

Doubts have been raised as to the effectiveness of the architectural design[15]. "The Holy Communion, essentially taking place in the hearts of the people gathered in a fraternal congregation, may be taken in any room, in a lounge, multi-purpose room, basement, in the open, in a private chapel; there is thus no intrinsic need for any sacral structure"[13]. This is reminiscent of Luther's words: "Even if you preached under a green linden-tree or willow, it would still be God's own abode and sanc-

37

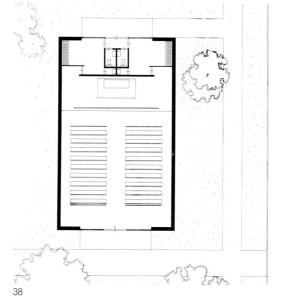

38

37, 38. Chapel of the Illinois Institute of Technology, Chicago, 1952; Architect: Ludwig Mies van der Rohe.
39. Vuoksenniska Church, Imatra, Finland, 1956–1959; Architect: Alvar Aalto.
40. Protestant parish centre, Stuttgart-Sonnenberg, 1963 to 1966; Architect: Ernst Gisel.
41. Kennedy Space Centre, Florida, USA.

a process which, in the Protestant church, basically began with the Reformation.

Nowadays, both denominations are mainly interested in promoting the unhindered and active participation of the whole congregation in the liturgy. Functional considerations call for optimum visibility and audibility from everywhere. As far as the congregation is concerned, the space characteristics depend on two factors: on the size of the congregation, and on the orientation of the seats towards the liturgical centres.

The number regarded as optimal by the ecclesiastical authorities is between 200 to 450 seats. The following considerations, unrelated to statistical and economic factors, play a role in determining the seating capacity: If the capacity is reduced, community participation is intensified, but the feeling of belonging to a large congregation is lost. If it is increased, this will give rise to acoustic and visual difficulties – acoustic amplification is required which does not make for improved personal contact between priest and congregation.

As the outer dimensions of churches are diminished, the altar is advanced (in keeping with the ideas of the 20's)

tuary, for God's Word reigns there. God's Word alone sanctifies the place and makes it His home and abode".[16]

The next step after the democratisation of the church is the "domestication"[6] of the church building. We no longer like to see the might of the Church *ecclesia triumphans* manifested in the church building; the church has assumed an historic dimension. A super-human scale is no longer recognised; such a scale may be needed for technical reasons, e.g. for the launching pad at Cape Kennedy (Ill. 41); for a church, however, such a scale seems inappropriate to us. Moreover, the time is past when the church could only be entered in one's Sunday suit. The distinctions between liturgy and life, between sacral and secular are outdated. If the churches are to be open to all people on all occasions, the design calls for a further modification: a social area should be linked directly with the church. Not unlike Frank Lloyd Wright's concept of the Unitarian Church, this room serves as an extended porch, foyer, parish hall and, on special occasions, as an extension of the church itself. Here, those taking part in the act of worship can, subsequently or at other times, come together.

39

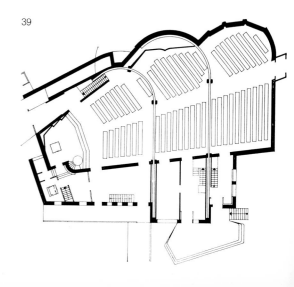

wendig, die den persönlichen Kontakt Priester–Gemeinde nicht eben intensiviert. Gleichzeitig mit der Verringerung der äußeren Abmessungen rückt in Anlehnung an Ideen der zwanziger Jahre der Altar immer entschiedener in das Zentrum der Gemeinde. Für die katholische Kirche, in der auch die anderen liturgischen Funktionsorte und der Ablauf des Gottesdienstes neu geordnet werden, ist damit eine geradezu revolutionäre Umformung des Kultes verbunden: Das Geheimnis wird geöffnet, der Priester verdeckt die Kulthandlung nicht mehr mit seinem Körper vor der Gemeinde, sondern er zelebriert im Angesicht der Gemeinde, »versus populum«, hinter dem Altar stehend. Dieser neuen Form der Kulthandlung zuliebe wurden sogar uralte Kirchen völlig umgebaut – beispielsweise wurde in Vorwegnahme der neuen liturgischen Vorstellungen im gotischen Dom zu Münster der Altar aus dem Hochchor herausgenommen und in die helle Vierung gestellt (Emil Steffan, 1955).

Zweifel an der Wirksamkeit der baulichen Gestalt kommen auf.[15] »Die Mahl-Feier, weil sie sich wesentlich in den brüderlich gegenwärtigen Menschen vollzieht, kann in jedem Raum stattfinden, im Wohnzimmer, im Mehrzweckraum, im Keller, im Freien, im eigenen Gottesdienstraum, das heißt, eine sakrale Anlage ist von der Sache her nicht erforderlich.«[13] Das hat Ähnlichkeit mit Luthers Wort: »Wenn auch unter einer grünen Linde oder Weide gepredigt würde, so hieße doch derselbe Ort Gottes Wohnung und Stätte, denn Gottes Wort regiert daselbst. Gottes Wort allein macht die Stätte heilig und zu Gottes Stätte und Hause.«[16]

Der nächste Schritt nach der Demokratisierung der Kirche ist die »Domestizierung«[6] des Kirchengebäudes. Die Macht der Kirche (ecclesia triumphans) möchten wir nicht mehr in einem Kirchenbau dokumentiert sehen, sie ist zu einer historischen Größe geworden. Ein übermenschlicher Maßstab wird nicht mehr anerkannt; er kann sich aus einer technischen Funktion ergeben wie beim Montageturm in Cape Kennedy (Abb. 41), beim Kirchenbau erscheint er uns unangemessen. Die Kirche kann auch nicht mehr so konzipiert sein, daß man sie nur im Sonntagsanzug betritt. Die Trennung von Liturgie und Leben, der Unterschied von sakral und profan wird aufgehoben. Wenn die Kirchen allen Menschen bei allen Gelegenheiten offen stehen sollen, ergibt sich eine weitere Änderung des Raumprogramms: Ein Sozialraum wird direkt an die Kirche angeschlossen. Nicht un-

41

ähnlich dem Konzept der Unitarierkirche von F. L. Wright dient er als erweiterter Windfang, Foyer, Gemeinderaum und als Erweiterung des Kirchenraums bei Festgottesdiensten. Hier können die Teilnehmer im Anschluß an den Gottesdienst und zu anderen Zeiten zusammenkommen und Kontakte finden.

Ein weiterer Schritt ist die Mehrfachnutzung des Kirchenraums. Er soll also nicht mehr ausschließlich dem Gottesdienst allein dienen, sondern es sollen auch alle anderen Aktivitäten der Gemeinde im gleichen Raum stattfinden. Ein solcher flexibler Raum (Abb. 42–44, 45) bietet dem Pfarrer Möglichkeiten spontaner Aktion. Es ist daran gedacht, außer den Gottesdiensten beispielsweise auch Gemeindevertretungswahlen, Kunstausstellungen, Konzerte, Feiern jeder Art im Kirchenraum stattfinden zu lassen. Die Ursache für diese Entwicklung zur Mehrfachnutzung ist nicht nur in dem unserer Zeit eigenen Sinn für Ökonomie zu suchen, sondern auch in der Phobie vor institutioneller, räumlicher Verfestigung, die der schnellen Wandelbarkeit der Anschauungen widersprechen würde. Wenn das Sakrale und das Profane zunächst gleichgesetzt wurden, so wird nun eine stärkere Gewichtung des Profanen deutlich.

Dementsprechend entsteht auch ein anderes Verhältnis von Kunst und Kirche. Die traditionellen Symbole kirchlicher Kunst werden meistens nur noch als Dekoration verstanden. Aus den neuesten Kirchen ist der Beitrag des Künstlers fast ganz verschwunden, und die Kunst wird erst dann ihren Platz in der Kirche wiederfinden, wenn die Kirche gewillt ist, die Kunst als eine der entscheidenden Möglichkeiten der Identifikation mit der eigenen Zeit zu sehen.

Zu den beschriebenen Tendenzen leisteten die europäischen Randländer England, Holland und Österreich einen besonderen Beitrag.

Zweifellos kommen in England die Einflüsse nicht allein aus einem artikulierten Bedürfnis der Religionsgemeinschaft. Vielmehr hat auch die Entwicklung anderer Bereiche ihren Anteil daran. Englische Schulen nach dem Krieg wurden überwiegend mit flexiblen Bausystemen errichtet. Die Anlage der Hall, also des zentralen Kommunikationsraumes, mag manchen Architekten zu einem analogen Kirchenraum angeregt haben. Auch die gelegentliche Verwendung von Bausystemen mag vom Schulbau her beeinflußt sein. Die anglikanische Kirche hat diese Ideen vor allem in Hodge Hill, Birmingham,

37, 38. Kapelle des Illinois Institute of Technology, Chicago, 1952; Architekt: Ludwig Mies van der Rohe.
39. Vuoksenniska-Kirche, Imatra, Finnland, 1956–1959; Architekt: Alvar Aalto.
40. Evangelisches Gemeindezentrum in Stuttgart-Sonnenberg, 1963–1966; Architekt: Ernst Gisel.
41. Kennedy Space Center, Florida, USA.

40

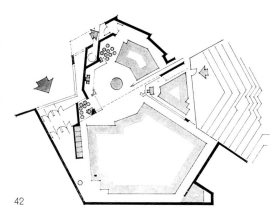

42

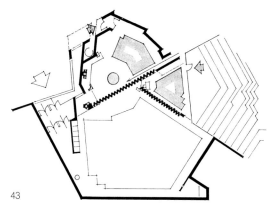

43

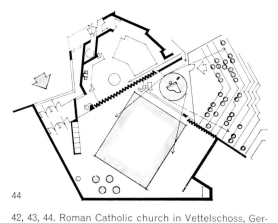

44

42, 43, 44. Roman Catholic church in Vettelschoss, Germany, 1970, Project; Architect: Justus Dahinden.
45. Parish centre of the Eisteichsiedlung, Graz, 1968 to 1970; Architect: Ferdinand Schuster.
46, 47, 48. St. Philips and St. James, Hodge Hill, Birmingham, England, 1963–1966; Architect: Martin Purdy.
49, 50. Church in Driebergen, Holland, Project; Architect: Aldo van Eyck.

A further step is the multi-purpose utilisation of the church interior itself which is no longer exclusively designed for divine service but also for all other activities of the congregation. Such a flexible space (Ill. 42–44, 45) offers the priest more opportunities for sponsoring spontaneous activities. The church might thus be used not only for public worship but also, e.g., for parish council elections, art exhibitions, concerts, celebrations of any kind. This trend towards the multi-purpose church is due not only to the economic mentality of our time but also to a modern aversion against "institutionalisation" which would not be in keeping with the rapidity with which our attitudes are liable to change. If, initially, the sacral and secular elements of community life were regarded as equally important, one is now inclined to place greater emphasis on the secular aspects.

Correspondingly, there is also a change in the relationship between art and church. In general, the traditional symbols of ecclesiastic art are merely regarded as pieces of decoration. From the latest churches, the artist's contribution has almost wholly disappeared, and art will only regain its place in the Church when the Church is willing to regard art as one of the vital means of identification with its own time.

In all these trends, certain countries on the fringe of Europe, such as England, the Netherlands and Austria, have made special contributions.

In England, these outgrowths undoubtedly do not stem solely from an articulation of the wants of the religious community; indeed, the development derives a large portion from other spheres. A predominate number of British post-war schools were erected with flexible building systems. The provision of a "hall", i.e. a central concourse, may have inspired some architects to adopt a similar spatial design for churches. Even the occasional use of building systems may have been influenced by school construction. The Anglican church has promoted these ideas mainly at Hodge Hill, Birmingham (Ill. 46–48). The main hall of this church centre is used for public worship as well as for theatre performances and dances; "Amen" and "Cheers" have equal rights.

In the Netherlands, religion has become a matter of national interest. In the long term, the non-conformist ideas of the Dutch Roman Catholics in opposition to the "established" Church have provided much inspiration to religious life and therefore also to modern church design. "A church suited for religiosity – a church also suited for the secular", this is how the architects van der Grinten and Heijdenrijk refer to their buildings. They try to comply with the paradoxical requirement of combining concentration with openness by placing the central space on a lower level than the outer concourse which anyone can use as an open passage. Aldo van Eyck attempted, in his competition design for a new church in

Driebergen (Ill. 49, 50), to place all functional premises on the same level yet so that they can be optionally segregated though remaining in communication with each other to form, if desired, a single large space. With inwards orientated, circular rooms lit up by narrow shed-type roofs rising at 45°, a corresponding conglomerate of premises has been created.

Of a more evolutionary character is the Austrian contribution to church design. Relatively few churches are built on the strength of profound theoretical preparatory work. The formal severity of the new buildings (Ill. 52) – symmetry is virtually obligatory – may well be interpreted as a confrontation with the traditions of a country abounding in old churches. Even the modern ideas of flexibility and variability of space become, in Austrian churches, a celebration in space. The ultimate consequence is the "mobile" church designed by Ottokar Uhl. The reason given by the architect for the preplanned dismantling of the church is that "the centres of gravity of residential areas have a tendency to shift rapidly"[17], and that his churches can then follow that shift. The mobile church should be adaptable to the mobility of society. A mentality based on technical and industrial principles has here been logically extended to church design.

In respect to town planning, the traditional trend has been reversed: If, up to the Middle Ages, European cities used to crystallise around the core of church and abbey, the modern church follows the modern town which owes its existence to different initiatives. This is reflected in the shape of the church: An impression of domesticity is aimed at (Steffan), the scale of the bungalow is adopted (v. d. Grinten and Heijdenrijk); the church is regarded as part of the leisure-time centre (Hodge Hill), or is erected as a prefabricated hall which can be assembled and dismantled as required (Uhl). The details, too, are regarded differently: For instance, the altar of the Roman Catholic Church – conceived in pre-Council days as a stone boulder or "mensa" firmly embedded in grown soil – has nowadays often become a table which can easily be removed (Ill. 51).

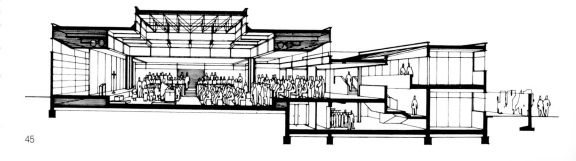

45

(Abb. 46–48) gefördert. Im Hauptraum dieses kirchlichen Zentrums finden sowohl Gottesdienst als auch Theateraufführungen und Tanzveranstaltungen statt, das »Amen und das Prost« sind hier gleichberechtigt.

In Holland ist die Sache der Religion zu einer Art nationalen Interesses geworden. Die zur institutionellen Kirche gegensätzlichen Auffassungen der holländischen Katholiken erwiesen sich auf die Dauer für das religiöse Leben und damit auch für den neuen Kirchenbau als außerordentlich anregend. »Eine Kirche, geeignet für das Religiöse – eine Kirche, geeignet für das Profane«, schreiben die Architekten van der Grinten und Heijdenrijk zu ihren Bauten. Sie versuchen der Paradoxie der Forderung, Konzentration mit Offenheit zu verbinden, nachzukommen, indem sie den Feierraum tiefer legen als den – für jeden Durchgehenden offenen – Umgang. Aldo van Eyck dagegen hatte in seinem Wettbewerbsentwurf für eine neue Kirche in Driebergen (Abb. 49, 50) den Versuch unternommen, alle Funktionsräume auf eine Ebene zu legen, sie bedarfsweise abtrennbar zu machen und sie in eine »interkommunikative« Beziehung zu setzen, um sie zu einem großen Raum zusammenziehen zu können. Durch nach innen orientierte kreisförmige Räume, die mit schmalen 45-Grad-Sheds beleuchtet sind, wird ein entsprechendes Raumkonglomerat geschaffen.

Von mehr evolutionärem Charakter ist der österreichische Beitrag zum Kirchenbau. Mit einer fundierten theoretischen Vorarbeit werden relativ wenige Kirchen gebaut. Die formale Strenge der neuen Anlagen (Abb. 52) – die Symmetrie ist beinahe obligatorisch – darf wohl als Auseinandersetzung mit den Traditionen des an alten Kirchen überreichen Landes gedeutet werden. Auch die neuen Raum-Ideen der Flexibilität und Variabilität werden in österreichischen Kirchen zur räumlichen Zelebration. Letzte Konsequenz sind die demontablen Kirchen von Ottokar Uhl. Als Grund für den eingeplanten Abbau gibt der Architekt an, daß sich »Siedlungsschwerpunkte rasch verschieben«[17] und seine Kirchen dann diese Verschiebung mitmachen können. Die mobile Kirche soll der Mobilität der Gesellschaft angepaßt werden können. Das Denken in technisch-industriellen Maximen ist hier konsequent auf den Kirchenbau übertragen worden.

In städtebaulicher Hinsicht ist eine Umkehrung der Entwicklung erreicht: Kristallisierte sich bis zum Mittelalter die europäische Siedlung um den kirchlich-klösterlichen Kern, so folgt heute die Kirche den sich aus anderen Initiativen bildenden Siedlungszentren. Damit geht die Gestalt der Kirche konform: So wird der Charakter des Häuslichen angestrebt (Steffan), der Bungalow-Maßstab übernommen (v. d. Grinten und Heijdenrijk), der Raum als Teil des Freizeit-Centers betrachtet (Hodge Hill) und die Kirche als Elementbau-Halle verwendet, um bei Bedarf auf- und abgebaut zu werden (Uhl). Auch das Detail wird anders aufgefaßt: So ist der Altar der katholi-

42, 43, 44. Katholische Kirche in Vettelschoß, Rheinland-Pfalz, 1970, Projekt; Architekt: Justus Dahinden.
45. Seelsorgezentrum der Eisteichsiedlung, Graz, 1968 bis 1970; Architekt: Ferdinand Schuster.
46, 47, 48. St. Philips and St. James, Hodge Hill, Birmingham, England, 1963–1966; Architekt: Martin Purdy.
49, 50. Kirche in Driebergen, Holland, Projekt; Architekt: Aldo van Eyck.

46

47

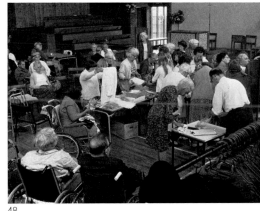

48

schen Kirche, bis zum Konzil als Natursteinblock oder -Mensa vorgeschrieben, dessen Fundament in die gewachsene Erde gegründet sein mußte, heute oft zu einem leicht wegräumbaren Tisch geworden (Abb. 51).

Die Kirche war in der Vergangenheit der größte Bau der Stadt, der Turm das Superzeichen des in die Welt wirkenden christlichen Glaubens. Ihr Informationsangebot bewegte sich in zwei Ebenen: Sie war die zentrale Vermittlerin von geistiger Information spekulativen Inhalts, und sie war eine ästhetische Realisation von hohem Informationswert. Für unseren Assoziationshorizont wurde in der Gotik die größte Übereinstimmung von Zeichen und Bedeutung erreicht. Nicht zuletzt deshalb ist für uns die gotische Kirche (Abb. 53) noch immer der Inbegriff des christlichen Sakralbaues, dessen semantische Norm[18] (Abb. 54).

Mit der Kirche des neuen Typs ist eine gewisse semantische Schwierigkeit zu überwinden: Sie sieht kaum

50

49

51

In the past, the church used to be the tallest building in town, its spire the supreme symbol of the world-dominating Christian faith. The information offered by the church was on two levels: The church served as the central exchange of spiritual information of a speculative nature, and it represented an aesthetic realisation of high informative values. Within the horizon of our associations, it was the Gothic style which achieved the greatest symbiosis of symbol and meaning. This may well be one of the most important reasons why, to us, the Gothic church (Ill. 53) still represents the embodiment of a Christian sacral building and its semantic standard[18] (Ill. 54).

With churches of the modern type, a certain semantic difficulty has to be overcome: The appearance of the building is hardly any longer that of a "church". It is no longer a super-building but just a building which may not even be as high as the four-storey blocks of flats surrounding it. Often, it tries to assume the external appearance of residential buildings, to assimilate to the "total housing environment" (Förderer), even to become an integral part of the residential structure, e.g. where in Sweden in the 1950s[19], the church was built into blocks of apartment houses. The information on offer – considered on both levels – is less strong or at least no longer so clear. The church no longer represents a central source of information of a speculative type, but just one of the sources of such information, – and at the same time, something else. It has become a bearer of variegated information contents. Even the spire – the super-symbol – has disappeared. The church has renounced its clear, semantic tenor and is content to feature certain building components such as attractive entrances and their links with pedestrian and shopping precincts.

In many of these churches, it is not only the spiritual-speculative purpose but also the aesthetic ambition which has faded. They try to escape aesthetic criticism and would like, first of all, to be judged by political and social criteria. This is in contrast to the criteria applied to the majority of the older churches. If one church wants to be judged by social criteria and the other by aesthetic criteria, is this not ultimately due to a split in our sense of values?

It is here that a future task of church design becomes apparent – a task which is, at the same time, incumbent on future society – to find a new inter-relation between social and aesthetic expressions.

Church Architecture of the Future

Forecasts must mainly take the form of conclusions drawn from the present stage of the process, now arrested. But who will deny that forecasts also contain an element of wishful thinking, reflecting our own ideas of future society.

From the theological aspect, the aim may well be to aspire to congregational activities which can be, and seek to be, appreciated also by a guest – and a guest not only from among people of the same creed. It is questionable whether, in that case, the church can still remain a mere parish church. Nowadays, the "believer" is no longer primarily concerned with his church but is also interested in a number of other institutions; in fact, his relationship to his church is generally confined to that of a "religion-consuming" and "contribution-paying" member[20]. The structure of the European churches is also liable to undergo changes for this further reason: Their role as a power supported from fiscal revenue will recede in favour of a service promoted by active participation. In the interest of a positive pluralism, each parish priest himself would then have to develop the programme of his congregation and to ensure its financial backing. From an architectural aspect, the church buildings may be expected to become more and more a spatial manifestation of the life of the congregation.

A word on the subject of transcendency: Especially in the Anglo-Saxon and Scandinavian countries, this notion is nowadays more and more eliminated from the church. But if, as a result of exclusive demands for the social activities of the congregation, the fundamental religious question of the meaning of Man's existence should become completely obscured, the Church will lose its *raison d'être* as a unique, irreplaceable institution; social activities alone can also be carried out by other benevolent institutions. Certainly, transcendental asceticism, just as much as aesthetic asceticism, is no doubt a reflection of the prevailing positivist rationalism. The more this mood affects the Church, the more important will it be to persist in that which defies rationalisation. One practical aid in keeping the basic religious tenets alive is to provide small cubicles for solitary meditation.

53

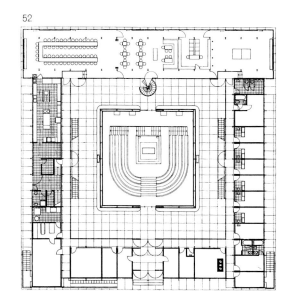

52

noch wie eine »Kirche« aus. Sie stellt sich nicht mehr als Superbau dar, sondern als Bau, der nicht einmal so hoch ist wie die viergeschossigen Wohnhäuser, die sie umgeben. Oft übernimmt sie Wohnbauformen, versucht sich dem »totalen Wohnmilieu« (Förderer) anzugleichen, wird womöglich Teil der Wohnstruktur, wenn sie beispielsweise wie im Schweden der fünfziger Jahre[19] in Wohnblocks eingebaut wird. Das Informationsangebot – in beiden Ebenen betrachtet – ist schwächer, oder mindestens nicht mehr so eindeutig. Kirche ist nicht mehr zentrale Information spekulativen Inhalts, sondern eine dieser Informationsquellen und zugleich anderes. Sie ist Träger unterschiedlicher Informationsgehalte geworden. Auch der Turm – das Superzeichen – ist verschwunden. Die Kirche verzichtet auf eindeutigen semantischen Gehalt und beschränkt sich auf die betonte Ausbildung einzelner Bauteile, wie zum Beispiel auf einladende Eingänge und deren Anbindung an die Fußgänger- und Einkaufszone.

In vielen dieser Kirchen tritt neben dem geistig-spekulativen auch der ästhetische Anspruch zurück. Sie versuchen, sich der ästhetischen Kritik zu entziehen, wollen vor allem mit politisch-sozialen Kriterien gemessen werden. Umgekehrt verhält es sich bei der Mehrzahl der älteren Kirchen. Wenn die eine Kirche mit sozialen und die andere mit ästhetischen Kriterien gemessen werden will, liegt das nicht zuletzt an einer Spaltung des Wertsystems?

Hier zeichnet sich eine Aufgabe des Kirchenbaues der Zukunft ab, die zugleich eine Aufgabe der zukünftigen Gesellschaft ist: zu einer neuen Interferenz zwischen sozialen und ästhetischen Äußerungen zu finden.

51. St. Jan, Eindhoven, Holland, 1964–1969; Architekten: G. J. van der Grinten, L. J. Heijdenrijk.
52. Kolleg St. Josef, Salzburg-Aigen, 1961–1964; Architekten: Arbeitsgruppe 4 (W. Holzbauer, F. Kurrent, J. Spalt).
53. Freiburger Münster.
54. Saint-Pierre, Firminy, 1963, Projekt; Architekt: Le Corbusier.

51. St. Jan, Eindhoven, Holland, 1964–1969; Architects: G. J. van der Grinten, L. J. Heijdenrijk.
52. Kolleg St. Josef, Salzburg-Aigen, 1961–1964; Architects: Arbeitsgruppe 4 (W. Holzbauer, F. Kurrent, J. Spalt).
53. Freiburger Münster.
54. Saint-Pierre, Firminy, 1963, Project; Architect: Le Corbusier.

Kirchenbau der Zukunft

Prognosen sind vor allem Folgerungen aus dem jetzt gestoppten Stadium des Prozesses. In Prognosen – wer will das leugnen – schlagen sich aber auch die Wünsche nieder, die man für die kommende Gesellschaft hegt.

Von theologischer Seite aus gesehen dürfte eine Gemeindeaktivität angestrebt werden, die auch als Gast erlebt werden kann und will, Gast nicht nur innerhalb der eigenen Religion. Es ist fraglich, ob Kirche dann noch Amtskirche sein kann. Heute engagiert sich der »Gläubige« nicht mehr überwiegend für seine Kirche, sondern für eine Menge anderer Einrichtungen; sein Verhältnis zur Kirche ist sogar meistens nur das des Beitrag zahlenden, Religion konsumierenden Mitglieds.[20] Möglicherweise werden sich die europäischen Kirchen in ihrer Struktur auch deshalb ändern: Sie werden weniger durch staatliche Steuereinnahme unterstützte Macht als vielmehr durch engagierte Teilnahme geförderter Dienst sein. Im Sinne eines positiven Pluralismus würde dann jeder Pfarrer selbst das Programm seiner Gemeinde entwickeln und auch für dessen Finanzierung sorgen. Auf die Architektur bezogen kann man erwarten, daß Kirchenbau immer mehr zur räumlichen Manifestation des Lebens der Gemeinde wird.

Ein Wort noch zur Transzendenz: Diese wird heute, besonders in den angelsächsischen und skandinavischen Ländern, mehr und mehr aus der Kirche ausgeschieden. Wenn jedoch unter einem total gewordenen Anspruch der sozialen Aktivität der Gemeinde die eigentlich religiöse Frage nach dem Sinn des Seins verschüttet wird, verliert die Kirche ihre Daseinsberechtigung als eigene, nicht zu ersetzende Instanz; Sozialarbeit allein wird ebensogut von anderen gemeinnützigen Institutionen betrieben. Sicherlich ist die transzendentale Askese, genauso wie die ästhetische, Ausdruck des herrschenden positivistischen Rationalismus. Je mehr dieser auf die Kirche übergreift, desto wichtiger wird gerade das Beharren auf dem Nichtrationalisierbaren. Baulich könnten kleine Meditationszellen dazu beitragen, den Urgrund des Religiösen offenzuhalten.

54

Notes

[1] L. J. Heijdenrijk, Description of the project for the church in Swalmen.
[2] W. Strolz, "Kann Gott wiederentdeckt werden?", *Neue Zürcher Zeitung,* 1970, 365.
[3] Alexander Mitscherlich, *Die Unwirtlichkeit unserer Städte – Anstiftung zum Unfrieden,* Frankfurt, 1965 (edition suhrkamp, 123).
[4] Max Scholch, "Alte und neue kirchliche Richtungen", in: Hanno Helbling (Ed.), *Kirche im Wandel der Zeit,* Zürich, 1969.
[5] Hubertus Halbfas, "Heute würde Jesus in der Kirche als Störenfried gehasst", *Der Spiegel,* 1970, 27.
[6] Lance Wright, in: *Architectural Review,* 877 (March, 1970).
[7] Reinhard Gieselmann und Werner Aebli, *Kirchenbau,* Zürich, 1960.
[8] *Der Volks-Brockhaus,* Wiesbaden, 1959.
[9] Romano Guardini, *Vom Geist der Liturgie,* 1918.
[10] cf.: Max Rosner, "Konzil und Kirchenbau", *Baumeister,* 1966, 1.
[11] Rudolf Schwarz, *Vom Bau der Kirche,* Heidelberg, 1947. The same, *Kirchenbau,* Heidelberg, 1960.
[12] Reinhard Gieselmann, "Eine Kirche ist eine Kirche", in: Erdmann Kimmig (selections and introduction), *Kirchen,* Stuttgart und Bern, 1968 (architektur wettbewerbe, 54).
[13] K. Ledergerber, "Das Heilige ist nicht mehr repräsentativ", *Publik Visuell,* 1969, 50.
[14] cf.: *Instruktionen zur ordnungsgemäßen Durchführung der Konstitution über die hl. Liturgie,* Regensburg, 1964.
[15] Siegfried Bachmann, in: Erdmann Kimmig, *op. cit.*
[16] from: Eisenhofer, *Handbuch,* 1912.
[17] Ottokar Uhl, "Erfahrungen mit einer demontierbaren Kirche", *Christliche Kunstblätter,* 1965, 2.
[18] cf.: Manfred Kienle, *Aesthetische Probleme der Architektur unter dem Aspekt der Informationsästhetik,* Quickborn, 1967.
[19] In Sweden, this was due to financial reasons; public funds for church construction were only obtainable in conjunction with housing developments.
[20] cf.: "Die Sendung des Christen", *Neue Zürcher Zeitung,* 1969, 373.

General Literature

G. E. Kidder Smith, *New Churches in Europe,* London, 1964.
Christliche Kunstblätter, Linz; this journal is particularly concerned with the development of Roman-Catholic church architecture after the Second Vatican Council.
Walter Förderer, *Kirchenbau für heute und morgen,* Würzburg, 1964.
H. Lamm, "Synagogenbau gestern und heute", *Baumeister,* 1966, 1.
Justus Dahinden, "Kirchenbau als gestalterische Aufgabe", *db – Deutsche Bauzeitung,* 1966, 3.
P. H. Muck, "Die Gestaltung des Kirchenraumes nach der Liturgiereform", *Lebendiger Gottesdienst,* 1966, 12.
Otto H. Senn, "Gestalt gehört zum Wesen der Kirche", *Bauwelt,* 1968, 9.

Anmerkungen

[1] L. J. Heijdenrijk, Projekterläuterung zur Kirche in Swalmen.
[2] W. Strolz, »Kann Gott wiederentdeckt werden?«, *Neue Zürcher Zeitung,* 1970, 365.
[3] Alexander Mitscherlich, *Die Unwirtlichkeit unserer Städte-Anstiftung zum Unfrieden,* Frankfurt, 1965 *(edition suhrkamp,* 123).
[4] Max Scholch, »Alte und neue kirchliche Richtungen«, in: Hanno Helbling (Hrsg.), *Kirche im Wandel der Zeit,* Zürich, 1969.
[5] Hubertus Halbfas, »Heute würde Jesus in der Kirche als Störenfried gehaßt«, *Der Spiegel,* 1970, 27.
[6] Lance Wright, in: *Architectural Review,* 877 (März 1970).
[7] Reinhard Gieselmann und Werner Aebli, *Kirchenbau,* Zürich, 1960.
[8] *Der Volks-Brockhaus,* Wiesbaden, 1959.
[9] Romano Guardini, *Vom Geist der Liturgie,* 1918.
[10] Vergl. hierzu: Max Rosner, »Konzil und Kirchenbau«, *Baumeister,* 1966, 1.
[11] Rudolf Schwarz, *Vom Bau der Kirche,* Heidelberg, 1947. Ders., *Kirchenbau,* Heidelberg, 1960.
[12] Reinhard Gieselmann, »Eine Kirche ist eine Kirche«, in: Erdmann Kimmig (Auswahl und Einleitung), *Kirchen,* Stuttgart und Bern, 1968 *(architektur wettbewerbe,* 54).
[13] K. Ledergerber, »Das Heilige ist nicht mehr repräsentativ«, *Publik Visuell,* 1969, 50.
[14] Vergl.: *Instruktionen zur ordnungsgemäßen Durchführung der Konstitution über die hl. Liturgie,* Regensburg, 1964.
[15] Siegfried Bachmann, in: Erdmann Kimmig, *op. cit.*
[16] Nach: Eisenhofer, *Handbuch,* 1912.
[17] Ottokar Uhl, »Erfahrungen mit einer demontierbaren Kirche«, *Christliche Kunstblätter,* 1965, 2.
[18] Vergl. hierzu: Manfred Kienle, *Ästhetische Probleme der Architektur unter dem Aspekt der Informationsästhetik,* Quickborn, 1967.
[19] In Schweden führten finanztechnische Gründe hierzu; öffentliche Mittel für Kirchenbau konnten nur in Verbindung mit Wohnbau erlangt werden.
[20] Vergl.: H. Ott, »Die Sendung des Christen«, *Neue Zürcher Zeitung,* 1969, 373.

Allgemeine Literatur

G. E. Kidder Smith, *New Churches in Europe,* London, 1964; deutsche Ausgabe: G. E. Kidder Smith, *Neuer Kirchenbau in Europa,* Stuttgart, 1964.
Christliche Kunstblätter, Linz; diese Zeitschrift setzt sich im besonderen Maße für die postkonziliare Bewegung im katholischen Kirchenbau ein.
Walter Förderer, *Kirchenbau für heute und morgen,* Würzburg, 1964.
H. Lamm, »Synagogenbau gestern und heute«, *Baumeister,* 1966, 1.
Justus Dahinden, »Kirchenbau als gesellschaftliche Aufgabe«, *db – Deutsche Bauzeitung,* 1966, 3.
P. H. Muck, »Die Gestaltung des Kirchenraumes nach der Liturgiereform«, *Lebendiger Gottesdienst,* 1966, 12.
Otto H. Senn, »Gestalt gehört zum Wesen der Kirche«, *Bauwelt,* 1968, 9.

Note to the Architectural Descriptions

All the buildings selected to be included in the following documentation stem from the time after 1960. During the decade from 1960 to 1970, the transformation of church design proceeded in an exemplary manner. In presenting the projects, a purely chronological order was not always found to correspond to a logical sequence. The examples have therefore been arranged in accordance with the morphology of their layout plans, and have been divided into three sections.

The first section comprises churches of predominantly longitudinal shape. Although the overall concepts of these churches may show many varieties, it is still derived from the traditional idea of the nave.

The second section brings churches where the plan shows a transverse emphasis. In these churches, the attempt has been made to obtain a closer association between congregation and altar. They also include compact structures (Disse, Rau) which do not contain a central space in keeping with this desire but can rather be regarded as a transitional form towards the transverse design.

Churches with centralised layout are combined in the third section. The term "central" must at once be qualified. Despite all the democratic attempts to make the altar rites visible, the space behind the altar is found to be unsuitable for the congregation. However closely the congregation may be gathered around the altar, the ring is hardly ever closed entirely. One exception, because of its dual function, is the Benedictine Church in Sarnen.

Zur Bautensammlung

Die in die folgende Dokumentation aufgenommenen Bauten stammen alle aus der Zeit nach 1960. In den Jahren von 1960 bis 1970 vollzieht sich die Wandlung des Kirchenbaus in exemplarischer Weise. Bei der Ordnung der Projekte erwies sich eine rein zeitliche Einteilung nicht immer als logische Abfolge. Deshalb wurden die Beispiele grundriß-morphologisch geordnet und in drei Abschnitte aufgeteilt.

Im ersten Abschnitt sind Kirchen mit einer Längstendenz des Raumes zusammengefaßt. Wenn auch ihre Gesamtform oft alle Freiheit hat, folgt sie doch der traditionellen Idee vom Kirchenraum.

Im zweiten Abschnitt sind Kirchen mit einer Quertendenz des Raumes versammelt. Es sind Räume, in denen eine breitere Beziehung der Gläubigen zum Altar gesucht wird. Es sind auch zentrale Baukörper (Disse, Rau) darunter, aus denen kein entsprechend zentraler Raum abgeleitet wird, sondern die Übergangsform des Querraumes.

Die zentralen Raumkonzeptionen sind im dritten Abschnitt zusammengefaßt. Der Begriff »zentral« muß gleich eingeschränkt werden: Bei aller demokratischen Sichtbarmachung des Altargeschehens erweist sich der Platz hinter dem Altar für die Besucher als unbrauchbar. Wie eng der Ring der Teilnehmer um den Altar gezogen wird – er wird fast nie ganz geschlossen. Eine Ausnahme bildet – wegen ihrer Doppelfunktion – die Benediktiner-Kirche in Sarnen.

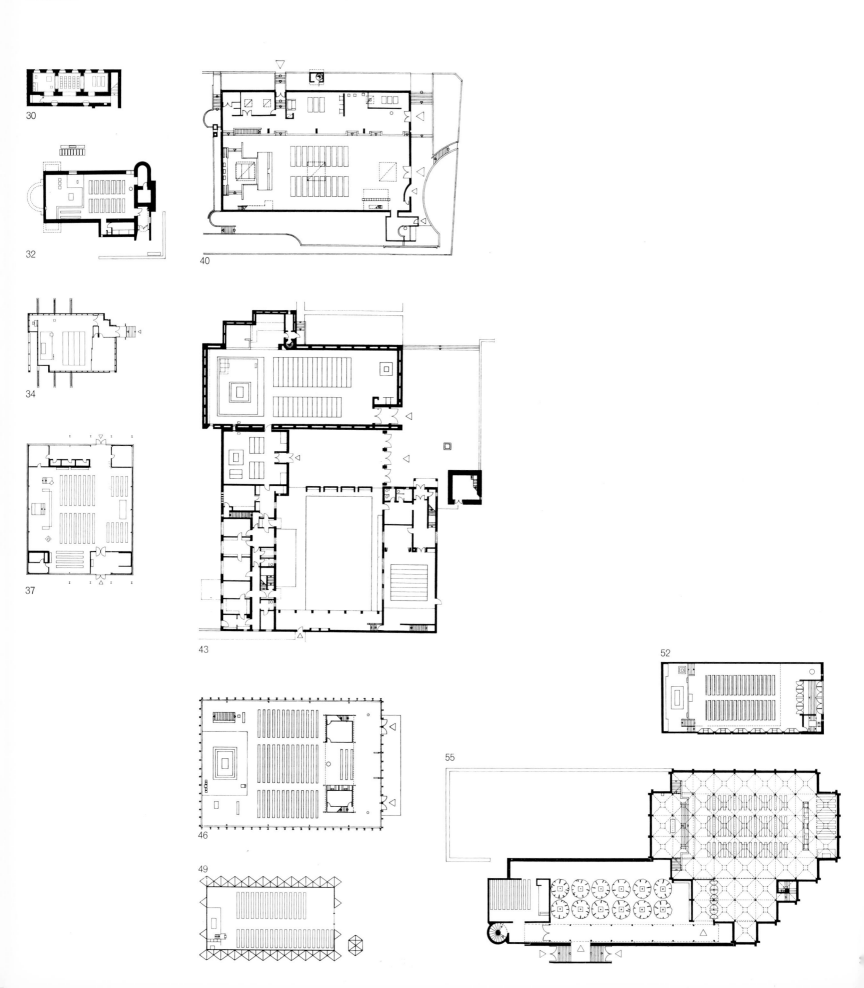

30

32

34

37

40

43

46

49

52

55

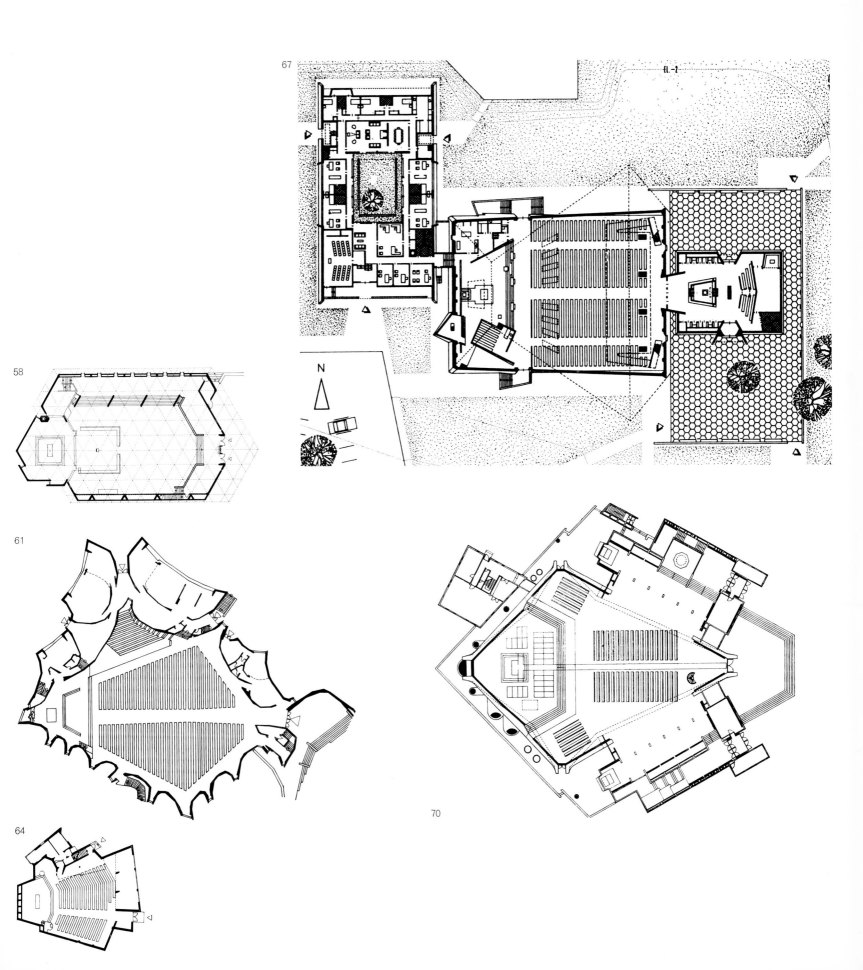

58

67

61

N

70

64

Chapel of the Capuchin Monastery in Bigorio,
Switzerland, 1969
Architects: Tita Carloni, Mario Botta

Kapelle des Kapuzinerklosters in Bigorio, Schweiz, 1969
Architekten: Tita Carloni, Mario Botta

1

The sub-structures of the monastery, which is situated on a slope, date back to the 18th century. They previously served as a shed for agricultural implements. The chapel was inserted in a matter-of-fact manner into the old rubble walls and brick vaults.

The porch is formed by an aisle integrated with the interior. The long chapel itself is divided into three parts in keeping with the given sub-structure. The altar room – with altar, tabernacle and ambo base made of concrete and with sedilia looking no different from the stools for the visitors – as well as the St. Mary's Chapel are placed a step higher. The stool seats in the middle section are varnished signal-red, the pews in St. Mary's Chapel radiantly blue. A black asphalt floor, detached from the walls, serves as an optical link for all the parts of the room, as does the rail carrying the light fittings and running through below the vaults.

Die Substrukturen des am Berghang liegenden Klosters stammen aus dem 18. Jahrhundert. Früher dienten sie zur Lagerung von landwirtschaftlichen Geräten. Die Kapelle wurde wie selbstverständlich in die alten Bruchsteinmauern und Backsteingewölbe eingefügt.

Ein zum Raum offener Gang bildet die Vorhalle. Der lange Kapellenraum selbst ist entsprechend der gegebenen Struktur dreigeteilt. Der Altarraum mit Altar, Tabernakel und Ambosockel aus Beton und mit Sedilien, die nicht anders aussehen als die Hocker der Besucher, liegt, ebenso wie die Marienkapelle, um eine Stufe erhöht. Die Hocker im Mittelteil sind signalrot, die Bänke in der Marienkapelle strahlend blau lackiert. Ein schwarzer, von den Wänden abgesetzter Asphaltboden hält optisch alle Raumteile zusammen, ebenso wie die unter den Gewölben durchlaufende Montageschiene mit den Serienleuchten.

1. Interior of the chapel with open gallery on the left·
The long room is smoothly articulated by a sunken middle section. Materials: Ochre-grey field stone walls, reddish brick vaults, black asphalt flooring, stools varnished in different colours, black seat cushions.
2. Plan and section. Key: 1 altar, 2 Chapel of the Virgin, 3 sacristy.
3. Altar space. Concrete cubes for altar, tabernacle stele, ambo and podium for the sedilia.
4. The brightly glazed windows give on an unobstructed view of the valley.

2

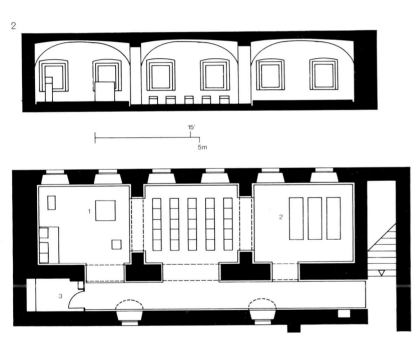

15'
5m

3

4

1. Kapellenraum, links anschließend der zum Raum offene Gang. Durch den abgesenkten Mittelteil wird der lange Raum angenehm gegliedert. Kräftig kontrastierende Farben und Materialien: ockergraue Feldsteinmauern, rötliches Backsteingewölbe, schwarzer Asphaltboden, farbig lackierte Hocker, schwarze Sitzkissen.

2. Grundriß und Schnitt. Legende: 1 Altar, 2 Marienkapelle, 3 Sakristei.

3. Altarraum. Betonkuben für Altar, Tabernakelstele, Ambo und Sedilienpodest.

4. Die hellverglasten Fenster geben den Blick in die Täler frei.

Notre-Dame, Sart-en-Fagnes, Belgium, 1965–1968
Architect: Roger Bastin

Notre-Dame, Sart-en-Fagnes, Belgien, 1965–1968
Architekt: Roger Bastin

Church architecture in Belgium shares the fate of general architecture in that country – the public is hardly interested in it. Modern buildings are noticed only if they are sensational. All the more valuable appears this little village church, designed by Roger Bastin.

This church is one of the few examples of an excellent restoration and an equally successful integration with the structure and scale of the village. The Neo-Gothic brick church was reduced in volume – spire, apse, roof over the nave – and its materials and shapes were adapted to the houses of the village. In this way, a building was created which is as simple as its surroundings without any romantic attempt to make itself more attractive.

The interior, with its visible roof structure and its simple cane chairs, holds no more than 140 people so that it has more the character of a devotional chapel than of a parish church.

Die Situation des Kirchenbaues in Belgien entspricht der dortigen Situation der Architektur – die Öffentlichkeit ist an ihr kaum interessiert. Moderne Bauten werden erst beachtet, wenn sie sensationell sind. Um so wertvoller erscheint die kleine Dorfkirche von Roger Bastin. Diese Kirche ist eines der wenigen Beispiele für eine hervorragende Restauration und für eine ebenso gelungene Einordnung in die Struktur und den Maßstab des Dorfes. Die neugotische Backsteinkirche wurde zum einen in den Volumina – Turm, Apsis, Dach über dem Schiff – reduziert, zum anderen im Material und in den Formen an die Häuser des Dorfes angeglichen. Es entstand ein Bau, der so einfach ist wie seine Umgebung, ohne sich ihr in romantischer Weise anzubiedern.

Der Innenraum mit seiner sichtbaren Dachkonstruktion und seinen einfachen geflochtenen Stühlen ist für nur 140 Personen bestimmt; dadurch hat er mehr den Charakter einer Andachtskapelle als den einer Gemeindekirche.

1, 3. The church in its village setting. The Neo-Gothic idea – no longer acceptable – has been replaced by a design well in keeping with the simple houses in the vicinity.
2. Plan and section with the outline of the old church shown in broken lines. Key: 1 altar, 2 choir, 3 baptistry, 4 confessional, 5 sacristy.
4. Daylight enters through a few windows and through sky-light ribbons on either side.

1

1, 3. Die Kirche im Dorf. Anstelle des – nicht mehr vorstellbaren – neugotischen Anspruches ist ein zu den einfachen Häusern gehörender Bau getreten.
2. Grundriß und Schnitt mit eingestricheltem Umriß der alten Kirche. Legende: 1 Altar, 2 Sänger, 3 Taufe, 4 Beichte, 5 Sakristei.
4. Wenige Fenster und beiderseitige Oberlichtbänder beleuchten den Kirchenraum.

2

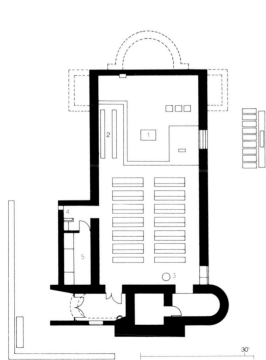

3

4

30'

10m

Heilig-Geist-Kirche, Schaftlach, Germany, 1966–1967
Architect: Hans Busso von Busse

Heilig-Geist-Kirche, Schaftlach, Bayern, 1966–1967
Architekt: Hans Busso von Busse

This church was designed for 80 people, with acommodation for another 30 people in the parish hall which can be combined with the church. From outside, the two parts can be discerned by the two opposing roofs.

Much of the plain, integral yet monumental effect of the church is derived from its compactness and from the masterly use of the material.

If the Protestant church aspires to a more intensive participation in divine worship, it will achieve its greatest success with small churches of this kind.

Für 80 Personen wurde diese Kirche gebaut, 30 weitere finden im Gemeindesaal Platz, der mit der Kirche verbunden werden kann. Beide Räume sind außen durch zwei gegenläufige Dachflächen ablesbar.

Die Kirche bezieht einen wesentlichen Teil ihrer schlichten, einheitlichen und monumentalen Wirkung aus ihrer Kompaktheit und aus der meisterhaften Anwendung des Materials.

Wenn die protestantische Kirche eine Intensivierung der Teilnahme am Gottesdienst anstrebt, wird sie den größten Erfolg in kleinen Kirchen wie dieser haben.

1

1. View from the forecourt. The roof is drained through two large spouts. On the right, the external supports of the high truss wall.

2. The timber boards are stained dark-brown, the doors are lacquered chestnut-brown.

3. Above the altar zone, the roof rises steeply. Most of the daylight enters through the high-level windows which are supplemented by a low-level window behind the altar (cf. Ill. 5).

4. The treatment of the facade detail is reminiscent of Norwegian timber structures.

1. Blick vom Kirchenvorplatz. Das Dach wird mit zwei großen Wasserspeiern entwässert. Rechts die Außenversteifung der hohen Fachwerkwand.

2. Die Verschalungen sind schwarzbraun imprägniert, die Türen kastanienrot lackiert.

3. Über dem Altarbereich steigt das Dach steil an. Der Raum wird vor allem durch die hochliegenden Fenster belichtet; ein »Unterlicht« hinter dem Altar ergänzt die Beleuchtung – vergleiche Abb. 5.

4. Die Fassade erinnert an norwegischen Holzbau.

2

3
4

5

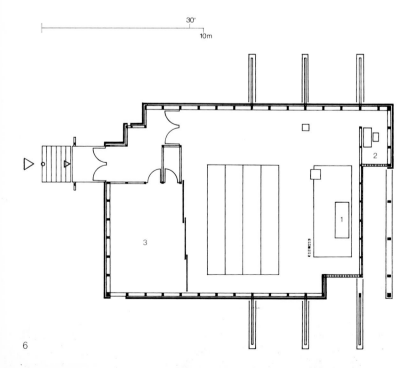

30'

10m

6

5. View from the parish hall into the very high interior of the church. The walls in the lower areas are lined with chestnut-brown panels.
6. Plan. Key: 1 altar, 2 sacristy, 3 parish room.

5. Blick aus dem Gemeindesaal in den sehr hohen Kirchenraum. Wandverkleidung im unteren Bereich mit kastanienroten Platten.
6. Grundriß. Legende: 1 Altar, 2 Sakristei, 3 Gemeinderaum.

Church in Haparanda, Sweden, 1964–1967
Architects: Alf Engström, Gunnar Landberg, Bengt Larson, Alvar Törneman

Kirche in Haparanda, Schweden, 1964–1967
Architekten: Alf Engström, Gunnar Landberg, Bengt Larson, Alvar Törneman

To achieve a dominating effect in the vastness of Northern Sweden, this church was given a great height.
The bearing structure is a steel framework. It is panelled with lightweight concrete slabs, externally insulated against the cold by mineral wool. The outer cladding consists of copper, chosen because of the difficult climatic conditions in the vicinity of the sea.
To prevent the formation of icicles and snow pockets, no eaves gutters have been provided. Rainwater can run off without hindrance on all the outer walls of the building, snow slides down the steeply sloped roofs or is blown away by the wind.
Inside, all the structural parts remain visible. Two huge wheels of lights suspended from the ridge set the scale for the height of the room and provide a link between the rows of pews which are separated by the central aisle.

Der Kirche wurde, um sie zu einem dominierenden Element in der Weite der nordschwedischen Landschaft zu machen, eine große Höhe gegeben.
Die Tragstruktur ist ein Stahlgerüst. Es wurde mit Leichtbetonplatten, die auf der Außenseite mit Mineralwolle gegen Kälte isoliert sind, ausgefacht. Für die äußere Verkleidung wählte man Kupfer – wegen der durch die Nähe der See bedingten schwierigen klimatischen Verhältnisse.
Um die Bildung von Eiszapfen und Schneetaschen zu verhindern, verzichtete man auf Dachrinnen. Der Regen kann ungehindert an allen Außenflächen des Baues ablaufen, und der Schnee rutscht von den stark geneigten Dachflächen oder wird vom Wind weggeblasen.
Im Inneren sind alle Konstruktionselemente sichtbar gelassen. Zwei mächtige Lichträder, die vom Dachfirst

herabhängen, relativieren die Höhe des Raumes und ziehen die durch den Mittelgang getrennten Bankreihen zusammen.

1. Forecourt, church and belfry.

1. Kirchenvorplatz Kirche und Glockenträger.

1

2
3

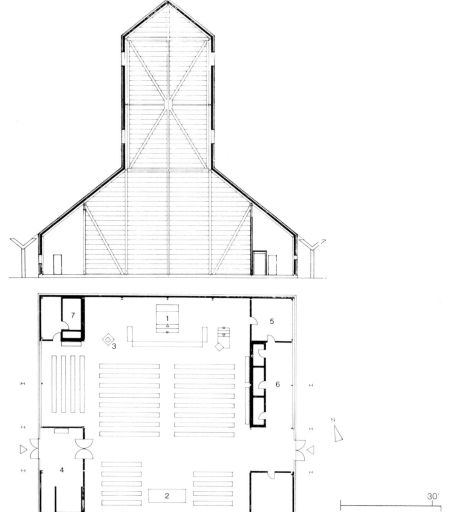

2. The church forms a landmark dominating the vast plain.

3. Plan and section. Key: 1 altar, 2 organ, 3 baptistry, 4 chapel, 5 sacristy, 6 coat room, 7 heating.

4, 5. Wheels of lights, held by steel cables, float above the basilica-like space.

2. Die Kirche als Landmarke und Superform in der Ebene.

3. Grundriß und Schnitt. Legende: 1 Altar, 2 Orgel, 3 Taufe, 4 Kapelle, 5 Sakristei, 6 Garderobe, 7 Heizung.

4, 5. Mit Stahlkabeln verspannte Lichträder schweben über dem basilikalen Raum.

1

The church is situated on the outskirts of Milan in a district known as Ponte Lambro. It is surrounded by some old houses rather than an identifiable town centre. The site is rectangular, bordering streets on two sides, and almost too small for the building. Nearly the whole of it is covered by a rectangular, two-nave church. In the lower floor are parish premises. The smaller aisle measures 8 × 40 metres and is placed three steps lower than the main nave; it contains a side altar, devotional chapels, confessionals, sacristy and side entrances, forming a subsidiary space in which all the ancillary functions take place. The main nave, twice as wide and nearly twice as high, thus becomes the church proper. Its plan is simple, governed by a main axis from the main entrance along the central aisle to the altar. It comes alive through the subtle distribution of the weights, through the lighting effect, and through the dignity with which the simple details are graced by austerity.

The pulpit by the side of the altar is related to the choristers' gallery in the entrance zone which has no pews. Light – natural as well as artificial – comes from the roof. Even the expansion joint between the two aisles, which had to be provided for structural reasons, is a source of daylight. A small baptistery, an austere belfry and a chimney breast project from the main building and, in common with some curved concrete walls, contribute to the plastic effect of the building.

The long, white wall of the main nave is decorated with Passion tablets. The ceiling is of white-washed exposed concrete, the flooring of red clinkers.

Die Kirche liegt an der Peripherie von Mailand in einem Gebiet, das Ponte Lambro genannt wird. Einige alte Häuser, nicht ein dezidierter Ortskern, bilden die Umgebung der Kirche. Das Grundstück ist rechteckig und an zwei Seiten von Straßen begrenzt – für den Bau beinahe zu klein. Der Architekt überbaute es fast ganz mit einer rechteckigen, zweischiffigen Kirche. Im Untergeschoß liegen die Gemeinderäume. Das schmalere Schiff ist 8 × 40 m groß, es ist niedriger und liegt drei Stufen tiefer als das Hauptschiff – hier sind Nebenaltar, Anbetungs-kapellen, Beichtstühle, Sakristei und Nebeneingänge. Es ist ein begleitender Raum, in dem alles Beiwerk un-tergebracht ist. Das Hauptschiff, doppelt so breit und fast doppelt so hoch, wird so zum eigentlichen Kirchen-raum. Dieser Raum ist im Grundriß einfach, mit einer Achse Haupteingang–Mittelgang–Altar; er lebt durch eine subtile Verteilung der Gewichte, durch seine Be-lichtung und die Würde, mit der seine Armut zur Anmut des einfachen Details gemacht wurde.

Mit der Predigt-Kanzel neben dem Altar korrespondiert die Sängerkanzel im bänkeleeren Eingangsbereich. Licht – natürliches wie künstliches – wird aus dem Dach geholt. Auch die zwischen den Schiffen notwendige Arbeitsfuge ist als Lichtschlitz ausgebildet. Eine kleine Taufkapelle, ein schlichter Turm und der Heizungs-kamin sind vom Hauptbau abgesetzt und tragen, ebenso wie einige geschwungene Betonwände, zur plastischen Belebung des Baukörpers bei.

Die lange weiße Wand des Hauptschiffes ist mit Kreuz-weg-Tafeln geschmückt. Die Decke ist geweißter Beton, der Boden wurde mit roten Klinkerplatten belegt.

1. Main elevation facing the Via Parea. The belfry stands in a central position in front of the building.
2. Plan and section. Key: 1 altar, 2 gallery, 3 baptistry, 4 confessional, 5 chapel, 6 sacristy.
3. Main entrance. Access is via a flight of stairs flanked by two high, curved walls. The solids and voids of the elevation are skillfully balanced.
4. External corner of the aisle.

1. Längsseite an der Via Parea. Der Turm steht in der Mitte vor dem Bau.
2. Grundriß und Schnitt. Legende: 1 Altar, 2 Empore, 3 Taufe, 4 Beichte, 5 Kapelle, 6 Sakristei.
3. Haupteingang. Zugang über eine Treppe zwischen zwei hohen, gebogenen Wänden. In der Fassade sind Flächen und Öffnungen meisterhaft abgewogen.
4. Außenecke des Seitenschiffes.

3

4

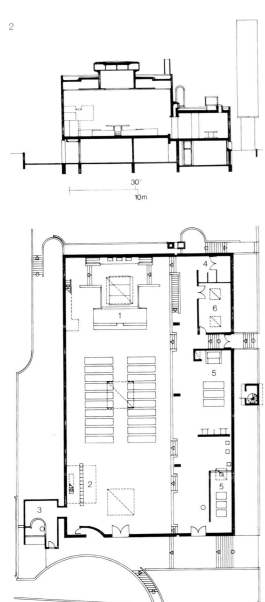

2

30'
10m

5, 6. Entrance, choristers' gallery and toplight. Ceiling of white-washed exposed concrete; white-plastered walls, red clinker flooring.
7. Guido Strazza's Passion tablets match the architecture particularly well. All the ancillary functions are concentrated in the lower aisle.
8. Devotional chapel in the aisle.

5, 6. Eingang, Sängerempore und Oberlicht. Gestrichene Sichtbetondecke, weißverputzte Wände, roter Klinkerplattenboden.
7. Der Kreuzweg von Guido Strazza fügt sich in die Architektur besonders gut ein. Im tieferliegenden Seitenschiff sind alle Nebenfunktionen untergebracht.
8. Anbetungskapelle im Seitenschiff.

5

6

7

8

St. Josef, Wels, Austria, 1960–1967
Architects: Franz Riepl, Othmar Sackmauer

St. Josef, Wels, Österreich, 1960–1967
Architekten: Franz Riepl, Othmar Sackmauer

The uniform appearance of this extensive group of buildings is due to the building materials used. Brick has been used for all the solid walls, for the floors of courtyard and church, and even for altar and sedilia. The brickwork forms a contrast to the dark timbering on the outside and the bright woodwork inside.

The church is of the longitudinal type, slightly asymmetric because of the position of the altar and of the aisle leading to it. The choir is accommodated in a kind of semitransept on one side. It is from here that the interior obtains most of its daylight. Additional daylight enters through a ribbon of skylight windows at the level of the roof beams which remain visible from the interior. Concepts of space and lighting are still in accordance with the notions which prevailed before the Second Vatican Council; in fact, the space proportions are reminiscent of much older periods. It is the imaginative yet unpretentious use of traditional building materials and methods which makes this parish centre attractive.

Die weitläufige Anlage erhält ihre Einheitlichkeit durch die verwendeten Materialien. Aus Backstein sind alle geschlossenen Wände, die Böden des Hofes und der Kirche, sogar der Altar und der Priestersitz. Dazu steht außen dunkles und innen helles Holz in Kontrast.
Die Kirche ist ein Langraum mit einer – durch die Stellung des Altars und des auf ihn zuführenden Ganges – leichten Andeutung von Asymmetrie. Der Chor ist seitlich in einer Art Halbquerschiff angeordnet. Hier ist die Hauptlichtquelle des Kirchenraumes. Auf der Höhe der im Raum sichtbaren Binder fällt zusätzlich Licht durch ein Oberlichtband ein.
Raumkonzeption und Lichtführung ergeben noch ganz die präkonziliare Kirche, wenn nicht durch die Raumproportionen sogar Bezüge zu viel älteren Zeiten gefunden werden können. Es ist die phantasievolle, unprätentiöse Anwendung traditioneller baumeisterlicher Mittel, die dieses Gemeindezentrum sympathisch machen.

1. Plan. Key: 1 altar, 2 sedilia, 3 choir, 4 baptistry, 5 confessional, 6 chapel, 7 sacristy, 8 rector's office, 9 parish hall.

1. Grundriß. Legende: 1 Altar, 2 Sedilien, 3 Sänger, 4 Taufe, 5 Beichte, 6 Kapelle, 7 Sakristei, 8 Pfarrbüro, 9 Gemeindesaal.

1

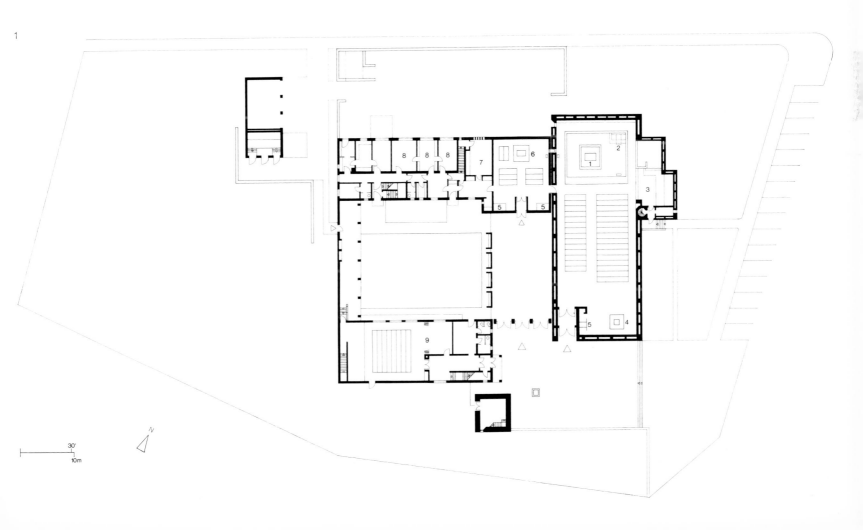

30'
10m

2

3

4

2. Narrow side of the church, belfry and rectory.

3. Half-transept, seen from outside. Copper roofing, two-ply brick walls.

4. Entrance to parish hall. Brick paving and walls.

5. Sedilia.

6. Interior of the church.

7. Interior of half-transept. Roof construction and covering of spruce-wood.

2. Schmalseite der Kirche mit Turm und Pfarrhaus.

3. Halbquerschiff von außen. Dachhaut aus Kupfer, Wände aus zweischaligem Ziegelmauerwerk.

4. Eingang zum Gemeindesaal. Der Boden des Hofes besteht wie die Wände aus Ziegeln.

5. Sedilien.

6. Kirchenraum.

7. Halbquerschiff von innen. Dachkonstruktion und Verschalung aus Fichtenholz.

6

7

5

Pius-Kirche, Meggen, Switzerland, 1964–1966
Architect: Franz Füeg

Pius-Kirche, Meggen, Schweiz, 1964–1966
Architekt: Franz Füeg

This church, which is exceptional in several respects, has been built not at the behest of a progressive clergyman but for the citizens of Meggen who approved the project with a two-thirds majority in a referendum. The building is distinguished by simplicity and clarity – features which according to Jürgen Joedicke, represent the ''purest manifestation for the potentialities of Mies van der Rohe's architecture''.

In the architect's opinion, the church is neither a house nor a parish hall but merely a wrapper, fixing the place at which the community becomes an ecclesiastic congregation. The wrapper is formed by a visible but almost dematerialised steel framework. The infilling of the bays between the uprights (spaced at 1.68 metres) consists of 28 mm thick Pentelicon marble slabs – the same material as that used for the Acropolis. This material is translucent and becomes a dominant feature of the interior. The colour shades range from gold-brown to grey-blue.

But for the noble material used for the diaphanous walls, the impression would be that of an attractive factory. It is the material which distinguishes this church from the secular.

The church forms part of a group of buildings with belfry, rectory and parish premises. It is situated on a slope rising above the St. Gothard road, facing the mountains which surround the Lake of Lucerne. By a terrace and piazza, this sacral precinct is clearly segregated from its environment. The entrances lie on a square, used for Easter celebrations, behind the church whilst the weekday chapel is built into the slope and can be entered from the forecourt facing the road.

Bauherr dieser in mancher Hinsicht außergewöhnlichen Kirche ist nicht ein progressiver Geistlicher gewesen, sondern die Bürgerschaft von Meggen, die dem Projekt mit Zweidrittelmehrheit zustimmte. Einfachheit und Klarheit zeichnen den Bau aus, der nach Jürgen Joedicke die »reinste Manifestation für die Möglichkeiten der Architektur von Mies van der Rohe« ist.

Die Kirche ist nach Meinung des Architekten kein Haus und kein Gemeindesaal, sondern eine einfache Hülle, die den Ort bestimmt, an dem die Gemeinschaft zur Kirche wird. Ein sichtbares, fast entmaterialisiertes Stahlskelett dient zur Umgrenzung. Die Felder zwischen den Stützen (Abstand 1,68 m) sind mit 28 mm starken Marmorplatten aus Pentelikon, dem Stein der Akropolis, ausgefacht. Dieser Stein ist lichtdurchlässig und bestimmt den Raumeindruck. Die Farbe spielt von goldbraun bis graublau.

Der Raumeindruck wäre der einer schönen Fabrikhalle, wenn nicht das edle Material der diaphanen Wand dazukäme. Dieses Material macht die Kirche zu mehr als einem beliebigen Ort.

Die Kirche ist Teil einer Gesamtanlage mit Turm, Pfarrheim und Pfarrhaus. Sie liegt auf einem von der Gotthardstraße ansteigenden Grundstück – vor sich die Berge am Vierwaldstätter See. Die Anlage ist durch eine Terrasse und einen vorgelagerten Platz als Sakralbezirk deutlich von der übrigen Bebauung abgesondert. Die Eingänge befinden sich an einem Osterfeier-Platz hinter der Kirche, während die in den Hang eingebaute Alltagskapelle vom straßenseitigen Vorplatz betreten werden kann.

1

1. The cube, consisting of grey steel and white marble.
2. Plan and section. Key: 1 altar, 2 gallery, 3 baptistry,
4 confessional, 5 chapel.
3. Stairs to the upper piazza.
4. Narrow side of the building.

1. Der Kubus aus grauem Stahl und weißem Marmor.
2. Grundriß und Schnitt. Legende: 1 Altar, 2 Empore, 3
Taufe, 4 Beichte, 5 Kapelle.
3. Treppe zum oberen Kirchplatz.
4. Ansicht der Schmalseite.

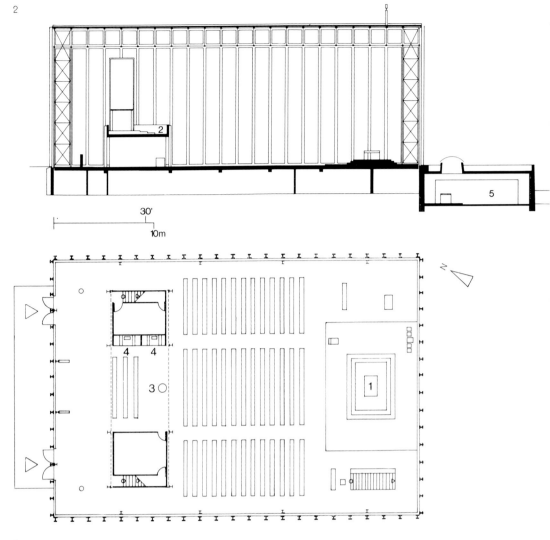

30'

10m

5

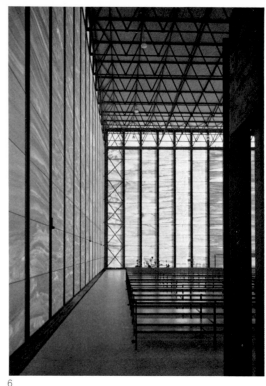

6

7

8

5. Altar side of the interior. By day, the marble walls admit a subdued light.

6. View toward the altar along the east nave wall, with the gallery columns on the right.

7. Gallery side of the interior. Built-in wooden sections below the gallery for confessionals, sacristy and storage area. In the centre, the font. Contrast of marble and exposed concrete surfaces.

8. Lower chapel. Passion tablets by Charles Wyrsch.

5. Altarseite des Innenraumes. Bei Tageslicht lassen die Marmorwände gedämpftes Licht ein.

6. Blick zur Altarseite entlang der östlichen Längswand, rechts eine Emporenstütze.

7. Emporenseite des Innenraumes. Holzeinbauten unter der Empore für Beichte, Sakristei und Abstellraum; in der Mitte der Taufstein. Gegensatz von Marmor und Sichtbeton.

8. Unterkapelle. Kreuzweg von Charles Wyrsch.

Jacobus-Kirche, Düsseldorf-Eller, 1962–1963
Architect: Eckhard Schulze-Fielitz

Jacobus-Kirche, Düsseldorf-Eller, 1962–1963
Architekt: Eckhard Schulze-Fielitz

The church has the appearance of a detail taken from the architect's concept of a "three-dimensional city", designed to overcome conventional notions of statics in town planning. The church too, is therefore a flexible structure which, if necessary, can easily be dismantled and re-built elsewhere (with the exception of the gallery which had to be built in concrete).

The three-dimensional steel framework consists of prefabricated MERO-tubes and connectors. The walls are transparent polyester panels bolted to the tubes. The south elevation has been enlivened by adding a second apron of polyester panels, mounted in rhythmic arrangement on the outer lattice work. When the lighting is right, the translucent walls produce a fascinating play of light and shade. This reinforces the impression of the temporary, tent-like character of the structure. In this church, not all the visitors may find it easy to concentrate on the sermon.

Artificial lighting too, is applied from outside through the polyester walls. Translucent polyester with colour inclusions has also been used for crucifix, pulpit, altar and font.

Die Kirche erscheint wie ein Detail aus der vom Architekten konzipierten »Raumstadt«, mit der die Immobilität im Städtebau überwunden werden soll. So ist auch sie ein flexibles Gebilde, leicht abzubauen, wenn es die Notwendigkeit erfordert, und anderswo wieder aufzustellen (bis auf die Empore, die betoniert werden mußte).

Das räumliche Stahltragwerk besteht aus fabrikfertigen MERO-Rohren und -Knoten; die senkrechten Raumabschlüsse sind durchscheinende Polyesterplatten, die auf die Rohre aufgeschraubt wurden. Eine Belebung der südlichen Außenwand wurde durch eine zweite Schicht von Polyesterplatten erreicht, die, rhythmisch angeordnet, auf den äußeren Traggittern befestigt wurden. Bei entsprechender Beleuchtung ergibt sich auf den durchscheinenden Wänden ein faszinierendes Spiel von Licht und Schatten. Das verstärkt den Eindruck des Auf-Zeit-Gebauten und des Zelthaften. Konzentration auf die Predigt wird in diesem Raum wohl nicht allen Besuchern möglich sein.

Die Beleuchtung bei Dunkelheit erfolgt von außen durch die Polyesterwände hindurch. Aus durchscheinendem Polyester mit Farbeinschlüssen sind auch Kreuz, Kanzel, Altar und Taufstein gemacht.

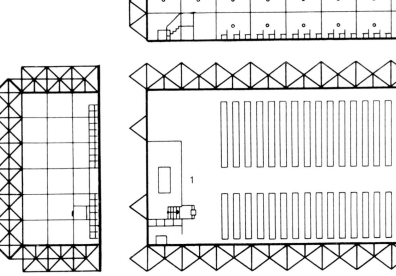

1. Plan, cross section and longitudinal section (the concrete gallery is not drawn in). Key: 1 altar.

1. Grundriß, Querschnitt und Längsschnitt (die betonierte Empore ist nicht eingezeichnet). Legende: 1 Altar.

2

3 4

5

2, 3. South side. The translucent polyester panels inserted into the triangular bays of the latticework serve as sun blinds.
4. South side by night.
5. Construction detail.
6. Daylight and artificial light generate a play of light and shade on the translucent polyester panels.
7. Detail of the gallery toward the altar. Crucifix, altar and baptismal font by André Thomkins.

2, 3. Südseite. Die in die Dreiecksfelder des Fachwerks gesetzten undurchsichtigen Polyesterplatten dienen als Sonnenblenden.
4. Südseite bei Nacht.
5. Konstruktionsdetail.
6. Tageslicht und künstliches Licht ergeben ein Schattenspiel auf den durchscheinenden Polyesterflächen.
7. Blick von der Empore zum Altar. Kreuz, Altar und Taufstein von André Thomkins.

6
7

Santa Maria de Belen, Malaga, Spain, 1962–1965
Architect: José M. Garcia de Paredes

In Spain, where traditions are still greatly respected, religious development and renewal proceed at a slower pace than elsewhere in Europe. Considering the circumstances under which this church has been built, its importance as a contribution to modern church design has to be acknowledged.

The architect had a site of 14.30 × 33.40 metres available, bordered by streets on three sides and by a fire-break wall on the fourth side. Apart from the church for the monks and parishioners, this site was also intended to accommodate a Carmelite monastery. Budget restraints led to an economic, yet imaginative solution.

The church occupies three storeys of the building which covers the entire site. Above the church are the common rooms of the monastery, above them an intimate, covered patio providing the only semi-open space, and still further up, already within the pent roof, the sixteen cells of the monks. The main entrance is from one of the roads. Here, steps lead directly up to the church where one faces a very long nave with central aisle. At its far end stands the sacramental altar at main floor level whilst the celebration altar is placed on a presbytery 1.70 metres above that level. The site is reminiscent of historic churches in the Mediterranean region. Where the old churches have a crypt, this church has a weekday chapel which has a level entrance from the road and can be used without disturbing the main church. Also on the lower floor is the sacristy. The presbytery can be reached by the monks from the staircase via a gallery. Below the latter are the six confessionals which provide a characteristic feature on the long side flanking the road. Daylight enters through glass joints which separate the steel structure from the non-bearing brick wall. At night, lighting is provided by glass candelabras which, with their crystalline shapes, form a decorative contrast to the otherwise austere interior. It is this very austerity which, in conjunction with its spaciousness, gives this church its timeless character.

By using a steel framework, it was possible to cater for the different spans required for the different functions of the building. The structural design is intelligible throughout.

The placing of the ecclesiastical building at a busy road in the middle of the town is a sign for the vitality of the Carmelite Order.

1

2

1, 2. The external view shows an architecture reminiscent of an industrial building. An opening to the outside was not desired. In the lower zone are the vertical slots of the church windows; in the centre, the covered patio; above it, the cells of the monks, accessible from an outside gallery.

3. Roof patio.

4. The space for the altar is placed like a theatre stage above the nave. The celebration altar is on the lower level.

Santa Maria de Belen, Malaga, Spanien, 1962–1965
Architekt: José M. Garcia de Paredes

3
4

In Spanien, einem Land, in dem die Traditionen hoch-
gehalten werden, schreitet die religiöse Entwicklung
und Erneuerung langsamer voran als im übrigen Europa.
Bei Würdigung der Bedingungen, unter denen diese
Kirche gebaut wurde, wird man sie als Beitrag zum
Kirchenbau unserer Zeit anerkennen.
Dem Architekten stand ein Areal von 14,30 × 33,40 m
zur Verfügung, das an drei Seiten von Straßen, an
der vierten von einer Brandmauer begrenzt ist. Hier
sollte außer der Kirche für Mönche und Pfarrangehörige
ein Karmeliterkloster errichtet werden. Ein begrenztes
Budget führte zu einer sparsamen, doch phantasievollen Lösung.
Die Kirche nimmt drei Geschosse des Gebäudes ein, das
die ganze Grundstücksfläche überdeckt. Über der Kirche befinden sich die Gemeinschaftsräume des Klosters,
darüber ein überdeckter intimer Dachhof als einziger
Freiraum der Anlage, darüber, und zwar bereits innerhalb der Dachschräge, die 16 Zellen der Mönche. Der
Haupteingang liegt an der Straße, von der aus Stufen
direkt zum Schiff emporführen. Man hat einen sehr hohen Langraum mit Mittelgang vor sich. Am Raumende
steht der Sakramentsaltar auf Raumebene, der Zelebrationsaltar dagegen ist auf dem 1,70 m über Raum-
niveau liegenden Presbyterium angeordnet. Ange-
sichts dessen fühlt man sich an historische Kirchen des
Mittelmeerraumes erinnert. Der bei alten Kirchen als
Krypta ausgebildete Raum ist hier eine Alltagskapelle,
die ebenen Zugang von der Straße aus hat. Sie kann
ohne Störung des Hauptraumes benutzt werden. Im
Untergeschoß liegt auch die Sakristei. Das Presbyterium
ist für die Mönche vom Treppenhaus aus über eine Sei-
tenempore erreichbar. Unter ihr liegen die sechs Beichtstühle, die der langen Straßenseite ihren charakteristi-
schen Sockel geben. Die Beleuchtung des Raumes erfolgt durch Glasfugen, die die Stahlkonstruktion vom
Füllmauerwerk trennen. Nachts wird der Raum durch
Glaslampen beleuchtet. Sie bieten mit ihren Kristall-
formen einen dekorativen Kontrast zu dem sonst nüch-
ternen Raum. Gerade diese Nüchternheit – in Verbindung mit den großzügigen Proportionen – macht diese
Kirche zu einem zeitlosen Bau.
Mit einer Stahlkonstruktion wurden die verschiedenen
Spannweiten für die verschiedenen Funktionen des Ge-
bäudes bewältigt. Die Konstruktion ist überall ables-
bar.
Die Einordnung des kirchlichen Gebäudes mitten in die
Stadt, an einer sehr belebten Straße, ist Zeichen der
Vitalität des Karmeliterordens.

1, 2. Die Außenansicht zeigt eine einem Industriebau
ähnliche Architektur. Eine Öffnung nach außen ist nicht
angestrebt. In der unteren Zone die senkrechten Schlitze
der Kirchenfenster, in der Mitte der überdeckte Hof,
darüber die von einem Laubengang erschlossenen Zellen der Mönche.
3. Dachhof.
4. Der Altarraum liegt wie eine Bühne über dem Schiff,
der Zelebrationsaltar steht unten.

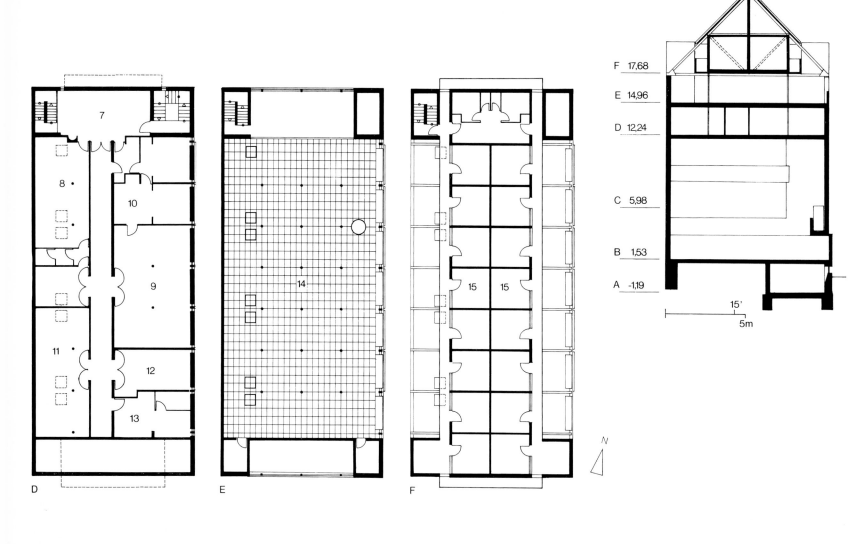

F 17,68
E 14,96
D 12,24
C 5,98
B 1,53
A -1,19

15'
5m

D   E   F

N

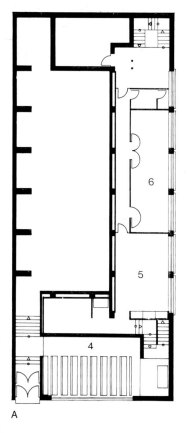

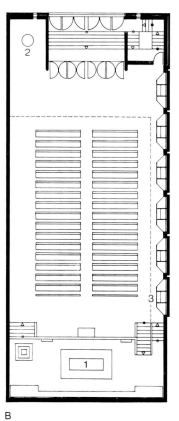

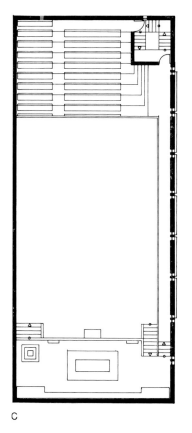

A   B   C

5. Plan and section. Key: 1 altar confessional, 2 baptistry, 3 confessional, 4 chapel, 5 sacristy, 6 conference room, 7 vestibule, 8 reception area, 9 dining hall, 10 kitchen, 11 library, 12 chapter hall, 13 guest room, 14 roof patio, 15 cubicles.

5. Grundrisse und Schnitt. Legende: 1 Altarbereich, 2 Taufe, 3 Beichte, 4 Kapelle, 5 Sakristei, 6 Sitzungsraum, 7 Vestibül, 8 Empfangsraum, 9 Speisesaal, 10 Küche, 11 Bibliothek, 12 Kapitelsaal, 13 Gastraum, 14 Dachhof, 15 Zellen.

Los Almendrales, Madrid, 1962–1965
Architect: José M. Garcia de Paredes

Los Almendrales, Madrid, 1962–1965
Architekt: José M. Garcia de Paredes

The project comprises a parish centre of which the present church and rectory form a part. The layout was partly influenced by a high-tension power line which cuts right across the site and precluded any buildings underneath it. That is why rectory and church had to be separated. The result of this, at first, difficult condition was a highly convincing design for the access. From the street, steps lead down to a low-level entrance platform which provides access to a quiet patio with regularly spaced trees. A long and narrow roof along the entrance side connects the entrances of church and rectory.

The church is described by the architect as a "continuous space". The roof is composed of identical truncated pyramids, crowned with skylight domes. The multiplicity of the tubular steel framework carrying these domes emphasises the continuity of the space which can be extended or reduced as desired. On the other hand, the brick-built altar zone, the gallery built into the entrance zone, and the completely solid outer wall of coarsely pointed brick provide a conventional wrapping.

The altar zone is placed on a relatively high level above the main floor; below it is a crypt – an arrangement still frequently encountered in present-day Spanish church design.

Geplant ist ein Gemeindezentrum. Zunächst wurden jedoch nur die Kirche und das Pfarrhaus gebaut. Eine Hochspannungsleitung, die mitten über das Grundstück führt, und die nicht unterbaut werden durfte, nahm Einfluß auf die Gestaltung der Baugruppe. Pfarrhaus und Kirche mußten getrennt werden. Ein sehr überzeugender Zugang war das Ergebnis dieser zunächst schwierigen Voraussetzung. Von der Straße führen Stufen auf ein tieferliegendes Eingangspodest. Dies öffnet sich auf einen stillen Hof mit regelmäßig gepflanzten Bäumen. Ein langes, schmales Dach entlang der Eingangsseite verbindet die Eingänge von Kirche und Pfarrhaus.

Die Kirche wird vom Architekten als »kontinuierlicher Raum« bezeichnet. Das Dach ist aus gleichartigen, von Lichtkuppeln bekrönten Pyramidenstümpfen zusammengesetzt. Die Vielzahl der sie tragenden Stahlrohre unterstreicht die Kontinuität des auf Erweiterung oder Verkleinerung angelegten Raumes. Die gemauerte Altarzone, die im Eingangsbereich eingebaute Empore und die völlig geschlossene Außenmauer aus grob verfugtem Backstein geben ihm allerdings wieder konventionelle Begrenzungen.

Der Altarraum liegt verhältnismäßig hoch über dem Gemeinderaum, darunter befindet sich eine Krypta – eine Anordnung, die im spanischen Kirchenbau auch heute noch beliebt ist.

1. The "continuity" of the building is apparent from the roof structure.

1. Der »kontinuierliche« Bau wird an der Struktur des Daches ablesbar.

1

2

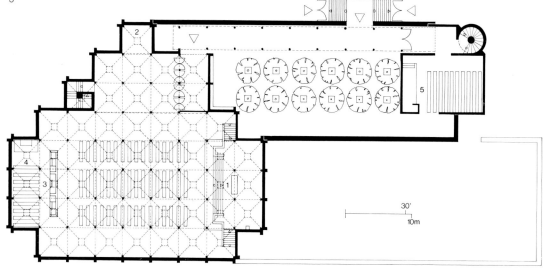

3

2. The surrounding church forecourt.

3. Plan. Key: 1 altar, 2 baptistry, 3 confessional, 4 chapel, 5 hall.

4. As in the previous church, the altar zone here is also placed high above the level of the nave; below it is the crypt.

5. The interior is exclusively illuminated by skylight domes.

30'

10m

4

5

2. Der umschlossene Kirchenvorhof.

3. Grundriß. Legende: 1 Altar, 2 Taufe, 3 Beichte, 4 Kapelle, 5 Saal.

4. Wie in der vorigen Kirche liegt auch hier der Altarraum hoch über dem Schiff, darunter befindet sich die Krypta.

5. Der Innenraum wird ausschließlich durch Lichtkuppeln beleuchtet.

Eglise de la Réconciliation, Taizé, France, 1960–1962
Architect: Denis Aubert

Eglise de la Réconciliation, Taizé, Frankreich, 1960–1962
Architekt: Denis Aubert

Volunteers of the German "Expiation Movement", together with a local building contractor, erected this building within eighteen months. The parish is under the guidance of a monastery.

The large, hall-like church with its slightly contracted choir is entered at the level of the gallery which flanks the room on two sides at an average height of 1.20 metres above the lower part. The altar zone is emphasised by its toplighting and by its staggered walls placed at irregular angles. The altar itself is placed on a podium surrounded by steps. The impression of a hall is mainly created by the waffle pattern of prefabricated concrete units which served as lost formwork when the concrete ceiling was cast. Prefabricated units have also been used for the eaves, fasc.a boards, window frames and the balustrade of the narthex. The walls are partly cast in concrete, partly erected as twoply panel walls between concrete columns; they are smooth on the outside and coarse-plastered on the inside.

The two-fold enclosure of the congregation, brought about by the gallery steps and again by the outer wall, has a concentrating effect. From the outside, the vertical orientation of the choir is deliberately opposed to the horizontal orientation of the nave (a contrast which here seems justifiable). It is from these features and from the large areas of walls and eaves that the church derives its impressive effect.

Freiwillige der deutschen Aktion »Sühnezeichen« haben diesen Bau zusammen mit einem örtlichen Bauunternehmer in eineinhalbjähriger Bauzeit errichtet. Die Gemeinde wird von einem Mönchskonvent geleitet.

Man betritt die große, saalartige Kirche mit dem leicht eingeschnürten Chor auf der Höhe der Empore, die zweiseitig um den Raum gelegt ist und im Mittel 1,20 m über dem tieferen Raumteil liegt. Der Altarraum ist durch Beleuchtung von oben und durch gestaffelte und geknickte Wände vom übrigen Raum abgesetzt. Der Altar steht auf einem Stufenpodest. Der saalartige Eindruck entsteht vor allem durch die Kassetten aus vorgefertigten Betonelementen, die beim Betonieren der Decke als verlorene Schalung dienten. Aus vorgefertigten Elementen wurden auch die Dachvorsprünge, die Gesimsbalken, die Fenstereinfassungen und die Balustrade des Narthex hergestellt. Die Wände wurden teilweise betoniert, teilweise als doppelwandige Ausfachungen zwischen Betonstützen ausgeführt, sie sind außen glatt, innen grobkörnig verputzt.

Die doppelte Zusammenfassung der Gemeinde, einmal durch die Emporenstufen und dann durch die Außenwand hat eine konzentrierende Wirkung. Außen ist der vertikal gegliederte Chor dem horizontalen Schiff (hier scheinen diese Termini berechtigt) deutlich entgegengesetzt. Aus diesen Momenten und aus der Großflächigkeit der Wände und Dachvorsprünge bezieht die Kirche ihre großzügige Wirkung.

1

1, 2. External view. The different component parts of the building – the enclosing wall, the roof composed of prefabricated units, the choir rising to a higher level – are clearly separated from each other.
3. Oecumenical youth gathering.
4. Plan. Key: 1 altar, 2 monks' choir, 3 organ, 4 chapel.

1, 2. Außenansichten. Die Elemente des Baues – die raumumschließende Wand, das Dach aus vorgefertigten Elementen, der höhergezogene Chor – sind deutlich voneinander abgesetzt.
3. Ökumenisches Jugendtreffen.
4. Grundriß. Legende: 1 Altar, 2 Mönchschor, 3 Orgel, 4 Kapelle.

2

3

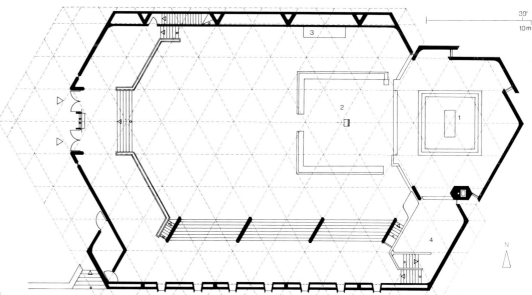

4

5. The church entrance is six steps above the main floor.
6. Glass mosaic by Frère Marc.
7. Chapel.

5. Der Eintretende steht 6 Stufen über dem Raum.
6. Eingangsverglasung von Frère Marc.
7. Kapelle.

Kaleva Church, Tampere, Finland, 1959–1966
Architects: Reima Pietilä, Raili Paatelainen

Kaleva-Kirche, Tampere, Finnland, 1959–1966
Architekten: Reima Pietilä, Raili Paatelainen

1. Entrance side. The vertical sub-division of the building volume is in contrast to the network formed by the joints of the ceramic lining.

1. Eingangsseite. Die vertikale Gliederung der Großform kontrastiert mit dem Fugennetz der Verkleidung.

This modern cathedral on the outskirts of Tampere, accommodating 1100 people, is one of the largest churches built during the last decade. Its walls are concave concrete shells which enclose an almost rhombic space. Daylight enters through vertical strips of windows, reminiscent of deep rock fissures which extend from floor to ceiling and also contain the floodlights for the artificial lighting. The concrete shells are painted white on the inside and lined with ceramic slabs on the outside. Timber-clad, convex concrete shells cover the space in the transverse direction. The interior is very bright. Its longitudinal emphasis in conjunction with the central aisle and the vertical emphasis of the shell walls are reminiscent of Gothic hall churches. As in the latter, the altar is moved into a mystical remoteness. In contrast, the exterior of the church has the appearance of an informally shaped monument. A turret placed on the roof serves as belfry; its three-dimensional crucifix represents the only Christian symbol – but its architectural effect is admittedly somewhat strange.
The part projecting from the slope contains meeting and club rooms.

Als eine der größten Kirchen des letzten Jahrzehnts bietet diese moderne Kathedrale am Rande von Tampere 1100 Personen Platz. Ihre Wände sind konkave Betonschalen, die einen fast rhombischen Raum begrenzen. Wie durch tiefe Felsspalten fällt das Licht aus raumhohen Fensterstreifen ein. Hier sind auch die Scheinwerfer für die künstliche Beleuchtung angebracht. Die Betonschalen sind im Inneren weiß gestrichen, außen mit keramischen Platten verkleidet. Konvexe Betonschalen mit Holzverkleidung überspannen den Raum in der Querrichtung. Der Raum ist sehr hell. Seine Längstendenz in Verbindung mit dem Mittelgang und der Vertikalität der Schalenwände läßt eine Assoziation an gotische Hallenkirchen aufkommen. Wie in diesen ist der Altar in mystische Ferne gerückt. Außen dagegen bietet die Kirche den Anblick eines frei geformten Monuments. Ein auf das Dach aufgesetzter Turmhelm ist der Glockenträger und mit seiner dreidimensionalen Kreuzform das einzige christliche Symbol – das architektonisch allerdings etwas fremd wirkt.
In dem aus dem Hang herausragenden Teil sind Versammlungs- und Clubräume untergebracht.

2

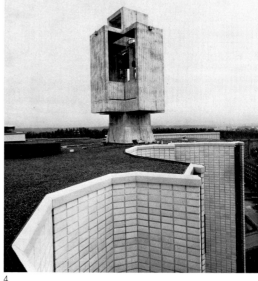

4

3

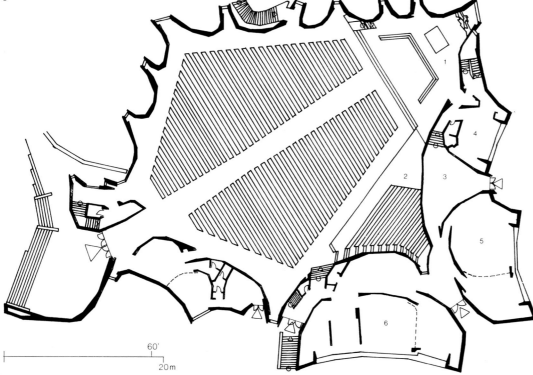

60'

20m

2. The horizontal curves, seen against the skyline.
3. Plan. Key: 1 altar, 2 choir, 3 chapel, 4 sacristy, 5 assembly room, 6 parish hall.
4. Belfry, placed on the ridge of the roof.
5. Wooden beams span the space between the high, small roof supports.
6, 7. The convex walls projecting into the interior space are reminiscent of Gothic hall churches.

5

6

7

2. Die Grundrißkurven gegen den Himmel.
3. Grundriß. Legende: 1 Altar, 2 Sänger, 3 Kapelle, 4 Sakristei, 5 Versammlungsraum, 6 Gemeindesaal.
4. Glockenträger als Dachreiter.
5. Zwischen die hohen, schmalen Deckenträger sind Holzelemente gespannt.
6, 7. Die in den Langraum hineingewölbten Wandschalen lassen Assoziationen an gotische Hallenkirchen wachwerden.

Heilig-Geist-Kirche, Wolfsburg, Germany, 1959–1962
Architect: Alvar Aalto

Heilig-Geist-Kirche, Wolfsburg, 1959–1962
Architekt: Alvar Aalto

1

2

3

In swinging curves, the three-dimensional vault of this church rises behind the altar from the floor, opening up widely towards the entrance side. The swinging movement of that curve is underlined by the rhythmically partitioned side windows. The dynamic impression is further enhanced by the conical taper in the plan towards the altar zone: Side walls, roof trusses and even the sacristy are orientated towards an imaginary point outside the building. Even the organ gallery – placed on one side – is governed by the same orientation. This three-dimensional dynamics leaves the visitor no choice; its orientation is clear enough. What does not quite accord with it is the lighting. The space around the altar is relatively dark whilst the font by its side is brightened up by the skylight.

The interior is full of surprising details, yet has a musical integrity of its own. The construction is simple: white-painted brick walls, white-plastered columns and walls. A rhythmically rising belfry of white-painted concrete forms a link between the church and the low-rise buildings for the parish premises.

Schwungvoll steigt das Raumgewölbe der Kirche hinter dem Altar aus dem Boden und öffnet sich weit zur Eingangsseite. Rhythmisch gegliederte Seitenfenster unterstützen die Bewegung der Raumkurve. Darüber hinaus gewinnt der Raum noch an Dynamik durch die konische Verjüngung des Grundrisses zur Altarzone hin: Seitenwände, Dachbinder und sogar die Sakristei sind auf einen imaginären Punkt außerhalb des Gebäudes gerichtet. Auch die – seitlich angeordnete – Orgelempore ist in diese Flucht gesetzt. Die Raumdynamik läßt dem Besucher keine Wahl: Seine Ausrichtung ist eindeutig. Nicht ganz korrespondiert die Beleuchtung damit. Am Altar ist es relativ dunkel. Der seitlich vom Altar stehende Taufstein dagegen hat ein hohes Oberlicht.

Der Raum ist voll von überraschenden Details, und doch hat er eine eigene musikalische Einheitlichkeit. Er ist einfach gebaut: mit weiß gestrichenem Mauerwerk, weiß verputzten Stützen und Wänden. Ein rhythmisch aufsteigender Glockenturm aus weiß gestrichenem Beton steht als Bindeglied zwischen der Kirche und den flachen Gemeindebauten.

4

5

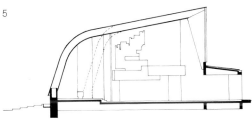

1. External view of the church. Brick walls painted white, belfry painted white, lantern with copper cladding.
2. View from the road.
3. Different designs are used for the kindergarten, parish hall, rectory and church.
4. The timber-clad segments of the ceiling seem to hurtle towards the altar.
5. Plan and section. Key: 1 altar, 2 baptistry, 3 sacristy.

1. Außenansicht der Kirche. Weiß gestrichene Backsteinwände, weiß gestrichener Betonturm, kupferverkleidete Laterne.
2. Außenansicht der Kirche von der Straße her.
3. Unterschiedliche Formgebung von Kindergarten, Gemeindesaal, Pfarrhaus und Kirche.
4. Holzverschalte Deckenfelder stürzen auf den Altar zu.
5. Grundriß und Schnitt. Legende: 1 Altar, 2 Taufe, 3 Sakristei.

30'
10m

6. Top light above the font. The light fittings are designed by the architect.
7. Organ gallery and glass wall over the entrance.
8. Interior, seen from the altar.

6. Oberlicht über dem Taufstein. Lampen vom Architekten.
7. Orgelempore und Glaswand über dem Eingang.
8. Innenraum vom Altar her.

6

7

8

St. Francis de Sales, Muskegon, Michigan, 1961–1967
Architects: Marcel Breuer, Herbert Beckhard

St. Francis de Sales, Muskegon, Michigan, 1961–1967
Architekten: Marcel Breuer, Herbert Beckhard

1. Plan and sections. Key: 1 altar, 2 monks' choir, 3 gallery, 4 baptistery, 5 confessional, 6 chapel, 7 sacristy, 8 assembly room, 9 offices, 10 dwelling area.

1. Grundriß und Schnitte. Legende: 1 Altar, 2 Mönchschor, 3 Empore, 4 Taufe, 5 Beichte, 6 Kapelle, 7 Sakristei, 8 Versammlungsraum, 9 Büros, 10 Wohnbereich.

The plan of this church is a simple rectangle whilst the shape of the elevation is more complicated. The side walls are surfaces of revolution, and front and rear walls lean across the room in trapezoidal form: the trapezoids are held by strongly profiled brackets which also support the longitudinal roof trusses. At its highest point, the structure attains the remarkable height of 24 metres.

The arrangement of the pews in the nave is conventional. The number of seats is in keeping with the size of the structure. The four groups of pews at ground level hold 972 people, another 231 persons can sit on the gallery. The space around the altar is built up like a stage, being six steps higher than the floor of the church. If, in our days, such distance-keeping can be regarded as unusual, the placing of the tabernacle – one storey above the altar floor – is incomprehensible. It is explained by the architects by the desire to provide "good visibility from everywhere".

The church provides a dominant feature, underlined by an excessively dynamic effect, of the whole group buildings. The low-rise building of the rectory stands close to the church on the altar side. The church entrance is reminiscent of early Christian times: From the road, one enters an open atrium surrounded by walls and displaying the stations of the Passion. Here are the main entrances to the narthex which has the form of a low-rise annex. Passing the sunken baptistry and the confessionals – where the penitential sacraments are combined – one enters the main nave from below the gallery.

The church has no windows; daylight enters through spherical skylights, and the floodlights used at night are mounted at the same points.

Der Grundriß dieser Kirche ist ein einfaches Rechteck, im Aufriß sind die Formen komplizierter. Die Seitenwände steigen als Rotationsflächen auf, und die Vorder- und Rückwände neigen sich als Trapeze über den Raum; die Trapeze werden von stark profilierten Vorlagen gehalten, die auch die Längsbinder des Daches abstützen. Die Kirche erreicht an ihrer höchsten Stelle die beachtliche Höhe von 24 m.

Das Schiff ist konventionell bestuhlt. Der Größe des Bauwerkes entspricht die Anzahl der Plätze. Die unteren vier Bankgruppen fassen 972 Menschen, die auf der Empore weitere 231. Der Altarraum ist bühnenartig aufgebaut, sechs Stufen höher als der Boden der Kirche. Wenn diese Distanzgebung in unseren Tagen ungewöhnlich genannt werden darf, so ist die Plazierung des Tabernakels – geschoßhoch über dem Altarraum – unverständlich. Die Architekten erklären sie mit »guter Sichtbarkeit von allen Punkten«.

Die Kirche ist die mit exzessiver Dynamik gesteigerte Dominante der Gesamtanlage. Ein flaches Pfarrhaus ist der Altarseite vorgelagert. Der Zugang in die Kirche erinnert an frühchristliche Zeiten: Von der Straße her betritt man ein ummauertes, offenes Atrium mit den Kreuzwegstationen, an ihm liegen die Haupteingänge zum Narthex, einem flachen Vorbau. Man geht an der versenkten Taufkapelle und den Beichtstühlen vorbei – die Poenitentia-Sakramente sind hier zusammengefaßt – und betritt den Hauptraum unter der Empore.

Die Kirche hat keine Fenster, die Beleuchtung erfolgt bei Tag durch Lichtkalotten im Dach und bei Nacht durch Scheinwerfer, die in den Kalotten installiert sind.

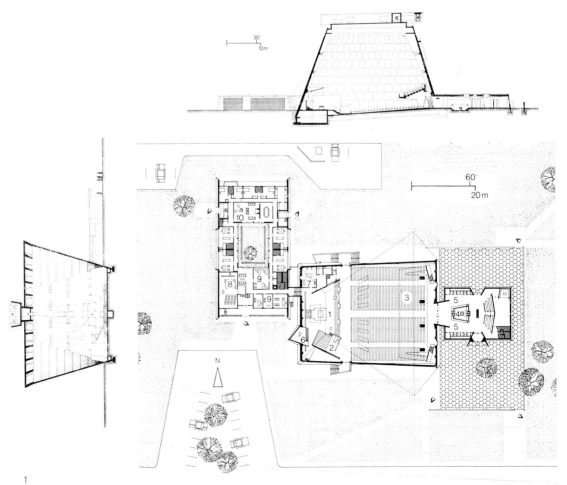

2

3

5

4

6
7

2. East elevation with belfry. The facades are of exposed concrete.

3. West elevation of the church with rectory. The tabernacle is inside the alcove projecting from the church wall. The concrete ladder leading to the roof forms an architectural feature of the facade.

4. The south elevation reveals the dynamism of the high-rising structure.

5. Facade detail.

6. Decorative display of the Passion stations on the east wall of the atrium.

7. Altar zone, seen from the gallery.

2. Ostseite der Kirche mit Glockenträger. Fassaden in Sichtbeton.

3. Westseite der Kirche mit Pfarrhaus. Im Erker an der Kirchenwand befindet sich das Tabernakel. Betonleiter zum Dach als Kompositionselement der Fassade.

4. Die Südansicht zeigt die dynamische Tendenz des hohen Baukörpers.

5. Fassadendetail.

6. Dekorative Ordnung des Kreuzwegs an der Ostwand des Atriums.

7. Blick von der Empore zum Altarraum.

St. Mary's Cathedral, Tokyo, 1967–1969
Architect: Kenzo Tange

Of the about 700,000 Roman Catholics living in Japan, 40,000 live in Tokyo, a metropolitan city with a population of 11 million. The cathedral has been erected close to the residence of the archbishop in the outskirts of the town.
The plan is rhomboidal. Eight twisted surfaces of revolution are composed to form four shell walls which are braced diagonally at the centre of the intersecting skylights. These skylights merge with the vertical slot windows to provide the only source of daylight. The concrete walls are left untreated on the inside whilst the outsides are covered by sheets of profiled high-grade steel with a slightly shiny surface which further emphasises the dynamic effect of the surfaces or revolution.
The architect has created a large structure overtowering all the buildings in the district – a shining super-structure which, with its unmistakable skyline, has become one of the landmarks in the endless sea of houses of the metropolis.
The cathedral has 800 seats, but another 2000 people can be accommodated standing. In the enormous interior, the altar zone claims a relatively large part. The altar is placed on a high podium. The present author was told by the Archbishop of Tokyo that Tange had rejected the idea of a community church with the words: "Fear of God should deter us from passing by the altar". Logically, the highest point of the church has been placed directly above the altar zone. For the same logical reason, the – very extensive – convent and parish premises have been deliberately played down inasmuch as they are removed from the main building, built of a less spectacular material, and designed in an entirely different formal language.

1. Aerial view. The layout plan was inspired by the shape of the site. The dual-curvature shells are tapered upwards to form a concave cross of skylight ribbons.
2. Plan and section. Key: 1 altar, 2 baptistry, 3 chapel, 4 sacristy.
3. The shining metal skin of the church is in contrast to the coarse surface of the low-rising annexes. The main entrance is several steps above the level of the piazza.

1. Luftbild. Die Grundrißform wurde durch den Grundstückszuschnitt angeregt. Die doppelt gekrümmten Schalen verjüngen sich zu einem konkaven Oberlichtkreuz.
2. Grundriß und Schnitt. Legende: 1 Altar, 2 Taufe, 3 Kapelle, 4 Sakristei.
3. Die schimmernde Metallhaut der Kirche kontrastiert mit der rauhen Oberfläche der niedrigen Anbauten. Der Haupteingang liegt mehrere Stufen über dem Platzniveau.

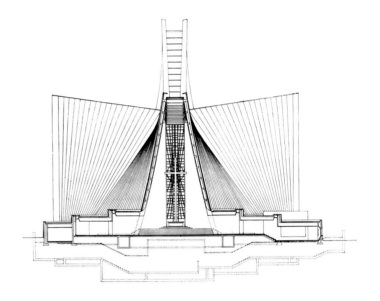

1

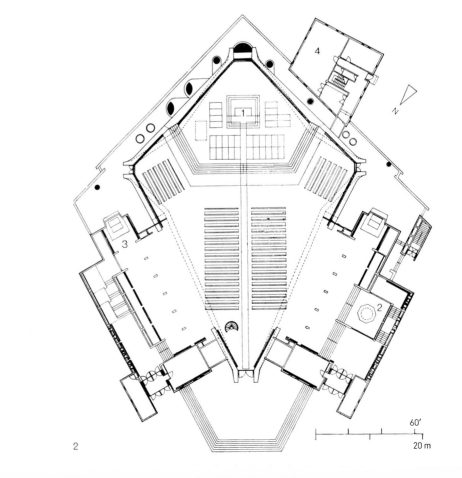

2

60'

20 m

Marien-Kathedrale, Tokio, 1967–1969
Architekt: Kenzo Tange

In Japan leben rund 700000 Katholiken, davon 40000 in Tokio, einer Stadt mit 11 Millionen Einwohnern. Die Kathedrale wurde bei der Residenz des Erzbischofs in einem Außenbezirk der Stadt erbaut.

Der Grundriß hat die Form eines Rhombus. Acht windschiefe Rotationsflächen ergeben vier schalenförmige Wände, die im Scheitelpunkt der kreuzförmigen Oberlichter diagonal gegeneinander abgestützt sind. Diese Oberlichtstreifen werden als senkrechte Lichtschlitze fortgesetzt; auf jede andere Art der Belichtung ist konsequent verzichtet. Die Wände sind innen Sichtbeton, außen haben sie eine Abdeckung aus profiliertem Edelstahlblech, dessen mattglänzende Oberfläche die Bewegung der Rotationsflächen unterstreicht.

Eine große Form, die alle Gebäude des Stadtteils weit überragt, ist geschaffen, ein schimmernder Superbau, der mit seiner unverwechselbaren Silhouette eine der Orientierungsmarken in der endlosen Bebauung der Millionenstadt ist.

Die Kathedrale hat 800 Sitzplätze, 2000 weitere Besucher können stehend an der Feier teilnehmen. In der riesigen Halle beansprucht die Altarzone einen relativ großen Raum. Der Altar steht auf einem hohen Postament. Der Erzbischof von Tokio erklärte dem Verfasser, daß Tange Anregungen zu einer Gemeinschaftskirche mit den Worten ablehnte: »Die Ehrfurcht vor Gott verbietet es, über den Altar hinwegzuschreiten.« Folgerichtig ist der Kulminationspunkt des Raumes über die Altarzone gelegt. Folgerichtig sind auch die – sehr umfangreichen – Konvents- und Gemeindebauten abgesetzt, untergeordnet, in einem weniger spektakulären Material und einer ganz anderen Formensprache gebaut.

4
5

4. Main nave, seen from the side aisle serving as entrance.
5. Chapel below the altar zone. Walls of exposed concrete, balustrade of white marble.
6. Altar space. The way in which the shell walls are supported by the cruciform intersection of concrete beams is vaguely reminiscent of the treatment of the nave intersection in historic churches.

4. Blick von der seitlichen Eingangshalle ins Kirchenschiff.
5. Kapelle unter dem Altarraum. Sichtbetonwände, Brüstung aus weißem Marmor.
6. Altarraum. Die Abstützung der Schalen durch einen kreuzförmigen Betonbalken erinnert entfernt an die Vierung historischer Kirchen.

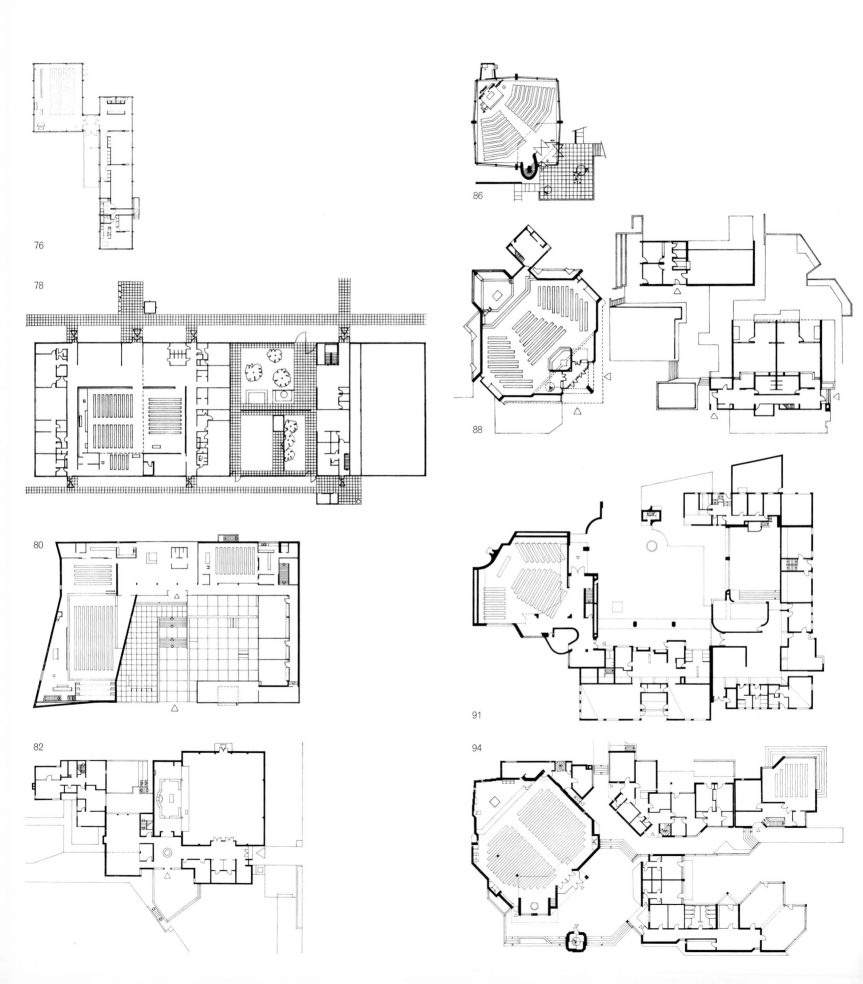

76

78

80

82

86

88

91

94

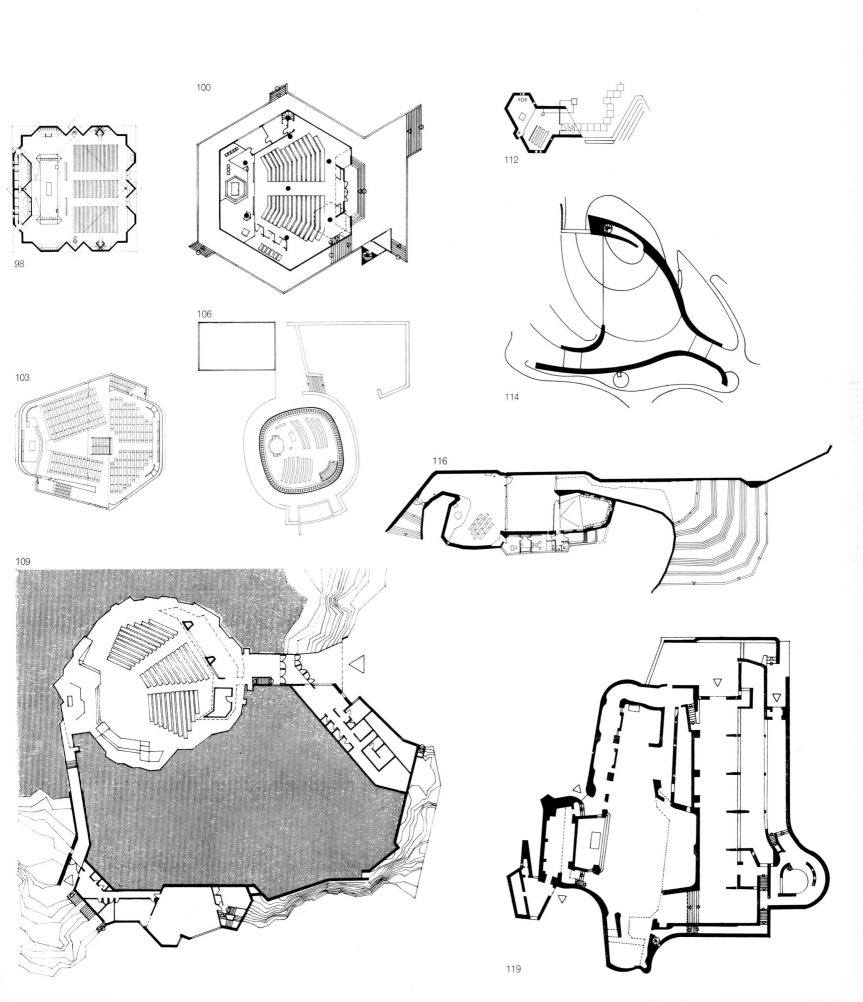

98

100

103

106

109

112

114

116

119

Parish Centre in Vuosaari, Finland, 1966–1969
Architects: Ola Laiho, Bengt-Vilhelm Levón

Gemeindezentrum in Vuosaari, Finnland, 1966–1969
Architekten: Ola Laiho, Bengt-Vilhelm Levón

This temporary parish centre, which can easily be dismantled, has been erected in the vicinity of Helsinki. Two buildings, connected by a short porch, contain the church and the parish premises, respectively. The two buildings are of similar construction (external steel frames with lightweight panels), but their proportions are different. The short church building, four panel units high, contrasts with the long three panels high parish hall. But both buildings have the same frame spacing and identical glass and wall units (plywood).

The only indication that the building is a church is provided by the crucifix cut into the disc which is mounted on the wall panel. The design is deliberately meant to suggest an assembly of mass-produced units which, without claiming originality or singularity, wants to be judged by the quality of the layout plan and the multifunctional use of each part.

Dieses provisorische, demontierbare Gemeindezentrum steht in der Nähe von Helsinki. In zwei mit einem knappen Eingangsgelenk verbundenen Baukörpern sind Kirche und Gemeinderäume untergebracht. Die Konstruktion beider Bauten ist gleich (außenliegende Stahlrahmen mit eingeschobener Leichtkonstruktion), die Proportionen jedoch verschieden. Gegen den kurzen, vier Platten hohen Kirchenbau ist der lange, drei Platten hohe Gemeindebau gesetzt. Beide haben den gleichen Rahmenabstand und die gleichen Glas- und Wandelemente (Sperrholz).

Den einzigen Hinweis darauf, daß es sich hier um einen kirchlichen Bau handelt, geben die auf die Füllwände aufmontierten Scheiben mit dem eingeschnittenen Kreuz. Der Bau ist bewußt ein Serienprodukt ohne Originalität und Singularität, das nach der Organisation des Grundrisses und der vielseitigen Verwendbarkeit der Elemente beurteilt werden will.

1

1. Externial view. On the left the church, on the right the parish premises. Steel frame structure with plywood panels.
2. Plan and section. Key: 1 church, 2 coat room, 3 club-room, 4 dwelling.
3. Altar zone.
4. Daylight enters through a glass wall in the rear of the room.

1. Außenansicht, links die Kirche und rechts das Gemeindehaus. Stahlrahmenkonstruktion mit Sperrholz-Füllungen.
2. Grundriß und Schnitt. Legende: 1 Kirche, 2 Garderobe, 3 Klubraum, 4 Wohnung.
3. Altarzone.
4. Der Raum wird von seiner Rückseite her durch eine Glaswand belichtet.

3

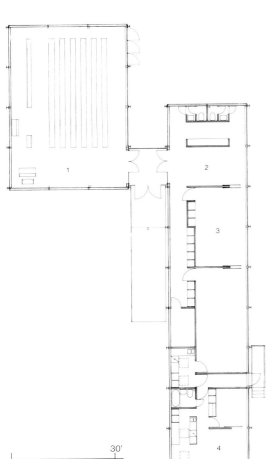

2

30'

10 m

4

Parish Centre in Hyrylä, Finland, 1965–1967
Architect: Kirmo Mikkola, Juhani Pallasmaa

Gemeindezentrum in Hyrylä, Finnland, 1965–1967
Architekten: Kirmo Mikkola, Juhani Pallasmaa

The entire parish centre is situated within an oblong, rectangular cluster of low-rise buildings where the low belfry is the only dominant feature, marking the entrance to the church. Church and parish hall have top lighting formed by a continuous ring of roof windows. The two interiors can be combined and have a joint entrance with porch and ancillary premises. The two-storey gymnastics hall and the clergymen's dwellings are separated from church and parish hall by a courtyard.
This centre has been conceived without semantic ambitions. The attempt was made to find a simple solution for the different programme tasks and to use the materials in a formal language suggested by Mies van der Rohe. Particularly attractive are the clarity and technical perfection of the group.

1. Entrances and belfry are the only elements outside the rectangular plan.
2. The severity of the long, single-storey elevations is mitigated by the variation of the materials.
3. Plan and section. Key: 1 altar, 2 sacristy, 3 rectory, 4 parish hall, 5 gymnasium.
4. Interior of the church.
5. Gymnastics hall with gallery.
6. A view of the courtyard.

Das gesamte Gemeindezentrum liegt in einer langen, niedrigen, rechteckigen Baumasse, aus der nur der kurze Glockenturm herausgenommen ist, um den Eingang zur Kirche zu kennzeichnen. Kirche und Gemeindesaal erhalten Oberlicht aus der ringsum verglasten Dachkonstruktion. Die beiden Räume sind zusammenlegbar und haben einen gemeinsamen Eingang mit Foyer und Nebenräumen. Die zweigeschossige Turnhalle und die Pfarrwohnungen sind vom Bereich der Kirche und des Gemeindesaals durch einen Hof getrennt.
Dieses Zentrum ist ohne semantische Ambitionen konzipiert. Es wurde die einfache Organisation der verschiedenen Programmpunkte gesucht und in die Material- und Formensprache Mies van der Rohes umgesetzt. Bestechend ist die Klarheit und technische Perfektion der Anlage.

1. Eingänge und Glockenturm sind als einzige Elemente aus dem Grundrißrechteck herausgenommen.
2. Die Strenge der langen, eingeschossigen Fronten ist durch den Wechsel der Materialien gemildert.
3. Grundriß und Schnitt. Legende: 1 Altar, 2 Sakristei, 3 Pfarrhaus, 4 Gemeindesaal, 5 Turnhalle.
4. Kirchenraum.
5. Turnhalle mit Empore.
6. Blick in den Hof.

1

2

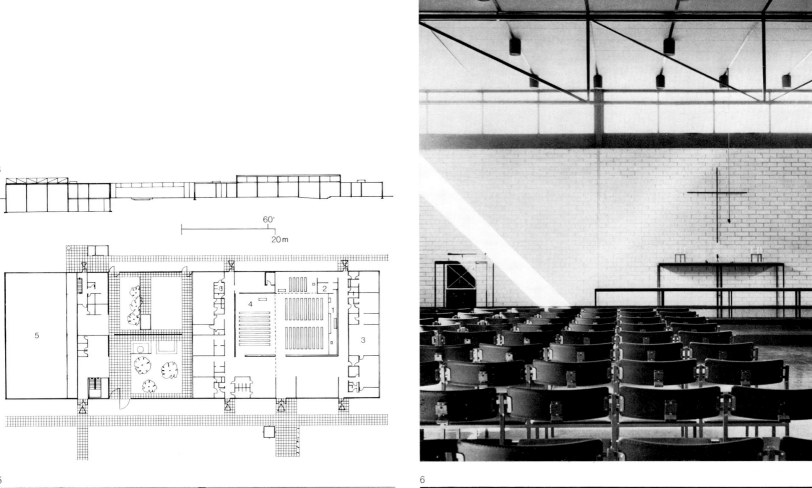

3

60'
20 m

5

6

This secluded parish centre has been placed on two levels around a central courtyard. A storey-high, open flight of stairs leads from the road to the entrance hall which serves as a vestibule for the chapel and several community rooms on one side, as well as for the church and the adjacent parish hall of the Finnish community on the other side. The Swedish parish hall and further community rooms are in the basement.

The plan of the church has been distorted into a rhomb. The rectangular space assigned to the congregation is surrounded by two steps and is reached via a ramp which begins at the entrance. All the liturgical zones are on the higher level; the choir is placed on an ascending flight of steps. Above the Finnish parish hall, which can be combined with the church, is a gallery. The room is very short and compact. Daylight enters mainly through a large, high-level window placed at the apex of the rhomb facing the road.

All the buildings are erected in concrete, the church being backed up with brickwork.

Dieses nach außen abgeschlossene Gemeindezentrum ist um einen zentralen Hof in zwei Ebenen angelegt. Eine geschoßhohe offene Treppe führt von der Straße aus in die Eingangshalle, die als Vorplatz für die Kapelle und einige Gemeinderäume auf der einen Seite sowie für die Kirche mit dem angeschlossenen finnischen Gemeindesaal auf der anderen Seite dient. Der schwedische Gemeindesaal und weitere Gemeinderäume befinden sich im Untergeschoß.

In dem zum Rhombus verzogenen Kirchengrundriß ist der durch zwei rechteckige Stufen fixierte Raum der Gemeinde eingelassen. Man betritt ihn über eine am Eingang beginnende Rampe. Alle liturgischen Orte sind auf dem oberen Niveau angeordnet, der Kirchenchor steht auf noch weiter ansteigenden Stufen. Über dem einbeziehbaren finnischen Gemeinderaum befindet sich eine Empore. Der Raum ist sehr kurz und kompakt. Die Hauptbelichtung bezieht der Raum aus einem großen, hochliegenden Fenster an der in die Straße vorspringenden Spitze des Rhombus.

Die gesamte Anlage wurde betoniert, die Kirche innen mit Backstein hintermauert.

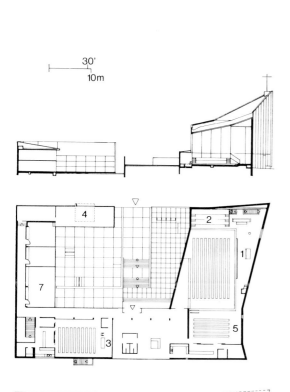

1. View from the street. The church building swings into the road.
2. Main entrance, with the belfry terrace on the right.
3. Innercourtyard, seen from the Swedish parish hall.
4. Plan and section. Key: 1 altar, 2 choir, 3 chapel, 4 belfry terrace, 5 Finnish parish hall, 6 Swedish parish hall, 7 community rooms.
5. Simple materials and a high-rising front wall determine the character of the room. Below the gallery on the right is the Finnish parish hall.

1. Straßenansicht. Der Kirchenbaukörper ist in die Straße hineingeschwenkt.
2. Haupteingang, rechts die Glockenterrasse.
3. Innenhof vom schwedischen Gemeindesaal aus.
4. Grundrisse und Schnitt. Legende: 1 Altar, 2 Sänger, 3 Kapelle, 4 Glockenterrasse, 5 finnischer Gemeindesaal, 6 schwedischer Gemeindesaal, 7 Gemeinderäume.
5. Einfache Materialien und eine überhöhte Stirnwand bestimmen den Charakter des Kirchenraumes. Rechts unter der Empore der finnische Gemeindesaal.

Chapel and Cultural Centre of the Rensselaer Newman
Foundation, Troy, N.Y., 1966–1968
Architects: Peter S. Levatich, John Clair Miller

Kapelle und Kulturzentrum der Rensselaer Newman
Foundation, Troy, N.Y., 1966–1968
Architekten: Peter S. Levatich, John Clair Miller

This group of buildings has been erected for the activities of the Roman Catholic students of the Rensselaer Polytechnic Institute and for meetings of other groups of the Parish of Troy. Apart from divine services for students, the centre also serves as a seminary, theatre, lecture room, concert hall, etc., with the idea of promoting a worldly student life with religious and cultural overtones. The creators of this centre saw no need for separating the sacral and secular activities.

The plan has three axes which govern the way in which the different premises can be combined. In the centre of the entrance axis is the font. At the far end, perhaps rather too remote from the entrance, are two smaller club rooms which can be combined. Along a second axis, parish hall and chapel can be combined for acts of worship. The chapel, comparable to the traditional choir, can be separated by a collapsible wall for different uses. A third axis, formed by chapel, baptistry and terrace, is used for open-air acts of worship and for theatrical performances.

Chapel and parish hall receive daylight through high-level skylights. With their concrete block walls, concrete floors, cedar wood ceilings and unconcealed steel structures, the premises have an austere, monastic appearance.

Für die Aktivitäten der katholischen Studenten des Rensselaer Polytechnic Institute und für Versammlungen anderer Gruppen der Gemeinde Troy wurde diese Baugruppe errichtet. Hier werden nicht nur Studentengottesdienste gehalten, sondern es finden auch Seminare, Theateraufführungen, Vorträge, Konzerte und so weiter statt. Ein weltoffenes, religiös-kulturelles Studentenleben soll auf diese Weise gefördert werden. Eine Trennung der Aktivitäten in sakrale und profane Bereiche schien den Schöpfern des Gebäudes unnötig.

Der Grundriß weist drei Achsen auf, mit denen die Kombinationsfähigkeit der verschiedenen Räume geordnet wird. In der Mitte der Eingangsachse steht der Taufstein. Am Ende, fast etwas zu weit vom Eingang, liegen zwei kleinere, zusammenlegbare Klubräume. Durch eine zweite Achse werden Gemeindesaal und Kapelle während des Gottesdienstes vereinigt. Die Kapelle, dem früheren Chor vergleichbar, kann für separate Nutzungen durch eine Faltwand abgetrennt werden. An der dritten Achse sind Kapelle, Taufkapelle und Terrasse aufgereiht – für Gottesdienste im Freien und Theateraufführungen.

Kapelle und Gemeinderaum erhalten Licht durch hochliegende Oberlichter. Betonblockmauerwerk, Betonböden, Zedernholzverschalungen und sichtbare Stahlkonstruktionen geben den Räumen einen strengen, mönchischen Charakter.

1

2

3

4

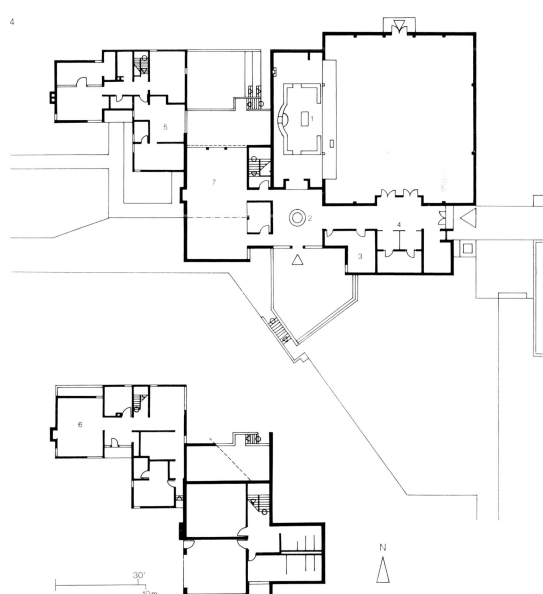

1. Entrance side. The annexes are subordinated to the
church building proper.
2. Adjacent buildings with assembly room (background,
far right) and dwellings.
3. The belfry and entrance to the baptistery.
4. Plans. Key: 1 chapel, 2 parish hall, 3 baptistry, 4
sacristy, 5 coat room, 6 rector's dwelling, 7 dwelling for
clerical assistant, 8 caretaker's dwelling, 9 assembly
room.

1. Eingangsseite. Dem Hauptbaukörper der Kirche sind
die Anbauten untergeordnet.
2. Nebengebäude mit Versammlungsraum (ganz rechts
im Hintergrund) und Wohnungen.
3. Glockenträger und Eingang zum Baptisterium.
4. Grundrisse. Legende: 1 Kapelle, 2 Gemeindesaal, 3
Taufe, 4 Sakristei, 5 Garderobe, 6 Pfarrwohnung, 7 Wohnung des Pfarrhelfers, 8 Hausmeisterwohnung, 9 Versammlungsraum.

30'

10 m

N

5

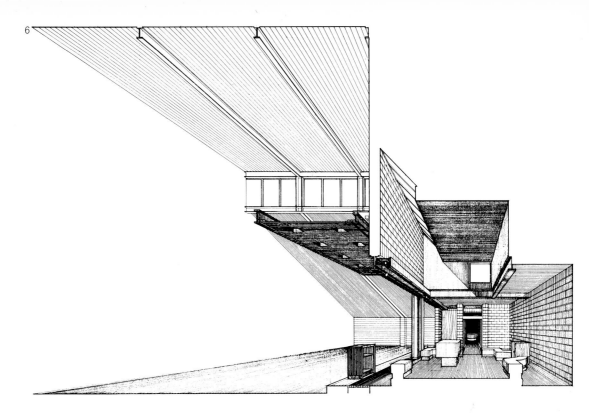

5. External view. In the centre, the chapel with its top-lighting.
6. Perspective section. An inclined skylight provides daylight for the chapel.
7. Parish hall, with furniture arranged for a theatre performance.

5. Außenansicht. In der Mitte die Kapelle mit Oberlicht.
6. Perspektivischer Schnitt. Belichtung der Kapelle durch ein schräges Oberlicht.
7. Gemeindesaal. Möblierung für eine Theater-Veranstaltung.

Pfingstberg-Kirche, Mannheim, 1958–1963
Architect: C. Mutschler (collaborator: Jürgen Bredow)

Pfingstberg-Kirche, Mannheim, 1958–1963
Architekt: C. Mutschler (Mitarbeiter: Jürgen Bredow)

This glass-encased church stands in a pinewood. With its minimum of walling, the interior seems to merge with the exterior, and with its differently sized vertical elements – columns, posts, mullions and light fittings – the building seems to become part of the woods. – A panentheistic space? Well, in any case, an integral space, visibly composed of supporting and supported units.

The plan is basically a square, but its outsides are slightly convex so that all the interior angles are obtuse. Orientation is provided by the diagonal axis: entrance – gallery – central aisle – altar. On either side are the pews, each of the straight rows being interrupted by one angle. The altar zone, placed in front of low relief walls in staggered arrangement, suggests concentration without impairing the transparency of the room. A strongly profiled ceiling spreads across the room like a roof of tree branches.

Placed in isolation are the simple structures of the belfry and of the parish-hall-cum-rectory. The belfry has a height of 24 metres, with an open loggia at 10 metres height for a trombone choir.

This church in the woods signifies a kind of primeval space experience: The segregation of a space from Nature is here achieved in a manner which befits the environment – without romantic overtones, without pathos and without symbolics, yet with workmanlike precision and artistic equivalence.

Der gläserne Kirchenraum steht in einem Kiefernwald. Ein Minimum an räumlicher Abgrenzung läßt den Raum nach außen fließen und durch die verschieden starken Vertikalelemente der Stützen, Zwischenstützen, Glassprossen und Beleuchtungslamellen zu einem Element des Waldes werden. – Ein panentheistischer Raum? Ein einhelliger Raum jedenfalls, sichtbar zusammengesetzt aus tragenden und getragenen Elementen.

Die Seiten des Grundrißquadrats sind in ihrer Mitte leicht nach außen gezogen – so entsteht ein Innenraum mit lauter offenen Winkeln. Als Raumrichtung wirkt die Diagonalachse: Eingang–Empore–Mittelgang–Altar. Seitlich stehen die einmal abgewinkelten Bankreihen. Der Altarbereich liegt vor lamellenartig verschobenen, niedrigen Reliefwänden; er wirkt als eine die Transparenz nicht störende räumliche Verdichtung. Eine stark profilierte Decke breitet sich wie ein Dach aus Zweigen über dem Raum aus.

Abgesetzt sind die einfachen Baukörper des Turmes und des Gemeinde- und Pfarrhauses. Der Turm ist 24 m hoch, in 10 m Höhe befindet sich eine offene Loggia für einen Posaunenchor.

Diese Kirche im Wald bedeutet eine Art räumlicher Urerfahrung: Das Abteilen eines Raumes von der Natur wird hier in der dem Platz angemessenen Weise vollzogen – ohne Romantik, ohne Pathos und ohne Symbolik, aber mit baumeisterlicher Genauigkeit und künstlerischer Äquivalenz.

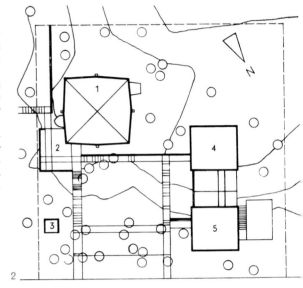

1. The church at night.
2. Site plan. Key: 1 church, 2 forecourt, 3 belfry, 4 youth center, 5 rectory.
3. Church, plan and section. Legend: 1 altar, 2 gallery, 3 baptistry.
4. Interior. The relief walls behind the altar are designed by H. O. Hajek.
5. A view from the gallery.

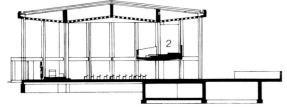

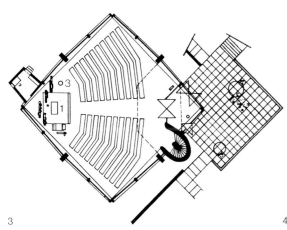

3

4

1. Die Kirche bei Nacht.
2. Gesamtanlage, Lageplan. Legende: 1 Kirche, 2 Vorplatz, 3 Glockenturm, 4 Jugendhaus, 5 Pfarrhaus.
3. Kirche, Grundriß und Schnitt. Legende: 1 Altar, 2 Empore, 3 Taufe.
4. Innenraum. Reliefwände hinter dem Altar von H. O. Hajek.
5. Blick von der Empore.

5

Roman Catholic Parish Centre in Korb, Germany,
1953–1966
Architects: Hans Kammerer, Walter Belz

Katholisches Gemeindezentrum in Korb, Baden-Württemberg, 1963–1966
Architekten: Hans Kammerer, Walter Belz

The plan of the church is a diagonally placed, modified square. With its mighty roof, the building is well integrated with the skyline of the new housing estate. The main source of daylight is at the apex: The altar is brightly lit through a north-light roof not visible to the congregation. At this point, the completely timber-clad roof extends right down to the ground. In contrast, the roof of the parish hall ends above concrete walls of 3 metres height. Roof and wall are separated by a horizontal ribbon of windows which, likewise invisible from the interior, allow the daylight to enter from below.

The spatial effect is that of a short hall with occult features in the lower part and a dramatic design near the roof. The altar zone in the diagonal axis of the church is not very large but forms an effective contrast to the pews. The church directly adjoins the road – its forecourt forms a natural enlargement of the sidewalk. All the more surprising is the emphasis given to the entrance by a hypertrophied concrete sculpture.

Die Kirche zeigt im Grundriß ein übereckgestelltes, abgewandeltes Quadrat. Mit der Überhöhung durch ein mächtiges Dach ist der Bau in die Formen des Neubaugebietes direkt eingegliedert. Über der Raumspitze ist die Hauptlichtquelle: Durch ein der Gemeinde nicht sichtbares Shed fällt das Licht voll auf den Altar. Das innen verschalte Dach wird an dieser Stelle bis zum Boden heruntergezogen, im Gemeinderaum dagegen endet es über 3 m hohen Betonwänden. Zwischen Dach und Wand liegt ein horizontaler Fensterstreifen, der ebenso unsichtbar Licht von unten hereinholt.

Die Raumwirkung ist die einer kurzen, im unteren Teil mystisch, in der Dachzone dramatisch gestalteten Halle. Der Altarbezirk in der Diagonale des Raumes ist nicht sehr groß, aber in wirksame Beziehung zu den Bankgruppen gesetzt. Die Kirche liegt direkt an der Straße – der Vorplatz ist eine einfache Verbreiterung des Trottoirs. Um so überraschender wirkt die Betonung des Eingangs durch ein hypertrophiertes Betonrelief.

1

1. The large roof is intended to suggest a relationship with the existing buildings.
2. Entrance. The toplight visible above the entrance roof illuminates the altar.
3. View of the church from the parish house. Asbestos cement cladding, concrete walls, steps formed by railway sleepers.
4. Plan. Key: 1 altar, 2 gallery, 3 confessional, 4 sacristy, 5 parish hall, 6 youth room, 7 kindergarten, 8 dwelling.

1. Mit dem großen Dach wird eine Beziehung zu vorhandenen Bauformen gesucht.
2. Eingang. Das über dem Eingangsdach sichtbare Oberlicht belichtet den Altar.
3. Blick vom Gemeindehaus auf die Kirche. Eternitverschaltes Dach, Betonwände, Stufen aus Eisenbahnschwellen.
4. Grundriß. Legende: 1 Altar, 2 Empore, 3 Beichte, 4 Sakristei, 5 Gemeindesaal, 6 Jugendraum, 7 Kindergarten, 8 Wohnung.

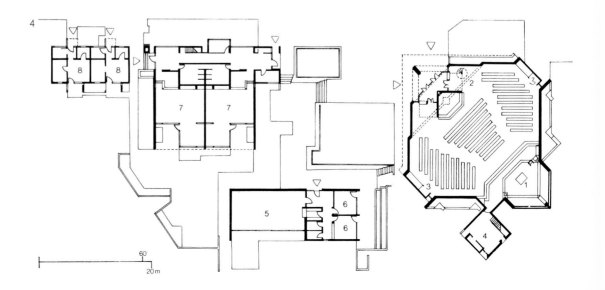

5. The interior receives indirect lighting through the sky-light and through the ribbons of windows above the concrete walls.
6. Gallery, with font below.
7. Altar, tabernacle, toplight, beam construction.

5. Der Innenraum erhält indirektes Licht aus dem Dachoberlicht und den Fensterstreifen über den Betonwänden.
6. Empore mit darunterliegendem Taufstein.
7. Altar, Tabernakel, Oberlicht, Binderkonstruktion.

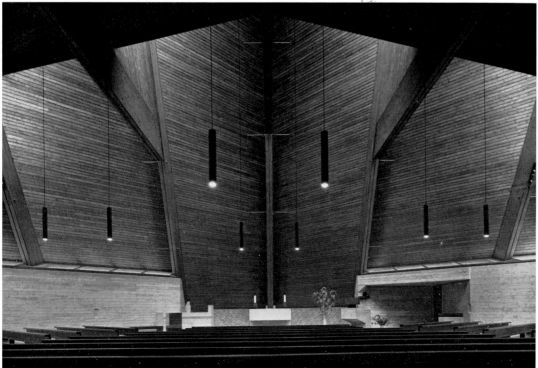

Protestant Parish Centre in Stuttgart-Sonnenberg, 1963–1966
Architect: Ernst Gisel

Evangelisches Gemeindezentrum in Stuttgart-Sonnenberg, 1963–1966
Architekt: Ernst Gisel

Sonnenberg is predominantly a low-rise dormitory suburb of Stuttgart. The proportions of the parish centre are adapted to the dimensions of the surrounding houses. Although the church forms the dominant feature of the group of buildings centred on a courtyard, its close relationship with the remaining buildings is preserved by the choice of design and materials. That is why the whole group is of such integral appearance.
The courtyard is removed from the road, and the slight differences in level are skilfully exploited, from the kerbstone through a strongly emphasised entrance zone to the interior of the church. Daylight enters the church through the roof; the only optical link with the outside is a small glass curtain wall facing the garden. Behind the altar is a convex wall, symbolising the "intrusion" of the liturgical rites into the room. This represents a reversal, used since Ronchamp, of the historic apse which tends to shift the liturgical rites into a mystical remoteness. In a similar way, the historic roof vault has here been used in reverse form, viz. as a suspended shell (consisting on a grid of steel bars with mortar covering) hanging convexly into the room. This is in contrast to the partly inclined, white-washed and rough-cast walls which are bordered and lit up by toplights. The elegant wooden pews, permanently mounted on iron supports, concentrate the congregation around the liturgical centre.
The church is deliberately designed for divine service only; social requirements are met by a number of separate premises (parish hall, two nurseries, display foyer, group premises, etc.).

Sonnenberg ist ein vorwiegend aus Einfamilienhäusern bestehender Vorort von Stuttgart; mit den Proportionen des Gemeindezentrums sind die Maße der umgebenden Bebauung aufgenommen worden. Die Kirche ist zwar Höhepunkt der um einen Hof gruppierten Anlage, jedoch durch Übereinstimmung von Form und Material integraler Bestandteil derselben. Daher wirkt die Baugruppe sehr geschlossen.
Der Hof ist von der Straße abgerückt, ein Höhenspiel mit dem Pflaster beginnt an der Straßenschwelle und setzt sich durch einen wuchtigen Eingang hindurch im Kirchenraum fort. Die Kirche erhält Licht aus dem Dach, nur eine kleine Glaswand zum Garten schafft optische Verbindung nach draußen. Der Altar steht vor einer konvex in den Raum gebuchteten Wand, die die liturgische

Handlung in den Raum »hineindrängt«. Dies ist die seit Ronchamp angewendete Umkehrung der historischen Apsis, die das liturgische Geschehen in eine mystische Ferne rückte. Genauso ist das historische Gewölbe hier in umgekehrter Form verwendet – eine Hängeschale (Rundeisennetz mit Mörtelbewurf) wölbt sich in den Raum hinein. Dagegen stehen durch Oberlichter abgesetzte und beleuchtete, teilweise geneigte, weiß und rauh verputzte Wände. Auf Eisenstützen fest montierte, elegante Holzbänke fixieren die Scharung der Gläubigen um die liturgische Handlung.
Die Kirche ist bewußt nur auf den Gottesdienst hin konzipiert – eine Reihe von Gemeinderäumen (Saal, zwei Kindergärten, Ausstellungsfoyer, Gruppenräume usw.) dienen den sozialen Ansprüchen.

1. Plan and section. Key: 1 altar, 2 gallery, 3 sacristy, 4 dwelling, 5 parish hall, 6 youth rooms, 7 clubrooms, 8 kindergarten.

1. Grundriß und Schnitt. Legende: 1 Altar, 2 Empore, 3 Sakristei, 4 Wohnung, 5 Gemeindesaal, 6 Jugendräume, 7 Klubräume, 8 Kindergarten.

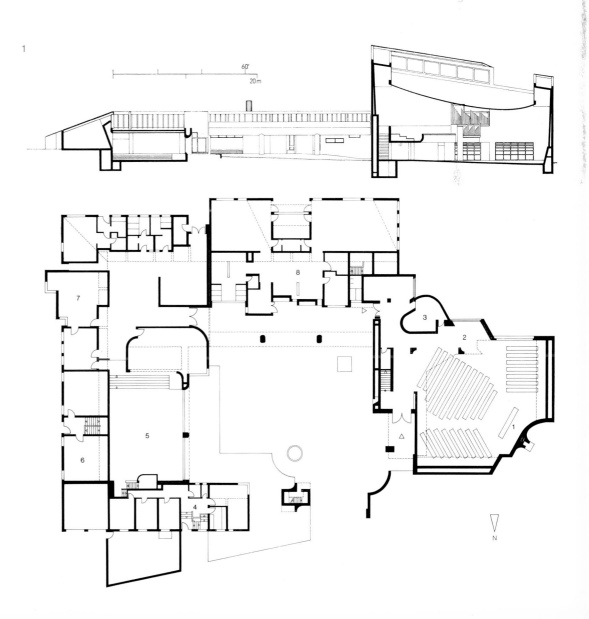

2. Rectory, church and belfry.
3. Kindergarten.
4. Well in the courtyard.
5. Passage connecting the church with the parish premises.
6. The ceiling, convexly suspended into the room, contributes measurably to the spatial effect. The apertures on the right are part of the hot-air heating system. In addition there is electric under-floor heating.
7. Gallery.

4

5

2. Pfarrhaus, Kirche und Turm.

3. Kindergarten.

4. Brunnen im Hof.

5. Verbindungsgang von der Kirche zu den Gemeindebauten.

6. Der Kirchenraum wird in seiner Wirkung maßgeblich
von der nach unten gewölbten Deckenschale bestimmt.
Rechts Öffnungen der Luftheizung (unter dem Pflaster
wurde außerdem eine Elektroheizung eingebaut).

7. Empore.

6

7

St. Stephanus, Bernhausen, Germany, 1964–1968
Architect: Reinhard Gieselmann

This church centre of a Roman Catholic diaspora community has been erected in a newly developed district amidst small factories and two-storey houses, enlivened by colour schemes. These surroundings form a contrast to the uniform design and materials of the church centre.

The parish centre comprises a church for 500 people, a belfry, rectory and kindergarten. The buildings surround a small piazza which, because of the sloping ground, is a few steps lower than the road. A parish hall is to be added later. The dominating church structure which turns and rises towards East, is counter-weighted by the kindergarten building which, though likewise rising, is orientated towards South, and by the planned parish hall. Between these structures are the low-rise buildings of the remaining premises. The belfry – in the picture still shown without louver windows – stands at the threshold between road and piazza, accentuating the skyline of the village.

The basic shape of the church is an irregular pentagon. The concrete walls facing the piazza are solid; those on the other sides, and increasingly towards the altar, are staggered and interrupted by slot windows. The conventional arrangement of the pews and the central aisle dates back to the time before the Second Vatican Council. Even so, the width of the room permits good visibility and audibility. Two reference axes can be discerned: one extending from the piazza through the entrance and central aisle to the altar, the other from the baptistry through the choristers' gallery to the pulpit. A weekday chapel envisaged in the first project has been reduced to a small devotional niche with a Madonna statue, and the supports originally intended for it now stand in the room in an isolated position.

The church forms a component part of the whole group. The integrity of the whole group may well help to clarify the semantic problem in modern church design.

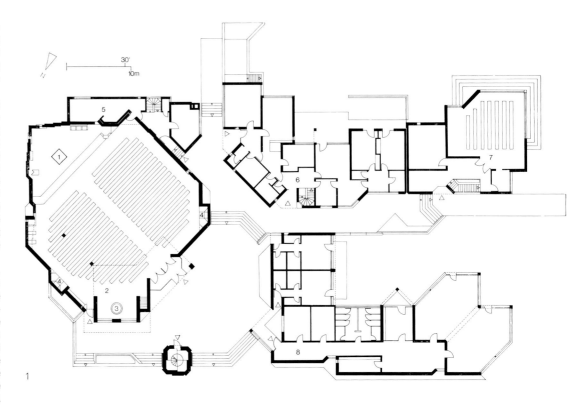

1

2

1. Plan. Key: 1 altar, 2 gallery, 3 baptistry, 4 confessional, 5 sacristy, 6 rectory, 7 parish hall, 8 kindergarten.
2. Kindergarten, belfry (not yet completed), church, rectory.
3. Glass windows behind the altar by Emil Kiess.

**St. Stephanus, Bernhausen, Baden-Württemberg,
1964–1968**
Architekt: Reinhard Gieselmann

Dieses Kirchenzentrum einer katholischen Diaspora-
gemeinde wurde in einem Neubaugebiet mitten zwischen kleinen Fabriken und farbig aufgemachten zweigeschossigen Wohnbauten errichtet. Dagegen kontrastiert die in Formgebung und Material einheitliche
Baugruppe.
Das Gemeindezentrum besteht aus einer Kirche für 500
Personen, einem Turm, Pfarrhaus und Kindergarten.
Die Bauten umgrenzen einen kleinen Platz, der – entsprechend dem Geländeabfall – gegen die Straße um
einige Stufen vertieft liegt. Später soll noch ein Gemeindehaus angebaut werden. Dem dominierenden,
nach Osten abgedrehten und ansteigenden Kirchenbaukörper sind als Gegengewichte die ebenfalls ansteigenden und nach Süden orientierten Kindergartenräume
und – später – der Gemeindesaal entgegengestellt. Die
übrigen Baumassen liegen flach dazwischen. Der Turm
– noch ohne das Schallgehäuse – steht an der Schwelle
zwischen Straße und Platz und bereichert die Silhouette
des Dorfes.
Die Grundform der Kirche ist ein unregelmäßiges Fünf-
eck. Die betonierten Wände sind an der Platzseite geschlossen, an den anderen Seiten zunehmend zum
Altarbezirk hin gestaffelt und geschlitzt. Die konventionelle Anordnung der Bestuhlung und des Mittelgan-
ges stammt aus vorkonziliarer Zeit. Die Breite des Raumes ermöglicht trotzdem gute Sicht- und Hörverhält-
nisse. Im Raum sind zwei Bezugsachsen spürbar: Die
eine reicht vom Vorplatz über Eingang und Mittelgang
zum Altar, die andere von der Taufkapelle und Sängerempore zur Kanzel. Von der Alltagskapelle des ersten
Entwurfes ist nur eine kleine Andachtsnische mit einer
Madonnenplastik übriggeblieben, und die Stützen, die
sie begrenzen sollten, stehen nun frei im Raum.
Die Kirche ist Element der Gesamtanlage. In der Geschlossenheit des Ganzen kann ein Beitrag zu einer
Klärung des semantischen Problems im neuen Kirchenbau liegen.

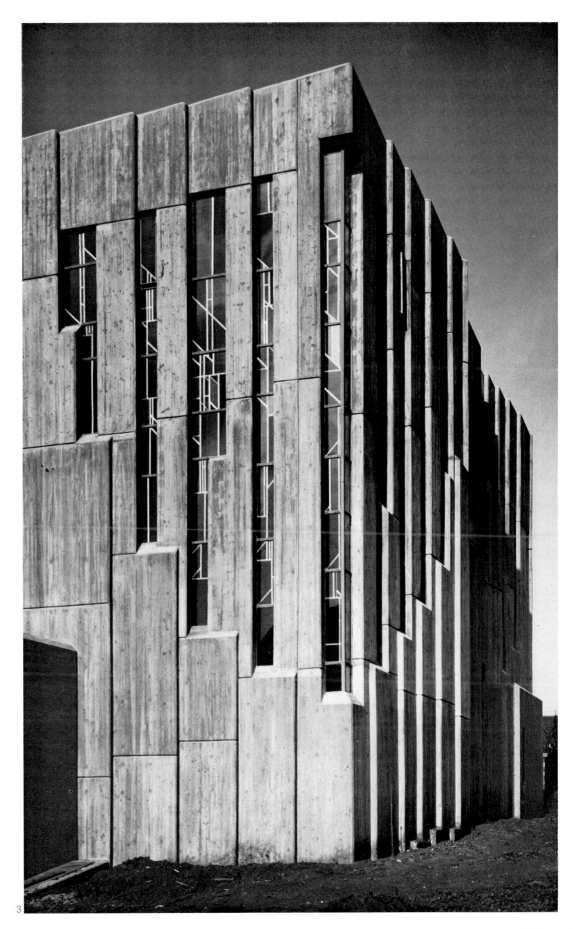

1. Grundriß. Legende: 1 Altar, 2 Empore, 3 Taufe, 4
Beichte, 5 Sakristei, 6 Pfarrwohnung, 7 Gemeindesaal,
8 Kindergarten.
2. Kindergarten, noch nicht vollendeter Turm, Kirche,
Pfarrhaus.
3. Verglasung hinter dem Altar von Emil Kiess.

3

4

5

6

4. South entrance, with the sacristy on the right.
5. View from the roof of the church towards the kindergarten. A parish hall is to be erected in the background, left.
6. Main entrance to the church. The doors are of cast aluminium.
7. Interior of the church. Wooden paving, rough-cast walls, wooden ceiling.
8. Details of roof cladding and columns. The intersections of supports and wooden ceiling are made points of visual conflict by the arrangement of the boards.
9. Altar and tabernacle are made of Londorf basalt. Candelabras and tabernacle door of cast aluminium.

4. Südlicher Zugang, rechts die Sakristei.
5. Blick vom Kirchendach auf den Kindergarten. Im Hintergrund links wird das Gemeindehaus entstehen.
6. Zugangsseite der Kirche. Türen aus Gußaluminium.
7. Kirchenraum. Holzpflaster, grob verputzte Wände, Holzdecke.
8. Die Stellen, an denen die beiden Kirchenraumstützen die hölzerne Deckenschale durchdringen, wurden durch die Anordnung der Schalung als Konfliktpunkte sichtbar gemacht.
9. Altar und Tabernakel aus Londorfer Basalt, Leuchter und Tabernakeltür aus Gußaluminium.

Parish Church in Völs, Austria, 1966–1967
Architect: Josef Lackner

Pfarrkirche in Völs, Österreich, 1966–1967
Architekt: Josef Lackner

This church has been erected by the side of the old village church to serve a rapidly growing congregation. The basically square layout is modified by diagonals so that the space is enlivened by angular projections and recesses. This zone extends to a height of 5 metres and provides a symmetrical orientation for all the liturgical points. In the upper zone, the basic square shape is again visible, the square being extended without further interruption up to the raised corners. Daylight enters through a ribbon of windows along the inner edge of the roof, falling on the rough-cast recesses and skew surfaces so that the interior has only indirect lighting. The white plaster and bright concrete flooring are in contrast to the wood of ceiling and pews.

The evocative contours of this church set a new scale for the village. With its multiple angles, the building seems to be related to the mountains. A touch of folklore has been associated with modern forms to create a modern church.

Neben der alten Dorfkirche wurde diese Kirche für eine stark wachsende Gemeinde errichtet.

Die quadratische Grundform ist durch die Diagonalen zu einem mit Winkeln und Nischen belebten Raum geworden. Diese Nischenzone reicht bis auf 5 m Höhe. Alle Funktionsorte werden durch sie symmetrisch fixiert. In der oberen Zone ist die Grundform wieder sichtbar, das Quadrat wird ungebrochen bis in die überhöhten Ecken hineingezogen. Licht fällt durch ein am inneren Dachrand herumgeführtes Fensterband auf die rauh verputzten Nischen und Schrägen ein, so daß der Raum nur indirekt erhellt wird. Zu dem weiß gestrichenen Putz und zum hellen Betonboden kontrastiert das Holz der Decke und der Bänke.

Der signifikante Umriß setzt im Dorf einen neuen Maßstab. Mit seinen Verwinklungen scheint er Beziehung zu den Bergen aufzunehmen. Ein Hauch Folklore verbindet sich mit modernen Formen zu einer modernen Kirche.

1

2

1. The church in its setting.
2. Exterior view showing the relationship of the dynamic mega-shape to the landscape.
3. Plan. Key: 1 altar, 2 choir, 3 baptistry, 4 confessional, 5 sacristy.
4. View toward the altar. The architect prefers to illuminate the outer walls by toplights along the edge. Deal-lined ceiling.
5. Altar zone. All walls and fittings are plastered white. Right, the rear wall of the priests' bench.
6. View over the altar into the church interior. The confessionals are designed as free-standing, glass-topped units.

1. Die Kirche im Ortsbild.
2. Außenansicht. Eine dynamische Großform nimmt Beziehung zur Landschaft auf.
3. Grundriß. Legende: 1 Altar, 2 Chor, 3 Taufe, 4 Beichte, 5 Sakristei.
4. Blick zum Altar. Der Architekt liebt es, die Außenwände seiner Kirchen durch Randoberlichter zu beleuchten. Decke aus Kiefernholz.
5. Altarzone. Alle Wände und Einbauten sind weiß verputzt. Rechts die Rückwand der Priesterbank.
6. Blick über den Altar in den Kirchenraum. Die Beichtstühle sind als frei stehende, mit Glas abgedeckte Türme ausgebildet.

3

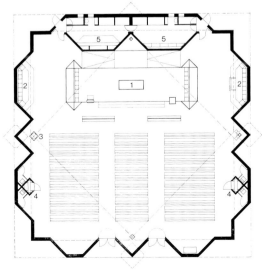

St. Johannes Baptist, Karlsruhe-Durlach, 1962–1965
Architect: Rainer Disse (collaborator: Immo Reinhold)

St. Johannes Baptist, Karlsruhe-Durlach, 1962–1965
Architekt: Rainer Disse (Mitarbeiter: Immo Reinhold)

This church stands in a large open space between low-rent blocks of flats. It gives the impression of an island, linked with its surroundings by narrow paths. Rectory and kindergarten are to be added later. The basic shape is an equilateral hexagon, emphasising the solitary character of the building. A visit to the church is not made easy. The visitor must cover a long distance in the open and then ascend numerous steps.

On entering the church, he is confronted with a strange sight: Mushroom-shaped columns with hexagonal canopies form the roof from which the sculptural non-bearing walls are clearly separated. White daylight enters through the triangular roof windows and through the gaps between the mushroom units, and strong red light through the horizontal slots above the walls. The sculptural walls consist of lightweight concrete with a greyish-mauve hue; the wooden pews are white-stained; the flooring consists of brownish no-fines concrete.

Partly-open and half-open rooms help to provide a reference scale. Separated by isolated confessionals is a weekday chapel; the choristers' gallery is formed by a

second mushroom canopy placed on a lower level of the same column. The sacristy, too, projects into the room. In contrast to the basic hexagonal shape, the central aisle provides a directional orientation. However, as a result of the consistent application of the same structural system, the central aisle is interrupted by a column.

A parish hall and premises at present used as a kindergarten are placed in a basement which receives daylight through an outer trench placed six steps below ground level. In the belfry, accessible from a separate stairwell tower, are premises for young people. The triangular shapes of the towers are in keeping with the triangular module on which the entire plan has been based.

The church reflects the controversy between the obligatory episcopal requirements for a central aisle, the new liturgical ideas, and an architectural personality inclined towards three-dimensional treatment. The social premises are unduly constrained by the monumental character and the rigid plan module of the building.

Die Kirche steht mitten in einer großen Grünfläche zwischen Blocks des sozialen Wohnbaues. Sie wirkt wie eine Insel, nur durch schmale Wege mit der Umwelt verankert. Pfarrhaus und Kindergarten sollen später einmal dazugebaut werden. Die Grundform ist ein gleichseitiges Sechseck, eine Form, die den Solitärcharakter des Gebäudes betont. Dem Gläubigen wird der Besuch nicht leicht gemacht. Er muß eine weite freie Strecke zurücklegen und zum Kirchenraum noch viele Stufen emporsteigen.

Den Besucher empfängt ein eigenartiger Raum: Pilzstützen mit sechseckigen Schirmen bilden das Dach, die raumbegrenzende, stark reliefierte Wand steht frei darunter. Weißes Licht fällt aus den dreieckigen Dachfenstern zwischen den Pilzschirmen ein, scharfes rotes Licht aus waagrechten Schlitzen über den Wänden. Die Reliefwände sind aus Ytong und schimmern graulila, die Holzbänke sind weiß imprägniert, der Boden ist bräunlicher Waschbeton.

Teil- und Halbräume tragen zur Maßstabbildung bei. Mit frei stehenden Beichthäuschen ist eine Alltags-

1

1. The church appears as a solitary building, isolated from its residential environment. The social premises are on the lower floor.
2. Plan. Key: 1 altar, 2 gallery, 3 confessional, 4 chapel, 5 sacristy.
3, 4. Views. The exposed concrete facades are divided by vertical grooves and concrete joints.

1. Die Kirche – ein von der Wohn-Umwelt abgesonderter Solitärbau. Im Untergeschoß befinden sich die Sozialräume.
2. Grundriß. Legende: 1 Altar, 2 Empore, 3 Beichte, 4 Kapelle, 5 Sakristei.
3, 4. Ansichten. Gliederung der Sichtbeton-Fassaden durch senkrechte Profilierung und Betonierfugen.

kapelle abgetrennt, die Sängerempore ist ein an der gleichen Stütze tiefersitzender zweiter Pilzschirm. Auch die Sakristei ist in den Raum hineingebaut. Der zentralen Form des Sechsecks widersprechend ist die Kirche durch den Mittelgang richtungsbetont. Durch die konsequente Anwendung des Konstruktionssystems steht im Mittelgang eine Stütze.

Ein Gemeindesaal und als Kindergarten benutzte Räume liegen im Untergeschoß, das Licht durch einen sechs Stufen unter Niveau liegenden Außengang erhält. Im Glockenturm, der durch einen weiteren Treppenturm erschlossen wird, befindet sich der Jugendraum. Die dreieckigen Türme folgen dem dreieckigen Grundraster, der dem ganzen Grundriß zugrunde gelegt ist.

Die Kirche spiegelt die Auseinandersetzung zwischen den bindenden bischöflichen Vorschriften für einen Mittelgang, den neuen liturgischen Ideen und einer zum Plastischen neigenden Architektenpersönlichkeit. Die sozialen Räume wurden dem monumentalen Charakter und dem strengen Grundrißschema des Baues zu stark unterworfen.

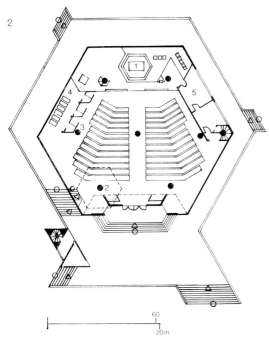

60
20m

5. Organ and choristers' gallery.
6. The interior walls are lined with lightweight concrete slabs, sculptured by Josef Weber. Roof consists of mushroom supports, intermediate bays covered by wired glass.

5. Orgel- und Sängerempore.
6. Die Innenwände sind mit Ytong-Platten verkleidet, die von dem Bildhauer Josef Weber reliefartig gestaltet wurden. Die Zwischenfelder zwischen den Sechseck-platten des Daches bestehen aus Drahtglas.

St. Bernadette, Nevers, France, 1963–1964
Architects: Claude Parent, Paul Virilio

Ste. Bernadette, Nevers, Frankreich, 1963–1964
Architekten: Claude Parent, Paul Virilio

The church at Nevers is part of a two-storey structure. In the lower floor are the main entrance, the parish premises and a chapel; on the upper floor is the church proper. The main stairs lead into the centre of the room – this immediacy of spatial experience is in keeping with the uncompromising directness which overwhelms the visitor even from the outside.

The architects, who have adopted the group description *Architecture Principe,* aim at the immediacy of the mega-shape. Their church, too, has an entirely sculptural, integrally cast, plastic shape. They do not conceal the fact that their phenotypes include the bunkers of the Atlantic Wall dating back to the time of the German occupation. This gives rise to the impression of a "castellated church".

The brutalistic shape is highly evocative, being equally distinguished by austerity and memorability. Compared with other examples of Brutalism, the design convinces through the harmony between interior and exterior.

Die Kirche von Nevers ist eine zweigeschossige Anlage. Im Untergeschoß befinden sich der Haupteingang, die Pfarräume und eine Kapelle, im Obergeschoß die Kirche. Die Haupttreppe führt mitten in den Raum – diese Unmittelbarkeit des Raumerlebnisses korrespondiert mit der kompromißlosen Direktheit, mit der der Besucher schon von außen überwältigt wird.

Die Architekten, die unter dem Namen »Architecture principe« hervorgetreten sind, erstreben die Unmittelbarkeit der Großform. So ist auch ihre Kirche eine rundum plastische Form aus einem Guß. Sie machen keinen Hehl daraus, daß zu ihren Phänotypen die Bunker des Atlantikwalls aus der deutschen Besatzungszeit gehören. So entsteht der Eindruck der Wehrkirche.

Die brutalistische Form hat eine hohe Aussagekraft. Schlichtheit und Einprägsamkeit zeichnen sie in gleicher Weise aus. Gegenüber anderen Beispielen des Brutalismus überzeugt sie durch die Konkordanz von innen und außen.

1

1. German bunker along the French Atlantic coast, built during the Second World War.
2. Entrance side of the church.

1. Bunker aus der Zeit des Zweiten Weltkrieges an der französischen Atlantikküste.
2. Eingangsseite der Kirche.

2

3. Detail of the recessed entrance.
4. On the ground floor, to the right of the entrance, is the baptistry. Font designed by Morice Lipsi. In the background, the entrance to the daytime chapel.
5. Glass has been used as a partition between staircase and the shell of the nave.
6. Plans and section. Key: 1 altar, 2 chapel.
7. View from the landing of the central stairs leading to the altar. Ambo, pulpit and tabernacle are designed by Lipsi.
8. Nave, side stairs, toplight.

3. Der zurückgesetzte Eingang.
4. Im Erdgeschoß befindet sich rechts vom Eingang die Taufkapelle; Taufstein von Morice Lipsi. Hinten Eingang zur Tageskapelle.
5. Glas als Trennung zwischen Treppenhaus und Schale des Schiffes.
6. Grundrisse und Schnitt. Legende: 1 Altar, 2 Kapelle.
7. Blick vom Austritt der mittleren Treppe zum Altar. Ambo, Kanzel und Tabernakel von Lipsi.
8. Schiff, Seitentreppe, Oberlicht.

7

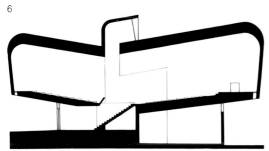

6

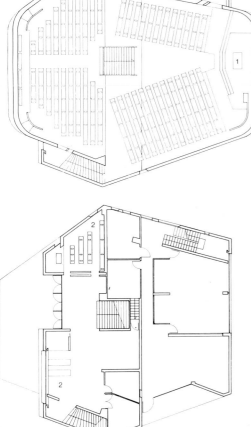

8

Synagogue of the Hebrew University, Jerusalem, 1956–1957
Architects: Ezra Rau, David Reznik

Synagoge der Hebräischen Universität, Jerusalem, 1956–1957
Architekten: Ezra Rau, David Reznik

Synagogues are not in every respect comparable with Christian places of worship. They have always been designed on more pragmatic principles as a house of prayer, of teaching, and of assembly. The latter function far exceeded the purpose of a purely religious community; it was here that the Jewish groups found their coherence. The ghetto synagogue was the centre of all community activities, in fact exactly what we nowadays aim at in the Christian church. In modern times, most of the synagogues have become more exclusive places of worship. With the synagogue, it is not possible to discern a historic development of a style, let alone a type, to the same degree as in church design. The awareness of being apart or different has always induced the Jews to keep a distance from Christian styles. Moreover, the liturgical requirements are comparatively simple – a place of sacrifice, for instance, is not needed. On the other hand, every synagogue must have a holy ark *(Aron ha-kodesch),* containing the scrolls of the Torah with the text of the Pentateuch. This text is read out publicly on the 52 sabbaths of the year. Such readings as well as prayers play a much more important role than lectures or sermons. For the reading, the synagogue must therefore have a further essential part, namely the reading desk *(almemor)* which is often identical with the desk of the prayer leader *(chasan).* Public worship may only be held in the presence of at least ten male persons over 13 years of age. Originally, divine service was confined to men, whilst women were relegated to a gallery.

The synagogue of the Hebrew University in Jerusalem forms, together with a small library, a precinct of its own which, in its seclusion, conveys a feeling of security.

A zone consisting of rooms and open spaces surrounded by rubble stones is covered by the independent, isolated structure of the white dome. The visitor enters the dome along the flanking walls. He is surrounded by a covered courtyard which provides a view framed by the arches. A curved flight of stairs leads to the place of worship on the upper level. Indirect light enters from below through the gap between the dome and the isolated floor slab. The white, seemingly infinite shell appears to float, conveying an impression of spacelessness which distinguishes the worship area from its secular surroundings.

Synagogen sind nicht in jeder Hinsicht mit christlichen Kultbauten vergleichbar. Sie waren von jeher mehr pragmatisch angelegt, als Haus des Gebetes, der Lehre und der Versammlung. Die letzte Funktion ging weit über den Rahmen der reinen Religionsgemeinschaft hinaus; in ihr fanden die jüdischen Gruppen ihren Zusammenhalt. Die Synagoge des Gettos war Mittelpunkt aller gemeindlichen Aktivitäten, also das, was wir uns heute für die christliche Kirche wünschen. Heute ist die Synagoge in den meisten Fällen nur Kultraum. Eine historische Stilentwicklung oder gar einen Typ kann man bei der Synagoge nicht in dem Maße feststellen wie im Kirchenbau. Das Bewußtsein des Abseits- und des Andersseins hat die Juden immer wieder Distanz zu christlichen Stilen nehmen lassen. Dazu kommt, daß der Kult vergleichsweise einfacher ist – ein Ort des Opfers wird zum Beispiel nicht benötigt. Jede Synagoge muß dagegen einen heiligen Schrein (Aron ha-kodesch) zur Aufbewahrung der Thora-Rollen haben, auf denen der Text der fünf Bücher Moses verzeichnet ist. Dieser Text wird im Laufe eines Jahres an 52 Sabbaten verlesen. Verlesung und Gebet spielten eine viel wichtigere Rolle

1. The precise shape of the synagogue forms a strong contrast to the rough surroundings.
2. The glass-encased entrance hall is recessed.
3. Plan and section. Key: 1 shrine, 2 lectern, 3 stairs, 4 library, 5 court.
4. The arches form a frame for the landscape. The ceiling is separated from the outer wall by an annular opening which admits daylight to the upper floor.

1

als Vortrag oder Predigt. Zur Verlesung dient das Vorlesepult (Almemor), das oft identisch mit dem Pult des Vorbeters (Chasan) ist. Zum Gottesdienst ist es notwendig, daß zehn über dreizehn Jahre alte Männer anwesend sind. Der Gottesdienst war ursprünglich reine Männersache – für Frauen wurde eine Empore vorgesehen.

Die Synagoge der Hebräischen Universität in Jerusalem bildet zusammen mit einer kleinen Bibliothek einen eigenen Bereich, der durch seine Intimität ein Gefühl der Geborgenheit vermittelt.

Über einer Zone von bruchsteinumgebenen Räumen und Freiräumen erhebt sich die unabhängige Einzelform der weißen Kuppel. Der Besucher wird durch die begleitenden Mauern unter die Kuppel geführt. Ein gedeckter Hof mit einer durch die Bögen gerahmten Aussicht umfängt ihn. Über eine gekrümmte Treppe gelangt er in den Kultraum der oberen Ebene. Indirektes Licht kommt von unten durch den Spalt zwischen Kuppel und frei stehender Bodenplatte in den Raum. Durch die weiße, scheinbar grenzenlose Schale entsteht der Eindruck des Schwebenden, Raumlosen, der den Ort aus seiner profanen Umgebung heraushebt.

1. Die präzise Form der Synagoge bildet einen starken Kontrast zu der rauhen Umgebung.
2. Die verglaste Eingangshalle ist zurückgesetzt.
3. Grundriß und Schnitt. Legende: 1 Schrein, 2 Vorlesepult, 3 Treppe, 4 Bibliothek, 5 Hof.
4. Die Bögen bilden Rahmen für die Landschaft. Von der Außenwand durch einen Lichtstreifen abgesetzte Decke.

3

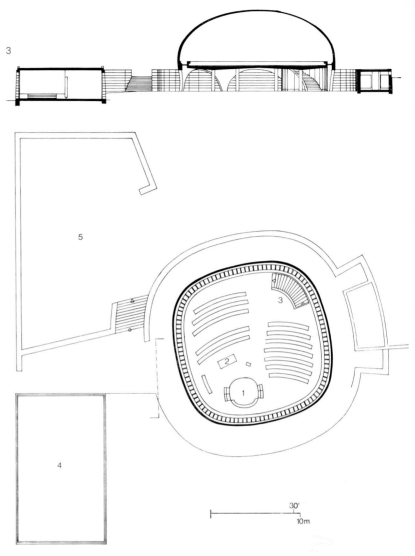

30'
10m

2

4

5

6

5. Aron ha-kodesch.
6. Stairway. On the left, the annular opening for daylight.
7. Lower entrance hall and walled courtyard.

5. Aron ha-kodesch.
6. Treppenaufgang, links das Unterlichtband.
7. Untere Eingangshalle und ummauerter Hof.

7

Taivallahti Church, Helsinki, 1961–1969
Architects: Timo and Tuomo Suomalainen

Taivallahti-Kirche, Helsinki, 1961–1969
Architekten: Timo und Tuomo Suomalainen

This church was blasted out from the rock on a site surrounded by tenement houses. Out of bed-rock and man-made walls, an almost circular space, covered by a flat dome, was created which is, in its austerity, reminiscent of early Christian religiosity. Daylight enters through the roof windows between the ribbons which support the flat, copper-lined dome. An underground passage connects the church with the parish premises. The service rooms are accessible from the main entrance. The cupola is surrounded by a rock garden.

The coarsely cut altar and the font consist of the same reddish stone as the walls. The traces of the blasting operations and drill holes in the walls are deliberately left unconcealed.

Here, a space has been created to suit modern theology. Young theologians had unsuccessfully demanded that the church should not be consecrated. They justified their demand by the fact that this room, financed from public funds, should be used not only for public worship but also for secular activities of the congregation.

Die Kirche wurde aus einem zwischen Wohnblocks liegenden Fels herausgehauen. Zwischen gewachsenem Stein und aufgemauerten Wänden entstand ein fast runder, nach oben durch eine flache Kuppel begrenzter Raum, der in seiner Schlichtheit den Eindruck frühchristlicher Religiosität erweckt. Licht fällt zwischen den verglasten Rippen ein, die die flache, mit Kupfer beschlagene Kuppel tragen. Ein unterirdischer Gang verbindet die Kirche mit den Gemeinderäumen. Um die Kirchenkuppel herum wurde ein Felsengarten angelegt. Aus dem gleichen rötlichen Stein wie die Wände sind auch der grob behauene Altar und der Taufstein. Die Spuren der Sprengungen und die Bohrlöcher an den Wänden sind bewußt erhalten.

Hier ist ein Raum für die moderne Theologie entstanden. Junge Theologen hatten sich vergeblich dafür eingesetzt, die Kirche nicht zu weihen. Sie begründeten ihren Wunsch damit, daß dieser mit öffentlichen Mitteln finanzierte Raum nicht nur dem Gottesdienst, sondern auch profanen Aktivitäten der Gemeinde dienen sollte.

1. The church is blasted into the rock; its flat dome is therefore only visible from the air.

1. Der aus dem Felsen herausgesprengte Raum wird mit seiner flachen Kuppel nur aus der Vogelschau sichtbar.

2

2. View from the gallery toward the altar.
3. Plan. Key: 1 altar, 2 gallery, 3 parish room.
4. Detail of the connection between the ribs of the dome and the rock wall. Key: 1 copper plate 0.5 mm, 2 base lining, 3 bitumen felt, 4 base lining, 5 windbreak, asbestos sheet, 6 heat insulation, light gravel concrete and mineral wool, 7 reinforced concrete shell, 8 acoustic surfaces, asbestos sheet. 9 wooden daises, 10 copper slat surface, slats 20 × 1 mm, holes 5 mm, 11 roof window, steel shell and heat glass units (lower pane triplex glass), 12 reinforced concrete beam (factory made), 13 copper-surfaced bitumen felting, 14 reinforced concrete slab with snow-melting resistors, 15 rainwater well, 16 heat insulation, hard mineral wool, 17 quarried stone wall, 18 rainwater pie, 19 external quarry line, 20 internal quarry line, 21 rock surface, 22 hole for outgoing air and water from rock, 23 ditching tubes.
5. Gallery.
6. Middle section of the church.

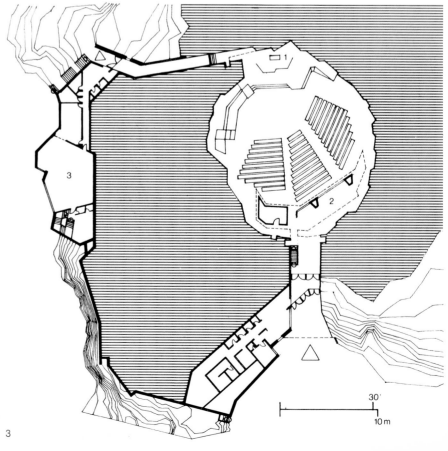

3

30'
10 m

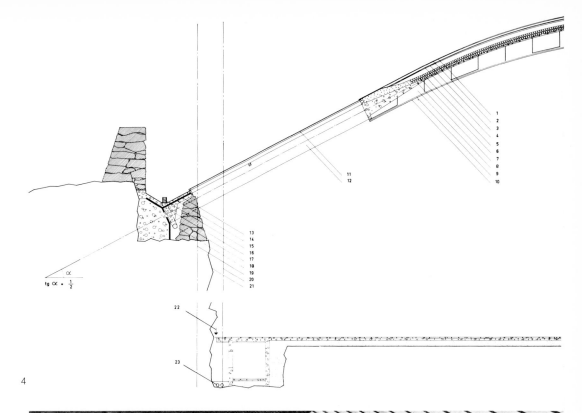

4

5

6

2. Blick von der Empore auf den Altar.

3. Grundriß. Legende: 1 Altar, 2 Empore, 3 Gemeinderaum.

4. Detail des Anschlusses der Rippen an die Felswand. Legende: 1 Kupferblech, 2 Unterfütterung, 3 Bitumenfilz, 4 Unterfütterung, 5 Asbestplatten als Windschutz, 6 Leichtbeton und Mineralwolle, 7 Stahlbetonschale, 8 Asbestplatten als Schallflächen, 9 Holzschalung, 10 Decklage aus Kupferleisten, 11 Oberlicht aus wärmedämmendem Glas, 12 vorgefertigter Stahlbetonbalken, 13 Bitumenfilz mit Kupferverkleidung, 14 Stahlbetonplatte mit Heizung zum Schneeschmelzen, 15 Regenwasser-Rinnenkasten, 16 verfestigte Mineralwolle, 17 Bruchsteinmauer, 18 Regenwasserrohr, 19 Außengrenze des Felsausbruchs, 20 Innengrenze des Felsausbruchs, 21 anstehender Fels, 22 Luft- und Wasserdurchlaß vor der Felswand, 23 Abzugsrohre.

5. Empore.

6. Mittelraum der Kirche.

Muttergotteskapelle, Niesenberg, Switzerland, 1962
Architect: Hans A. Brütsch

Muttergotteskapelle, Niesenberg, Schweiz, 1962
Architekt: Hans A. Brütsch

This chapel has been erected on a hill top near the Monastery of Muri in the Swiss Canton of Aargau. The plan shows an oblong hexagon which is enlarged by the rhombic porch. Altar step and pews are placed parallel to the contour lines of the roof which has its lowest point at the forecourt and its highest point behind the altar. From the glass wall of the entrance, the whole of the high room can be taken in at once, with its wooden pews, the statue of the Holy Virgin, and the sandstone altar. At the same time, the glass curtain makes the forecourt appear to be a natural extension of the chapel. The forecourt is bordered by the steps of the approach paths. In this simple manner, platforms have been created which serve as a venue for summerly celebrations attended by large congregations. A concrete altar marks the focal point of the forecourt. At the top of the building, the walls rise to form a small belfry.

As in many modern churches, the glazing of the narrow windows is indifferently non-committal. In such a small room, designed with so much architectural care, one might have expected either a colourless glazing or, alternatively, precious mosaic windows.

Die Kapelle steht auf einer Hügelkuppe im Aargau in der Nähe des Klosters Muri. Der Grundriß zeigt ein langgezogenes Sechseck, das um die rhombische Vorhalle erweitert ist. Altarstufe und Bänke sind parallel zu den Gefällelinien des Dachs gesetzt, das mit seiner tiefsten Stelle am Vorplatz beginnt und bis zum höchsten Punkt hinter dem Altar ansteigt. Von der Glaswand des Eingangs aus erfaßt man sogleich den hohen Raum mit den Holzbänken, der Marienstatue und dem Sandsteinaltar. Die Glaswand läßt andererseits den Vorplatz als natürliche Raumfortsetzung erscheinen. Die Stufen der Zu-

1

2

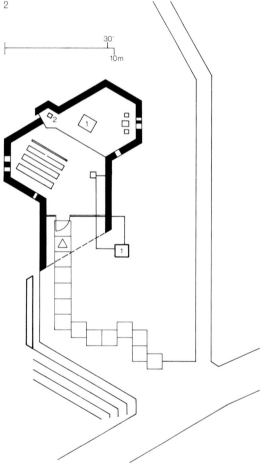

gangswege begrenzen den Außenraum. Auf einfache Weise sind hier Estraden entstanden, die sommerlichen Feiern mit einem größeren Personenkreis dienen. Ein Altar aus Beton ist Mittelpunkt des Außenraumes. Die Mauern sind am Kulminationspunkt des Gebäudes zu einem Glockenträger hochgezogen.

Die Verglasung der kleinen Lichtschlitze ist – wie in vielen neuen Kirchen – von einer dürftigen Unverbindlichkeit. Gerade in diesem kleinen, architektonisch so sorgfältig gestalteten Raum hätte man eine farblose Verglasung oder aber kostbare Glaskunstfenster erwartet.

1. The glass curtain wall has the effect of integrating the piazza with the interior of the church.
2. Plan. Key: 1 altar, 2 statue of the Virgin.
3, 4. The forecourt is flanked by an inclined wall which takes up the slope of the pent roof.
5. Interior with forecourt.

1. Durch eine Glaswand wird der Vorplatz in den Kirchenraum einbezogen.
2. Grundriß. Legende: 1 Altar, 2 Marienstatue.
3, 4. Eine abgeschrägte Wand schließt den Vorplatz ab. Sie hat die gleiche Neigung wie das Pultdach.
5. Innenraum mit Vorplatz.

Centre Oecuménique de Chamrousse, Roche-Béranger, France, 1966–1967
Architect: Pierre Jomain

Centre Oecuménique de Chamrousse, Roche-Béranger, Frankreich, 1966–1967
Architekt: Pierre Jomain

One of the few examples of a place of public worship shared by Roman Catholics and Protestants alike has been created in the holiday region near Chamrousse. The denominations jointly built a twin church which was placed on two levels: a Roman Catholic church for 500 to 2,000 people on the upper level, and a Protestant church for 100 to 200 people on the lower level.

The interior of the upper church which slopes down to the altar, is enclosed by two walls which are informally curved in the plan and rise in the elevation. The ceiling rises in the opposite direction. The south wall is mainly of glass so that the skiers – who are numerous on winter Sundays – can take part in the service from outside. The liturgical furnishings and the floor consist of rubble stone and thick gravel; the walls are coarsely treated on the inside, and clad with reddish cedar boards on the outside.

The smaller chapel on the lower floor has a different character. Its plan is oval, the floor is level and paved with circular setts of wood. The thick wall is composed of heavy, sculpturally treated laminations which keep the interior in the shade.

Eines der wenigen Beispiele für einen gemeinsamen Kultbau von Katholiken und Protestanten ist im Erholungsgebiet bei Chamrousse entstanden. Die Konfessionen erbauten zusammen ein zweigeschossiges Kirchengebäude mit Kulträumen für 500–2000 Katholiken im Obergeschoß und 100–200 Protestanten im Untergeschoß.

In der Oberkirche fassen zwei im Grundriß frei gekurvte, im Aufriß ansteigende Wände den zum Altar abfallenden Raum ein. In entgegengesetzter Richtung steigt die Decke an. Die Südwand ist in Glas aufgelöst, so daß die an Wintersonnentagen zahlreichen Skifahrer von außen am Gottesdienst teilnehmen können. Die Kulteinrichtungen und der Boden bestehen aus Feldsteinen und dicken Kieseln; die Wände sind innen grob bestochen, außen mit rötlichen Zedernschindeln verkleidet.

Die kleinere Kapelle im Untergeschoß hat einen von der Oberkirche abweichenden Charakter. Der Grundriß ist eiförmig, der Boden eben und mit runden Holzabschnitten gepflastert. Die dicke Wand ist in kräftige, plastische Lamellen aufgelöst, die den Raum in Schatten tauchen.

1. A view of the north entrance.
2. Towards south, the building opens up with a glass curtain wall.
3. Plans. Key: 1 Catholic room, 2 Protestant room.
4, 5. Catholic room in the upper-storey. The character of the room is determined by the coarsely treated wall and the rubble stone flooring, together with the boulders serving as altar and tabernacle.
6, 7. The Protestant church on the lower floor. Here, the flooring consists of wood paving. The windows are negative moulds cut out of the walls.

1

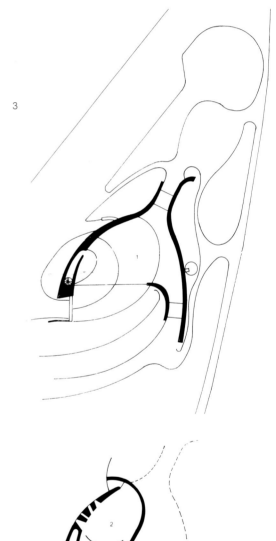

3

2

1. Blick zum Nordeingang.
2. Der Bau ist mit einer Glaswand nach Süden geöffnet.
3. Grundrisse. Legende: 1 Katholischer Raum, 2 evangelischer Raum.
4, 5. Katholischer Raum im Obergeschoß. Die grob bestochene Wand und der Boden aus Feldsteinen bestimmen zusammen mit den Findlingsformen von Altar und Tabernakel den Charakter des Raumes.
6, 7. Evangelischer Raum im Untergeschoß. Boden aus Holzabschnitten. Die Fenster sind aus der Wand herausgeschnittene Negativformen.

Protestant Atonement Chapel in the former KZ
Dachau, Germany, 1965–1967
Architect: Helmut Striffler

Evangelische Versöhnungskirche im ehemaligen KZ
Dachau, 1965–1967
Architekt: Helmut Striffler

With great care, the notorious concentration camp in Dachau has been restored; the watch towers have been freshly painted, the barbed wire renewed, the gravel paths freshly covered, creating an oppressively perfect monument to the atrocities of the Nazi period. In addition, the three religious denominations have built memorial chapels. The last to be erected was the Protestant chapel which was built in 1967. The architect was required to build a monument, yet wanted to do so without monumentality. He saw in the rectangularity of the camp a ''symbol of a deathly police regime'' so outrageously abused that he would not wish to use it for his chapel.
The memorial chapel is ''dug like a trace of life in the pitiless realm of the camp''. A path leads down over large steps, becomes narrower, expands again to form a patio of tranquility and contemplation, passes through the chapel before returning through another bottleneck into the open. The three premises – an ante-room for information purposes, the patio and the chapel – form an optical unit which can also be made real by pushing aside the glass partitions which separate them.

Das Konzentrationslager Dachau wurde mit großer Gründlichkeit wiederhergestellt, die Wachtürme frisch gestrichen, der Stacheldraht erneuert, die Kieswege neu bestreut; es entstand ein bedrückend perfektes Denkmal an die hier verübten Greuel der Nazi-Zeit. Zusätzlich haben die drei Konfessionen Gedenkkapellen gebaut. Die evangelische Kapelle wurde 1967 als letzte errichtet. Der Architekt hatte ein Monument zu bauen und wollte es ohne Monumentalität tun. Er glaubte, in der Rechtwinkligkeit des Lagers »Symbol der tödlichen Polizeiordnung« zu sehen, mit der zuviel Mißbrauch getrieben worden war, um sie auch noch für seinen Bau anwenden zu können.
Die Gedenkstätte ist wie eine »lebendige Spur in die unbarmherzige Fläche des Lagers eingegraben«. Ein Weg führt mit großen Treppen hinab, wird enger, erweitert sich zu einem Platz der Ruhe und Stille und findet – durch den kirchlichen Raum hindurch – wieder halseng ins Freie. Die drei Räume – Sozialraum mit Informationen, der Hof und die Kapelle – bilden, durch Glaswände verbunden, eine optische Einheit, die auch durch Wegschieben der Glaswände real hergestellt werden kann.

1. Concentric stairs lead down to the entrance.
2. Plan. Key: 1 altar, 2 sacristy, 3 community room, 4 court.
3, 4. External views.

1. Zum Eingang führen sammelnde Treppen hinab.
2. Grundriß. Legende: 1 Altar, 2 Sakristei, 3 Gemeinschaftsraum, 4 Hof.
3, 4. Außenansichten.

1

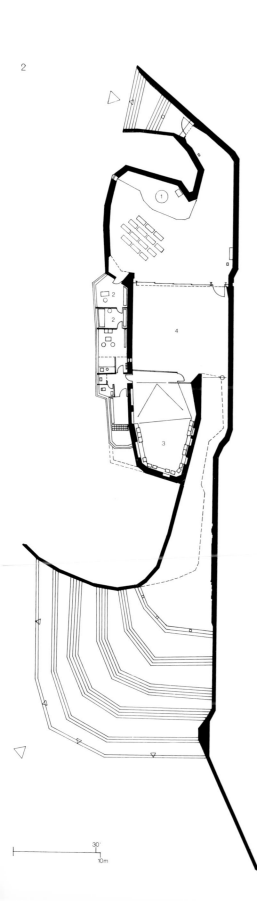

2

3

4

30'
10m

5. Passage to the patio. Relief by Hubertus v. Pilgrim.
6. Entrance door.
7. Patio, with view on the social area.
8. Chapel. The round altar enables the priest to chose his position depending on the number and grouping of the congregation.

5. Gang zum Innenhof. Relief von Hubertus v. Pilgrim.
6. Eingangstor.
7. Hof mit Blick in den Sozialraum.
8. Kapelle. Der runde Altar ermöglicht dem Geistlichen eine nach Zahl und Gruppierung der Zuhörer verschiedene Standortwahl.

1. Plan and section. Key: 1 altar, 2 gallery, 3 cloister, 4 baptistry, 5 sacristy.
2. Entrance side. The materials of the church are rubble stone, exposed concrete and copper sheeting.

1. Grundriß und Schnitt. Legende: 1 Altar, 2 Empore, 3 Kreuzgang, 4 Taufe, 5 Sakristei.
2. Eingangsseite. Die Materialien der Kirche sind Bruchstein, Sichtbeton und Kupferblech.

This church monument, visible from afar, has been erected for passing motorists by the side of the Autostrada del Sole near Florence. It is dedicated to the memory of the workers who came to grief during the construction of the motorway. In his "Justification of an architectural design", Michelucci writes as follows: "I was given the opportunity to develop my own ideas in searching for means and forms which (as I thought) should convey such an expressive eloquence that they would, even apart from any aesthetic or technical interest, find an echo and approval with people – also, and especially, with those who are not familiar with theory, plan, technological problems and aesthetic questions". Michelucci's semantic reference is the "tent", symbolising a transient passage not only of the passing motorist but also of the Christian on his way from this world to the next. Yet the architect emphasises that the notion of the "tent" was not the point of departure of his project; it was first after the internal structure had evolved that the shape of the tent had become apparent.
Michelucci was one of Italy's leading Functionalists. The railway station at Florence (1936) is one of the most convincing buildings of that period. The church is the late creation of a man who had apparently developed doubts in the cause of Rationalism – he built a church which primarily appeals to the emotions.

Für durchreisende Touristen wurde an der Autostrada del Sole bei Florenz dieses weithin sichtbare Kirchenmonument errichtet. Gewidmet ist der Bau den beim Bau der Autobahn verunglückten Arbeitern. Michelucci schreibt in seiner »Rechtfertigung einer architektonischen Form«: »Mir wurde die Möglichkeit gegeben, meinen Geist frei zu entfalten bei der Suche nach den Mitteln und Formen, die (wie ich dachte) eine derart ausdrucksvolle Beredsamkeit entwickeln sollten, daß sie außerhalb jeglichen ästhetischen oder technischen Interesses Widerhall und Zustimmung bei den Menschen fänden, auch und überhaupt bei solchen, denen Theorie, Grundriß, technologische Probleme und Formfragen fremd sind.« Micheluccis semantischer Bezug ist das Zelt, das »Durchreise« bedeuten soll, also das transitorische Moment sowohl des Autobahnreisenden als auch des Christen auf seinem Weg vom Diesseits zum Jenseits. Der Architekt betont, daß jedoch die Vorstellung »Zelt« nicht der Ausgangspunkt des Entwurfes war, sondern daß zuerst die innere Struktur entstand und die Form des Zeltes sich anschließend herausgeschält hat.
Michelucci war einer der führenden Funktionalisten Italiens. Der Bahnhof von Florenz (1936) ist einer seiner überzeugendsten Bauten aus jener Zeit. Die Kirche ist das Spätwerk eines Mannes, den offenbar Zweifel am Rationalismus befallen haben – er baute eine Kirche, die primär an die Gefühle appelliert.

1

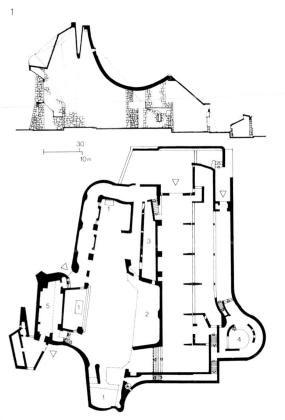

30
10m

2

3

4

3. Roof structure with the ramified concrete supports.
4. A view of the smaller gallery leading to the baptistry.
5, 6, 7. The expressive forms of the supports are obviously inspired by timber-construction.
8. Interior of the church, to the left behind, the entrance.

3. Dach mit sich verzweigenden Betonstützen.
4. Die kleinere, zur Taufkapelle führende Galerie.
5, 6, 7. Die expressive Formung der Stützen wurde offensichtlich vom Holzbau inspiriert.
8. Kirchenraum, links hinten der Eingang.

5

6

7

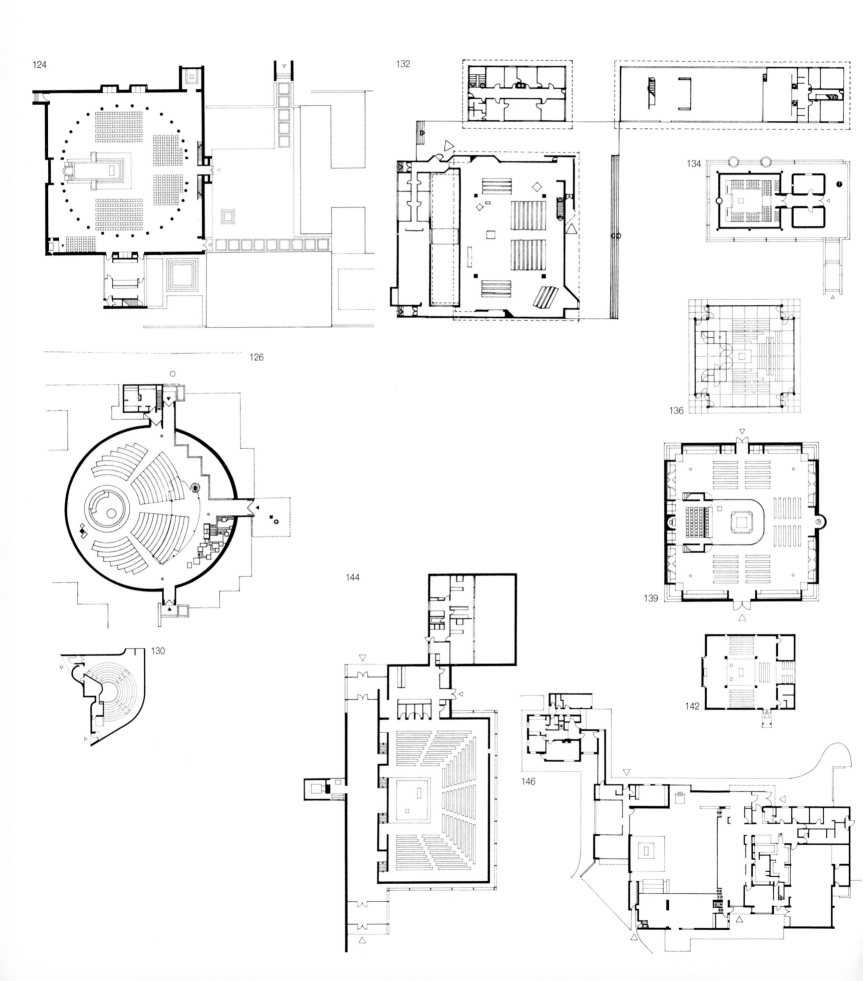

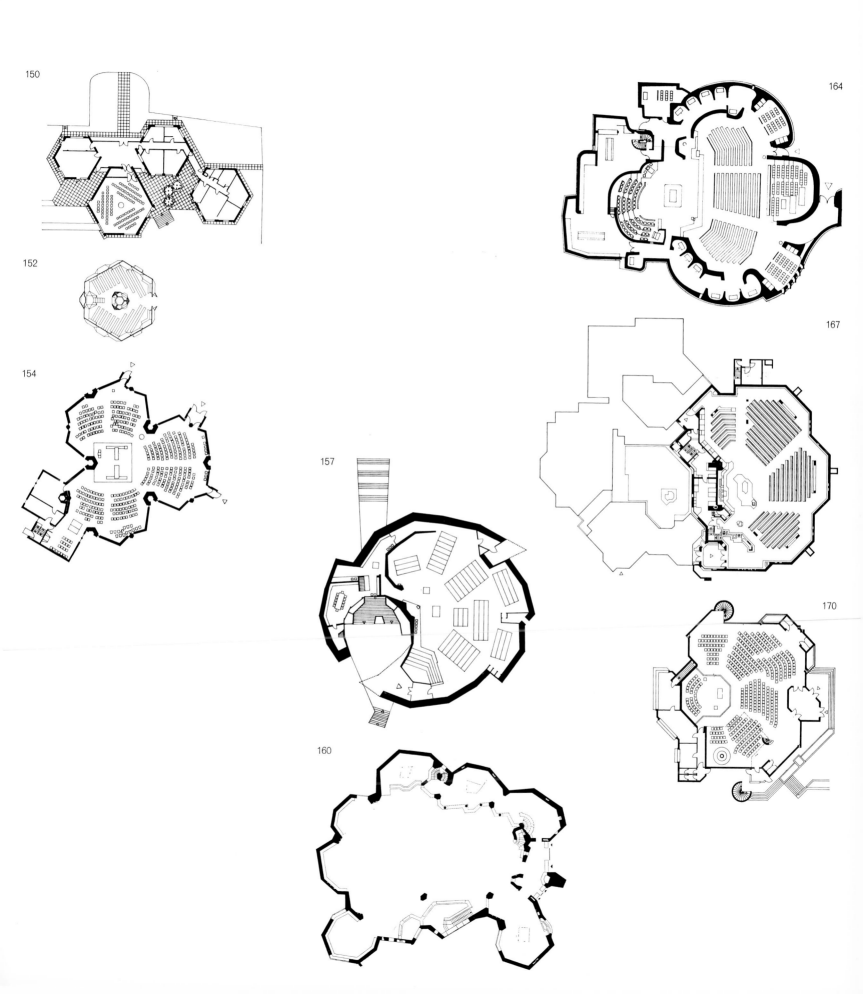

150

164

152

154

167

157

170

160

St. Matthias, Fürstenried, Munich, 1962–1965
Architect: Alexander Freiherr von Branca

St. Matthias, München-Fürstenried, 1962–1965
Architekt: Alexander Freiherr von Branca

The different zones of this parish centre are combined in an integrated group. Each zone has its own enclosed patio; the priest has his own garden, the parish hall has its own open space, and the youth premises, too, have their own garden plots. The result is a whole sequence of patios assigned to specific premises; even so, the cohesion of the whole group is clearly noticeable. This arrangement forms a pendant, albeit on a much larger scale, to the structure of the adjacent low-rise housing estate of patio houses. The desired compactness almost assumes the character of castle-like seclusion.

The church itself makes an even more robust impression than the parish centre. Above a square plan rises a high rotunda to form a solemn place of worship. Its conception is governed by the rules of the new liturgy – the pews surround the altar on three sides.

Die Bereiche des Gemeindezentrums sind in einer geschlossenen Anlage zusammengefaßt. Jeder Teilbereich hat seinen eigenen geschlossenen Hof; der Pfarrer hat seinen Garten, dem Pfarrsaal ist ein eigner Freiraum zugeordnet, auch die Jugendräume haben eigene Gartenteile. Eine ganze Folge von Höfen, die bestimmten Räumen zugeordnet sind, ist so geschaffen, trotzdem ist die Zusammengehörigkeit des Ganzen deutlich spürbar. Mit dieser Anordnung wurde das Zentrum der Struktur der benachbarten Atriumhaus-Siedlung angepaßt – die Maße sind jedoch stark überhöht. Die angestrebte Geschlossenheit wird fast zur burgartigen Abgeschlossenheit.

Noch wuchtiger als das Gemeindezentrum wirkt die Kirche. Über einem quadratischen Grundriß erhebt sich ein hoher Rundbau als feierlicher Zelebrationsraum. Er ist nach den Regeln der neuen Liturgie konzipiert – die Bänke stehen in großem Abstand um den Altar.

1

2

3

4

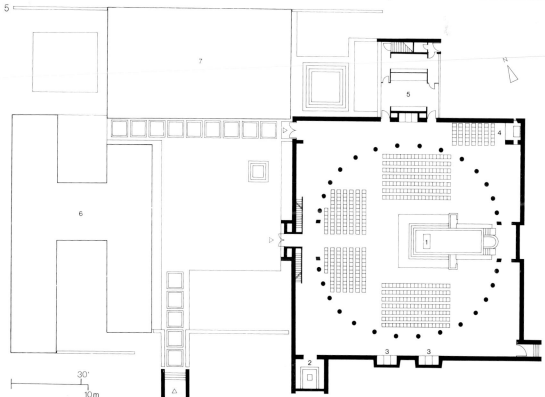

5

1, 2. Brick walls and exposed concrete for lintels and water spouts are the building materials used for church and parish centre.

3, 4. The high room is surrounded by a circle of cylindrical columns, interrupted by columns of rectangular cross-section at one end of each quadrant. Heavy beams span the room, intersecting above the altar.

5. Plan. Key: 1 altar, 2 baptistry, 3 confessional, 4 chapel, 5 sacristy, 6 rectory, 7 parish house.

1, 2. Mauerwerk aus Backstein sowie Stürze und Wasserspeier aus Sichtbeton sind die Bauelemente von Kirche und Gemeindezentrum.

3, 4. Die beiden Rundsäulenreihen, die den hohen Raum begrenzen, werden an ihren Enden von Vierkantpfeilern abgeschlossen. Schwere Unterzüge überspannen sich kreuzend den Raum und markieren den Ort des Altars.

5. Grundriß. Legende: 1 Altar, 2 Taufe, 3 Beichte, 4 Kapelle, 5 Sakristei, 6 Pfarrhaus, 7 Gemeindehaus.

30'

10 m

Maria-Regina, Fellbach, Germany, 1961–1967
Architect: Klaus Franz

Maria-Regina, Fellbach, Baden-Württemberg, 1961–1967
Architekt: Klaus Franz

The truncated cone rising out of the ground forms a logical wrapping for the church space designed for *circumstantes*. The pews are arranged in a three-quarters circle around the slightly eccentric altar island. The axis of the cone is inclined correspondingly. Its truncated top is exactly above the altar zone where it dispenses the brightest light. A subtle tension between the different liturgical zones is created by the off-centre position of the altar in the altar island. Altar and sedilia are of white marble, the slightly removed tabernacle is gilded.

In the entrance zone, a gallery painted in bright orange stands in an isolated position. In this way, the room also acquires, as it were, a downwards dimension. The church floor is detached from the wall shell so that a spatial link is created with the lower church which is used as a weekday chapel and baptistry. This chapel is accessible from a spacious flight of stairs and receives daylight through the top of the upper church. The main entrance forms a bridge across it.

The building is somewhat reminiscent of Le Corbusier's project for a church at Firminy. In that project, however, the cone was over-sized, suggesting a Gothic mystique, whilst in the present church, its scale is adapted to the task of supporting the active participation of the congregation in the act of worship.

The cone is an in-situ cast concrete shell; its outside is lined with asbestos cement shingles, its inside rough-cast in order to improve the acoustics. The top lighting is a polyester construction. Ventilation is through three small cowls.

The parish house, standing in front of the church, is adapted to the narrowness of the site. It is a two-storey building where public and private premises are horizontally segregated.

Der aus der Erde heraussteigende Kegelstumpf ist eine logische Begrenzung für den Kirchenraum der »circumstantes«. In einem Dreiviertelkreis stehen die Bänke um die aus der Mitte gerückte runde Altarinsel. Entsprechend ist die Achse des Kegels geneigt. Seine abgeschnittene Spitze befindet sich genau über der Altarzone und spendet ihr das hellste Licht. Ein subtiles Spannungsverhältnis zwischen den liturgischen Orten entsteht dadurch, daß der Altar nicht in die Mitte der Altarinsel gerückt ist. Altar und Sedilien sind in weißem Marmor ausgeführt, die etwas abgerückte Tabernakelstele ist vergoldet.

Eine in leuchtendem Orange gestrichene Empore steht frei im Eingangsbereich. Hier gewinnt der Raum auch Dimension nach unten. Der Kirchenboden ist von der Wandschale abgelöst, so entsteht ein räumlicher Zusammenhang mit der Unterkirche, die mit einer weitläufigen Treppe erschlossen wird und Licht vom Oberlicht des Hauptraumes erhält. Die Unterkirche wird als Werktags- und Taufkapelle benutzt. Der Haupteingang ist als Brücke darübergelegt.

Der Bau fordert zu einem Vergleich mit dem Entwurf von Le Corbusier für eine Kirche in Firminy (1963) heraus. Dort hat der Kegel eine gotisch-mystische Überhöhe, während er hier im Maßstab auf die Aufgabe, die aktive Teilnahme der Gemeinde am Gottesdienst zu unterstützen, zugeschnitten ist.

Der Kegel ist als Ortbetonschale gegossen, mit Asbestzementschindeln verkleidet und innen zur Verbesserung der Akustik rauh verputzt. Das Oberlicht ist eine Polyester-Konstruktion. Der Raum wird durch drei kleine Gauben entlüftet.

Der vor der Kirche errichtete Gemeindebau ist dem schmalen Grundstücks-Zuschnitt angepaßt. Mit der zweigeschossigen Anlage sind die öffentlichen von den privaten Bereichen horizontal getrennt.

1, 2. Church and two-storey parish house, with upper-floor dwellings facing the patio.
3. Church, seen from the parish centre.
4. Plans and section. Key: 1 altar, 2 gallery, 3 confessional, 4 weekday chapel, 5 sacristy, 6 parish hall, 7 kindergarten, 8 dwelling.

1, 2. Kirche und zweistöckiges Gemeindehaus mit Hofwohnungen im Obergeschoß.
3. Kirche vom Gemeindezentrum aus.
4. Grundrisse und Schnitt. Legende: 1 Altar, 2 Empore, 3 Beichte, 4 Werktagskapelle, 5 Sakristei, 6 Gemeindesaal, 7 Kindergarten, 8 Wohnung.

2

3

4

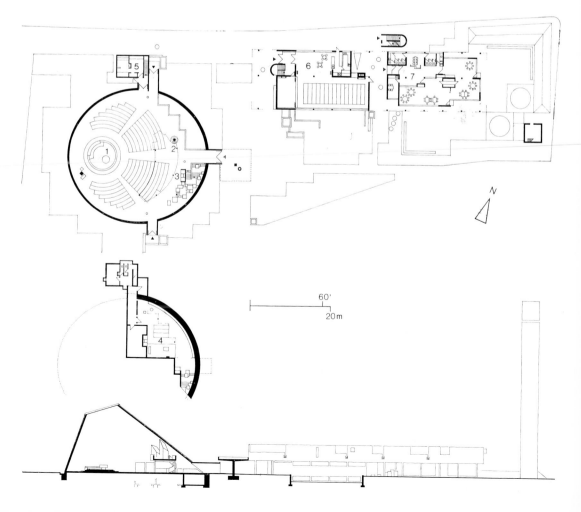

60'

20 m

N

5. A view of the gallery from the tabernacle.
6. A view from the bridge-like main entrance towards the altar. Below the bridge is a weekday chapel.
7. Weekday chapel on the lower level.
8. Altar island, seen from the gallery. The waffle-shaped partition of the skylight is not recognisable.

5. Blick vom Tabernakel zur Empore.
6. Blick vom brückenartigen Haupteingang auf die Empore und den Altar. Unter der Brücke befindet sich die Werktagskapelle.
7. Werktagskapelle im Untergeschoß.
8. Altarinsel von der Empore aus. Die waffelartige Aufteilung des Oberlichtes ist nicht zu erkennen.

Place of Worship of the Pestalozzi Children's Village in Trogen, Switzerland, 1966–1968
Architect: Ernst Gisel

Kultraum des Pestalozzi-Kinderdorfes in Trogen, Schweiz, 1966–1968
Architekt: Ernst Gisel

"The place is not intended to remind you of a Roman Catholic or Protestant church, or of a synagoge or mosque. The only purpose which can here be valid is the foregathering of the community itself", writes the architect about this building. It is destined for the community of children and their wardens. It is not only intended as a place of worship for the different denominations but also for other activities (concerts, amateur shows, etc.).

The seats are amphi-theatrically arranged on benches around the sunken centre. The strictly circular core is surrounded by a more informally aligned outer wall. The carefully planned conducted tour for the visitor begins at the doors on the sides and continues along the curved outer walls to the seats. This route is also marked out by the lighting from the two windows which extend from floor to ceiling. The light falls sideways on the strongly profiled, vertically boarded walls, giving them a plastic appearance and filling the room with reflected light.

Altar zone and outer passage are paved with red porphyry; steps and benches are conceived as an entity and consist of reddish mahogany wood; walls and ceiling are boarded with white firwood. The dark-stained outer cladding forms a contrast to the white-enamelled entrance doors.

The visitor, impressed by the beauty of the gently undulating Appenzell landscape, is suddenly confronted with an introvert place of concentration. But the undulations of the landscape are also reflected in this building. With its materials, its sparse apertures and its flat roof covering the curved walls, the building has that degree of self-confident modesty which we desire for a modern church placed in a beautiful landscape.

»Der Raum soll nicht an eine katholische oder reformierte Kirche oder an eine Synagoge oder Moschee erinnern. Das einzige, was hier Gültigkeit haben kann, ist die Zusammenfassung der Gemeinde selbst«, schreibt der Architekt zu diesem Bau. Er ist bestimmt für die Gemeinde der Kinder und ihre Betreuer. Er soll nicht nur als Andachtsraum der verschiedenen Konfessionen dienen, sondern auch für andere Aktivitäten (Konzerte, Laienspiele und so weiter) benutzt werden.

Die Sitze sind auf amphitheatralisch abgetreppten Bankreihen um die Aktionsmulde in der Mitte angeordnet. Um den streng kreisförmig angelegten Kern des Raumes ist eine freier geformte Außenwand gelegt. Die sorgfältig bedachte Führung des Besuchers beginnt bei den an den Seiten liegenden Türen. An den gekurvten Außenwänden entlang wird er zu den Sitzplätzen geleitet. Die Lichtführung durch die beiden raumhohen Fenster entspricht der Führung der Besucher. Auf die kräftig reliefierten, senkrecht verschalten Wände fällt Streiflicht, es modelliert sie und gibt reflektiertes Licht in den Raum.

Die Altarzone und der äußere Umgang sind mit rotem Porphyr gepflastert, Stufen und Bänke sind als Einheit aufgefaßt und aus rötlichem Mahagoniholz, dagegen stehen Wände und Decken aus weißem Tannenholz. Zur dunkel imprägnierten Außenverschalung kontrastieren weiß emaillierte Eingangstüren.

Der von der lieblichen Bewegtheit der Appenzeller Landschaft erfüllte Besucher findet einen nach innen gerichteten Raum der Konzentration. Bewegt wie die Landschaft ist dieser Bau. Das Material, die sparsamen Öffnungen und das flache Dach über den geschwungenen Wänden geben ihm die selbstbewußte Bescheidenheit, die wir uns für die heutige Kirche in der Landschaft wünschen.

2

3

1

1. Entrance side. The white-enamelled doors form a contrast to the dark timber cladding.
2, 3. Valley sides of the building. A robust, yet subtle shape.
4. Ceiling in the vestibule to the sacristy.
5. Plan. Key: 1 altar, 2 sacristy.
6, 7. The ³/₄ circle around the altar is surrounded by a ring of standard lamps.

1. Eingangsseite. Die dunkle Holzschalung steht in Kontrast zu den hell emaillierten Türen.
2, 3. Talseiten des Gebäudes. Eine kräftige, doch subtile Form.
4. Decke im Vorraum zur Sakristei.
5. Grundriß. Legende: 1 Altar, 2 Sakristei.
6, 7. Ein Kranz von Stehleuchten umschließt das Dreiviertelrund um den Altar.

6

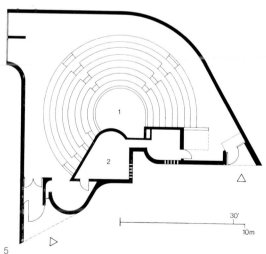

4

5

7

30'
10m

1

2

Heilig-Kreuz-Kirche, Langholzfeld, Austria, 1965–1966
Architect: Ernst Hiesmayr

Heilig-Kreuz-Kirche, Langholzfeld, Österreich,
1965–1966
Architekt: Ernst Hiesmayr

The thick concrete roof seemingly floating above the church is carried by four internal columns. The walls stand freely below the roof and leave room for a ribbon of windows which surround the church and provide uniform brightness. The introvert appearance of the interior is enhanced by a mazelike entrance.

Altar steps, altar, font, tabernacle base and ambo step as well as the floor slabs depicting the stations of the Passion have been created by the sculptor Karl Prantl. It is through these features that the church has attained its specific character.

Weekday chapel and sacristy are separated from the church by an inner patio but connected with it by passageways.

Das dicke Betondach, das über der Kirche schwebt, wird von vier innenliegenden Pfeilern getragen. Die Wände stehen frei unter dem Dach und lassen Platz für ein umlaufendes, den Raum gleichmäßig erhellendes Lichtband. Ein labyrinthartiger Eingang verstärkt die Introvertiertheit des Raumes.

Altarstufe, Altar, Taufwasserbecken, Tabernakelsockel, Ambostufe sowie die im Asphaltboden eingelassenen Kreuzwegsteine sind das Werk des Bildhauers Karl Prantl. Mit ihnen erhielt der Bau seinen spezifischen Charakter.

Alltagskirche und Sakristei sind – durch einen Innenhof getrennt – mit Gängen an die Kirche angeschlossen.

1, 2. A wall of complex shape is covered by a simple rectangular roof.
3. Isometric drawing.
4. Plan. Key: 1 altar, 2 baptistry, 3 confessional, 4 week-day chapel, 5 rectory, 6 parish hall.
5. Altar, designed by Karl Prantl.
6. Interior. White-plastered walls, grey concrete ceiling, black asphalt flooring.

1

2

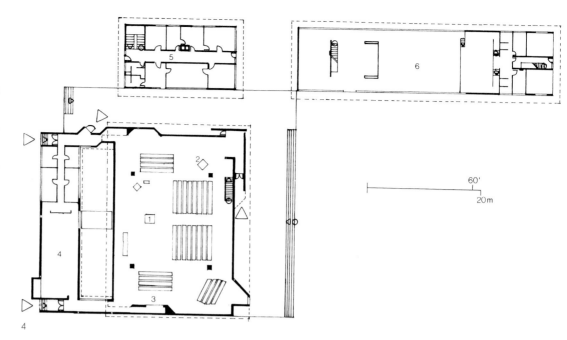

1, 2. Ein einfaches rechteckiges Dach schwebt über den kompliziert geformten Wänden.
3. Isometrie.
4. Grundriß. Legende: 1 Altar, 2 Taufe, 3 Beichte, 4 Alltagskirche, 5 Pfarrhaus, 6 Gemeindesaal.
5. Altar von Karl Prantl.
6. Innenraum. Weiß verputzte Wände, graue Betondecke, schwarzer Asphaltestrich.

4

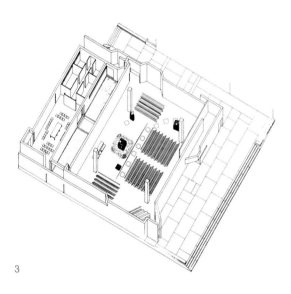

3

5

6

Synagogue in Linz, Austria, 1967–1968
Architect: Fritz Goffitzer

Synagoge in Linz, Österreich, 1967–1968
Architekt: Fritz Goffitzer

The synagogue in Linz has been erected on the site of the old synagogue which had been destroyed. The east-west orientation is required for liturgical reasons.

The size of the building is on an exemplary scale in that it realistically corresponds to the smallness of the congregation. Unfortunately, in the course of the restitution process, a number of synagogues have been built at great expense and of excessive size – witnesses to well-meant efforts at atonement which were, however, lacking a realistic appreciation of the situation.

The building is placed on a granite-paved platform six steps above ground level – a simple means of lifting it above the secular environment. The visitor crosses a low vestibule which is axially orientated towards reader's desk and ark. The different ceiling heights of the premises are adapted to their different finctions. The synagogue proper has been given a comparatively great height, an a convex "countervault" projecting from the walls creates a feeling of security. The roof proper – separated from this counter-vault by toplight ribbons – appears to float; it has a wide overhang and is supported by external circular columns. It admits daylight without permitting an outward view. Artificial lighting, too, is confined to indirect light which is reflected from the ceiling into the room. The pews, placed on a floor rising by steps, surround the desk in horse-shoe fashion.

The architect has based the design on a module system which relates all the components to a given scale. Using the means of Functionalism in a personally inspired version, he has created a place of worship which convinces through its proper size and shape.

Die Linzer Synagoge wurde auf dem Platz der alten, zerstörten errichtet. Die Ost-West-Achse des Gebäudes folgt den liturgischen Bedingungen.

Der Bau ist von einer vorbildlichen – nämlich der Kleinheit der Gemeinde realistisch entsprechenden – Größe. Leider sind im Zuge der Wiedergutmachung einige Synagogen mit viel Aufwand und von unangemessenem Umfang entstanden – Zeugen ernstgemeinter Sühneanstrengungen, die aber der konkreten Einschätzung der Lage entbehrten.

Die Anlage steht auf einem sechs Stufen über Niveau gelegten Podest, das mit Granit gepflastert ist – ein einfaches Mittel, das Gebäude aus dem Bereich des Alltäglichen abzuheben. Der Besucher durchquert einen niedrigen Vorraum, der axial auf Pult und Schrein zuführt. Die verschiedenen Höhen der Räume sind ihren verschiedenen Funktionen angepaßt. Der Betraum ist stark überhöht – ein aus den Wänden auskragendes »Gegengewölbe« schafft ein Gefühl von Geborgenheit. Das eigentliche Dach – durch Oberlichtstreifen von diesem Gegengewölbe getrennt – scheint zu schweben, es kragt weit aus und wird von außenstehenden Rundstützen getragen. Es läßt Licht ein, ohne den Blick ins Freie zu ermöglichen. Auch das künstliche Licht wird nur indirekt, über die Decke, in den Raum reflektiert. Die Bestuhlung, auf abgetrepptem Fußboden, ist U-förmig um das Pult angeordnet.

Der Architekt hat dem Gebäude ein Modulmaß zugrunde gelegt, das alle Teile in maßlichen Zusammenhang bringt. Mit den persönlich variierten Mitteln des Funktionalismus ist eine Kultanlage entstanden, die durch die Angemessenheit in Größe und Form überzeugt.

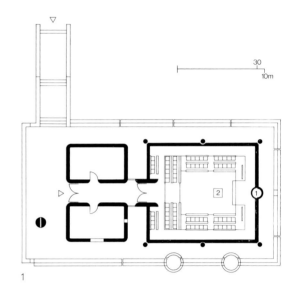

30
10m

1

2

1. Plan. Key: 1 shrine, 2 lectern.
2. Exterior of the synagogue; on the right, the annex with the ancillary premises.
3. Facade details. Contrast formed by the alternation of hard and soft corners.
4. Main building, seen through the corridor of the vestibule. Doors of cast aluminium.
5. Interior with indirect lighting from windows above the caunter-vaults. The frescos are by Fritz Fröhlich.

1. Grundriß. Legende: 1 Schrein, 2 Pult.
2. Die Synagoge von außen, rechts der Vorbau mit den Nebenräumen.
3. Außenecke. Kontrast von harten und weichen Ecken.
4. Blick durch den Gang im Vorbau in den Hauptbau. Tore aus Gußaluminium.
5. Der Betraum wird durch ein zwischen Dach und »Gegengewölbe« liegendes Fensterband beleuchtet. Fresken von Fritz Fröhlich.

Heilig-Kreuz-Kirche, Vienna, 1965–1967
Architect: Ottokar Uhl

Heilig-Kreuz-Kirche, Wien, 1965–1967
Architekt: Ottokar Uhl

The motivation for this "portable" church is derived from recent social surveys which indicate that the centres of gravity of housing estates are liable to shift rapidly. It was intended to create a church building which would be relatively inexpensive, would have a life of approximately forty years, and would be capable of being dismantled and re-erected at least twice.

From these conditions sprang a number of consequences: To allow for mobility, the maximum dimension was confined to 15 metres. To provide for future extensions, the architect designed a number of structural units which can be used for enlarging the building in different ways. The main room, with 250 seats, measures 15 × 15 metres and is spanned by trusses of 1.25 metres depth. Daylight comes through a ribbon of high-level windows surrounding the entire room; the low side passages have no windows.

In this way, a very simple, tidy and austere room has been created, lacking any fanciful details, and not letting you forget for a moment that it is a building of a temporary character.

Similar notions of a church that can be dismantled had been applied to an earlier structure in Siemensstraße, Vienna, planned in 1962 and erected in 1964. In this case, the structure consists of a MERO-grid system, windowless concrete wall panels and a roof with toplight dome.

Begründet mit neuen Sozialuntersuchungen, nach denen sich Siedlungsschwerpunkte schnell verschieben können, wurde diese »mobile« Kirche geplant. Es war die Absicht, einen möglichst kostensparenden Kirchenbau zu schaffen, der etwa vierzig Jahre Lebensdauer haben und mindestens zweimal aufgestellt und wieder abgebaut werden könnte.

Viele Konsequenzen ergaben sich aus diesen Prämissen: Wegen der Transportfähigkeit beschränkte man sich auf ein Maximalmaß von 15 m. Wegen der Erweiterungsfähigkeit konzipierte der Architekt mehrere Bauelemente, die zu einer Vergrößerung des Raumes in verschiedener Form verwendet werden können. Der Hauptraum mißt 15 × 15 m und enthält 250 Plätze; er wird von 1,25 m hohen Bindern überspannt. Ein ringsum gelegtes Oberlicht leuchtet den Hauptraum aus, der niedrige Umgang dagegen ist ohne Fenster.

Ein sehr einfacher, klarer und strenger Raum ist entstanden, jedes phantasievolleren Details bar, der keinen Moment vergessen läßt, daß es sich um einen Bau auf Zeit handelt.

Ähnliche Gedanken von einer demontablen Kirche lagen einem früheren Bau an der Siemensstraße in Wien zugrunde. Er wurde 1962 geplant und 1964 ausgeführt. Die Konstruktion besteht hier aus einem MERO-Gitter-System, fensterlosen Wandelementen aus Beton und einem Lichtkuppeldach.

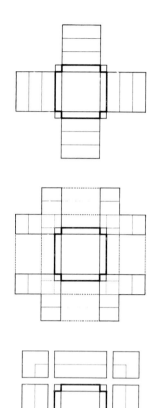

1

2

1. The architect's sketches, indicating the way in which the church could be extended.
2. Exterior. The low parts of the building, capable of extension, are inserted between the load-bearing structures at the corners.
3. Isometric view.
4. Plan and section. Key: 1 altar, 2 tabernacle, 3 choir, 4 confessional, 5 sacristy.
5. Exterior.

1. Skizzen des Architekten zur Erweiterbarkeit der Kirche.
2. Außenansicht. Die niedrigen, erweiterbaren Raumteile sind zwischen die winkelförmigen Eckglieder geschoben.
3. Isometrie.
4. Grundriß und Schnitt. Legende: 1 Altar, 2 Tabernakel, 3 Chor, 4 Beichte, 5 Sakristei.
5. Außenansicht.

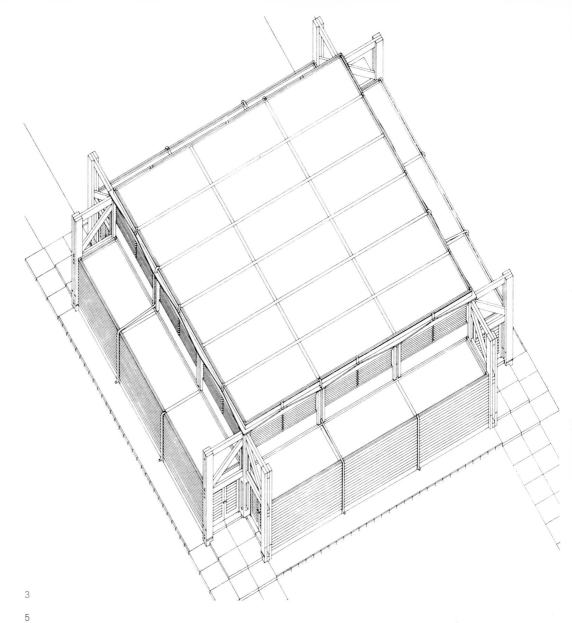

3

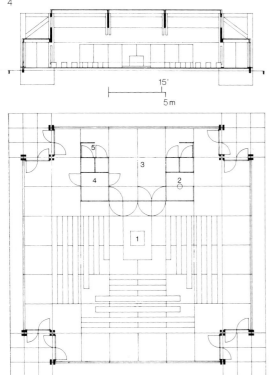

4

15'

5 m

5

6. The church during the consecration by the archbishop.
7. Interior. Uniform materials have been used for load-bearing structure, fittings, furniture and altar.
8, 9. Church at Siemens-Straße, Vienna, assembled from simple materials – precast concrete units and skylight domes. Roof and walls of the interior are supported by the MERO-grid.

6. Der Kirchenraum während der Weihe durch den Erzbischof.
7. Tragwerk, Einbauten und Möblierung zeigen eine konsequente Einheitlichkeit in Material und Form.
8, 9. Kirche an der Siemens-Straße in Wien. Innenliegendes Tragwerk im MERO-System, fensterlose Wände, Oberlichtdach.

1. The church is part of a group of buildings, forming a social and cultural centre. Lackner's contribution is confined to the church.
2. Plan and section. Key: 1 altar, 2 exit to the gallery, 3 baptistry, 4 confessional, 5 chapel.

1. Gesamtanlage des »Sozialen Bildungshauses«. Von Lackner stammt nur die Kirche.
2. Grundriß und Schnitt. Legende: 1 Altar, 2 Aufgang zur Empore, 3 Taufe, 4 Beichte, 5 Kapelle.

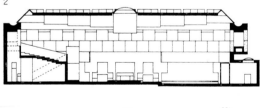

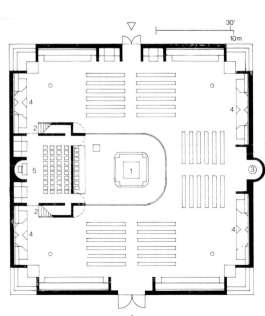

This building is one of the first Roman Catholic hall-type churches built after the Second Vatican Council. It serves not only as a parish church for Lainz but also as headquarters of the Order of the Jesuits. The column-free interior has a symmetric layout and is orientated towards the altar zone in the centre. The church has 350 seats and can, altogether, accommodate 800 people.
The altar is placed on a platform raised by two steps in the centre of the room. Behind the altar, the wall of the weekday chapel, which also forms the balustrade of the choir, serves as an effective backcloth. It is flanked by two robust staircases. The choir provides access to a gallery which surrounds the entire room and provides an internal connection to the offices of the Order. Below this gallery are entrances, confessionals, and celebration altars for the Jesuit priests. The forecourt forms an extension of a bury arterial road; because of the traffic noise – writes the architect – the windows were placed in the central and lateral zones of the roof.
The unconventional composition of materials has been chosen with much care: waffle-type ceiling, pulpit, confessionals and pews are of white-varnished steel sheeting; the walls are of smooth-cast untreated concrete and Leca precast concrete blocks, contrasting with the yellow floor carpeting and hassocks.
With its refined details, the building represents a logical realisation of the notions stemming from the Second Vatican Council.

Der Bau ist eine der ersten nachkonziliaren katholischen »Saalkirchen«. Er ist sowohl für das Ordenshaus der Jesuiten als auch für die Pfarre Lainz bestimmt. Der stützenfreie Raum wurde symmetrisch angelegt und auf den zentralen Altar-Bereich orientiert. Die Kirche hat 350 Sitzplätze; insgesamt kann sie 800 Personen aufnehmen.
Der Altar steht um zwei Stufen erhöht mitten im Raum. Hinter ihm liegt als wirkungsvolle Folie die Wand, die die Werktagskapelle abschließt, und die die Brüstung der Sängerempore bildet. Sie wird flankiert von zwei wuchtigen Treppenaufgängen. Die Empore erschließt einen um den Raum herumlaufenden Gang, der die interne Verbindung zum Ordenshaus herstellt. Unter diesem Gang sind Eingänge, Beichtstühle und Zelebrationsaltäre für die Ordensgeistlichen angeordnet. Die Kirche liegt an der platzartigen Erweiterung einer stark belebten Ausfallstraße; wegen des Verkehrslärms, schreibt der Architekt, wurde die Belichtung des Raumes in die Mittel- und Randzonen des Daches gelegt.
Mit Sorgfalt erfolgte die eigenwillige Zusammenstellung der Materialien: Kassettendecke, Kanzel, Beichtstühle und Bänke sind aus weiß lackiertem Stahlblech, die Wände aus glattgeschaltem Sichtbeton und Lecabeton-Fertigteilen; dazu kontrastiert ein gelber Teppichbelag auf Boden und Kniebänken.
Der Bau ist – in raffinierter Detaillierung – eine konsequente Realisierung der Ideen des 2. Vatikanischen Konzils.

3

3. Interior, seen from the gallery. Daylight enters through the high-level windows surrounding the room.
4. The heavy concrete walls form an impressive contrast to the graceful fittings of sheet-lacquered steel.
5. Altar, seen from the gallery.
6. Font.

4

5

6

3. Innenraum von der Galerie aus. Der Raum erhält Licht durch die umlaufenden Randoberlichter.
4. Die wuchtigen Betonwände stehen in einprägsamem Kontrast zu den grazilen Einbauten aus lackiertem Stahlblech.
5. Altar von der Galerie aus.
6. Taufbecken.

Churchill College Chapel, Cambridge, England,
1963–1967
Architects: Richard Sheppard, Robson & Partners

Churchill College Chapel, Cambridge, England,
1963–1967
Architekten: Richard Sheppard, Robson & Partners

The original plan was for the chapel to be placed directly at the college entrance so that all the students would have had to pass it on entering or leaving the building. A later committee then decided not to integrate the chapel with the college buildings but to place it in an isolated position, though not far from the quarters of married students. The architects emphasise that they were anxious to adapt the structure, material and design of the chapel to the college. Because of the noise coming from the nearby sports grounds, the building is fairly inclosed.

The plan reveals the shape of a Greek Cross. Four concrete columns carry four concrete beams of considerable depth; the roof of the central bay among the nine bays formed by the beams is glazed. Here stand the portable altar table, a reader's desk and four candelabras. The brick walls are lit up by high-level ribbons of windows. Four vertical slot windows below the projecting concrete beams represent the only windows in the lower part of the room. They will eventually be fitted with glass mosaic. As in the college itself, floors and walls are of clinkers.

The isolated position underlines the severance of the chapel from the college tradition. "It is not part of the furniture", as the officiating priest writes. It serves as a religious as well as a cultural and social centre for students of all denominations. According to the priest, even the Moslem has no objection to saying his prayers here.

Zunächst wurde die Kapelle direkt am College-Eingang geplant, so daß alle Studenten beim Betreten oder Verlassen des College an ihr hätten vorbeigehen müssen. Ein später eingesetzter Kirchenbau-Ausschuß entschloß sich dann, sie nicht in die College-Bauten zu integrieren, sondern sie ganz abseits, jedoch nicht weit von den Wohnungen der verheirateten Studenten, anzusiedeln. Die Architekten betonen, daß ihnen daran lag, die Kapelle in Struktur, Material und Form dem College anzupassen. Wegen des Lärms von nahe gelegenen Sportplätzen entstand ein sehr geschlossener Bau.

Im Quadrat des Grundrisses zeichnet sich ein griechisches Kreuz ab. Vier Betonstützen tragen vier hohe Betonbalken; das mittlere der neun von den Balken gebildeten Deckenfelder wird durch ein Oberlicht erhellt.

1

Hier steht die transportable Altar-Mensa, ein Buchpult und vier Leuchter. Die Backsteinwände werden von oben durch Lichtbänder beleuchtet. Vier senkrechte Fensterschlitze unter den herausschießenden Betonbalken sind die einzigen Fenster im unteren Teil des Raumes. Sie sollen einmal farbig verglast werden. Böden und Wände sind wie das College aus Klinkern gemauert.

Die abseitige Lage unterstreicht die Unabhängigkeit der Kapelle von der College-Tradition. Sie ist nicht »part of the furniture«, wie der amtsführende Geistliche schreibt. Sie dient Studenten aller Konfessionen als religiöses und auch als kulturelles und gesellschaftliches Zentrum. Der Geistliche betont, daß sich auch der Moslem nicht geniert, hier sein Gebet zu sprechen.

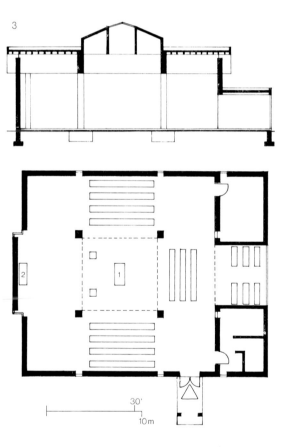

1, 2. Exterior. A markedly plastic effect. Brick cubes, concrete beams, copper-clad toplights, belfry of timber.
3. Plan and section. Key: 1 altar, 2 organ.
4. Interior. Portable liturgical furniture. The central zone is illuminated by toplights.

1, 2. Außenansichten. Stark plastische Baumasse. Backsteinkuben, Betonträger, kupferverkleidete Oberlichter, hölzerner Glockenträger.
3. Grundriß und Schnitt. Legende: 1 Altar, 2 Orgel.
4. Innenraum. Transportable liturgische Möbel. Beleuchtung der zentralen Zone durch Oberlichter.

**"Het Woord Gods" Church, Swalmen, Holland,
1964–1966**
Architects: G. J. van der Grinten, L. J. Heijdenrijk

**»Het Woord Gods«-Kirche, Swalmen, Holland,
1964–1966**
Architekten: G. J. van der Grinten, L. J. Heijdenrijk

With their churches at Eindhoven, Amsterdam-North and Swalmen, the architects have created a new type. To achieve openness and accessibility for everybody, yet at the same time to create a feeling of security and concentration for the celebrating congregation, they conceived premises on two levels: A surrounding passage at ground level provides direct connections with street and shopping centre; from it, stairs lead down to the place of worship which is about 1 metre lower. L. J. Heijdenrijk describes this space effect as follows: "A secluded pit at the wayside – a hole in the ground, a traditional screen against the happenings around us". From the level of the passage, one is able to participate in the activities in the "pit". In this way, every visitor is able to make his own decision as to the distance which he wants to keep – as a spectator or as an active participant.

The building volume can be described as a kind of agglomeration: Adjoining the church, which is accentuated by its mighty roof, are the social premises, and by adding further cultural, leisure-time and school premises, the architects look forward to an even greater vitalisation of the whole complex.

The *rue intérieure* which, even with Le Corbusier, merely represented a traffic artery and which, with Bakema, assumed the further function of a communication medium or contact zone, here becomes an integral part of the space.

Die Architekten haben mit ihren Kirchen in Eindhoven, Amsterdam-Nord und Swalmen einen neuen Typ geschaffen. Um Offenheit und Zugänglichkeit für jedermann zu erreichen, gleichzeitig Geborgenheit und Konzentration für die feiernde Gemeinde, konzipierten sie Räume auf zwei Ebenen: Ein ebenerdig liegender Umgang schafft direkte Verbindung mit Straße und Einkaufszentrum; Treppen führen von ihm zum Feierraum hinab, der um etwa 1 m tiefer liegt. L. J. Heijdenrijk beschreibt diese Raumwirkung so: »Eine geschlossene Grube längs des Weges – das Loch in der Erde, eine traditionelle Abschirmung gegen das Geschehen ringsum.« Von der Ebene des Umgangs aus kann man an dem Geschehen in der »Grube« teilnehmen. So kann jeder Besucher seine Distanz dazu – Zuschauer oder aktiver Teilnehmer – selbst bestimmen.

Die Baumasse kann man als eine Art Agglomeration bezeichnen: An die durch ihr mächtiges Dach herausgehobene Kirche sind die sozialen Bauteile herangeschoben – die Architekten versprechen sich von einer weiteren Hinzufügung von Kultur-, Freizeit- und Schulräumen eine noch größere Vitalisierung des Komplexes. Die rue intérieure, die noch bei Le Corbusier ein Verkehrs-Element war, bei Bakema zum Kommunikations-Medium, zur Kontakt-Zone aufstieg, wird hier zu einem integrierten Teil des Raumes.

1, 2. Exterior. The proportions of glass, stone and wooden faces are neatly balanced.
3. The "rue intérieure" by night.
4. The sacristy also serves as a weekday chapel and a room for minor assemblies.
5. Plan. Key: 1 altar area, 2 sacristy, 3 interior street, 4 dwelling.
6. Service in the "liturgical pit". Portable chairs, portable wooden altar, fixed tabernacle.

1

2

1, 2. Außenansichten. Proportionsspiel der gläsernen, steinernen und hölzernen Flächen.
3. Die Innenstraße bei Nacht.
4. Die Sakristei dient auch als Werktagskirche und kleiner Versammlungsraum.
5. Grundriß. Legende: 1 Altarbereich, 2 Sakristei, 3 Innenstraße, 4 Wohnung.
6. Gottesdienst in der »liturgischen Grube«. Lose Bestuhlung, transportabler Holzaltar, fixes Tabernakel.

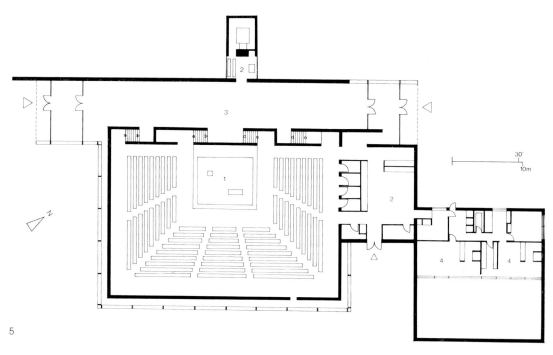

3

5

4

6

St. Philip and St. James Hodge Hill, Birmingham, England, 1963–1968
Architect: Martin Purdy

Hodge Hill is situated in the eastern outskirts of Birmingham. It is one of those typical suburbs without centre or boundaries, of the kind encountered not only in England.

Amidst this undefined environment stands the new church centre for the Birmingham diocese. The building is remarkable not so much because of its architectural design but rather because of its social and functional significance. Here, architecture has wholly become a means to an end, namely to serve a social purpose, and the creation of a specifically ecclesiastic type of building has not even been attempted.

The democratisation of the church centre had already been aimed at during the planning stage. Initially, the project was entrusted not to an architect but to the Institute for Worship and Religious Architecture of the University of Birmingham and to the Live Project Department of the Birmingham School of Architecture. Following one year's preparatory planning work for the extension of the existing parish centre, architect Martin Purdy was commissioned to act as co-ordinator. But the old parish centre burned down before the new building was commenced. Despite the loss of time caused by the necessary revision of the project, even the new plans were exhaustively debated in discussion meetings with all the parishioners which were preceded by a series of lectures on the subject of church architecture. Meanwhile, the University of Birmingham had carried out surveys into the structure of the population and its social and devotional needs. From the consensus of these preliminary surveys and from the co-ordination of the different funds, the project crystallised in this conglomerate of premises designed partly for specific purposes (altar zone, baptistry) and partly for multi-functional use. For instance, the lounge as well as the nursery can be used as extensions to the parish hall during acts of worship.

The parish hall itself, taking the place of the traditional "nave", becomes a meeting room of the congregation not only for acts of worship but also for meetings of the parish council, theatre performances and dances. Its size has been governed by the normal maximum number of 250 persons attending a Sunday service. By including the adjacent rooms, the accommodation can be doubled. On certain days, the centre is open for 14 hours. During the week, it is attended by about 3,000 people.

Simple timber and brick structures provide the robust background for the continuous and variegated use of the building and a permanent weather protection against the industrial atmosphere of the city.

1. Entrance side. The materials of the unpretentious group of buildings are brick, wood and glass.
2. There is nothing to distinguish the group from a non-ecclesiastical community centre.
3. Isometric view.
4. Plan. Key: 1 altar, 2 choir, 3 baptistry, 4 sacristy, 5 platform, 6 storage area, 7 lounge, 8 multi-purpose hall, 9 kitchen, 10 dwellings.

Hodge Hill liegt am östlichen Rand von Birmingham. Es ist eine der typischen Vorstädte ohne Zentrum und ohne Begrenzung, wie man sie nicht nur in England findet. Mitten in dieser undefinierten Umgebung steht das neue Kirchenzentrum für die Diözese Birmingham. Der Bau ist wegen seiner architektonischen Form sicher nicht so bemerkenswert wie wegen seines sozial-funktionalen Gehalts. Die Architektur ist hier völlig Mittel zum sozialen Zweck geworden, es wird gar nicht erst der Versuch gemacht, eine spezifisch kirchliche Bauform zu kreieren.

Die Demokratisierung des Kirchenzentrums wurde bereits mit dem Planungsvorgang angestrebt. Mit der Planung wurde zunächst nicht ein Architekt, sondern das Institute tor Worship and Religious Architecture der University of Birmingham und das Live Project Department der Birmingham School of Architecture betraut. Nach einjähriger Planung einer Erweiterung des bestehenden Gemeindehauses wurde als Koordinator der Architekt Martin Purdy beigezogen. Das Gemeindehaus brannte ab, bevor der Neubau begann. Trotz des mit der Umplanung verbundenen Zeitverlustes wurden auch die neuen Pläne in Diskussionsveranstaltungen mit allen Pfarrangehörigen ausgiebig besprochen, nachdem eine Serie von Vorträgen über das Thema Kirchenbau vorangegangen war. Inzwischen waren von der Universität Birmingham Untersuchungen über die Struktur der Bevölkerung und deren soziale und kirchliche Ambitionen gemacht worden. Aus dem Konsensus dieser Vorarbeiten und der Koordinierung der verschiedenen Finanzquellen entstand dieses Konglomerat von Räumen, die teilweise für spezifische Zwecke (Altarzone, Taufkapelle), teilweise für multifunktionalen Gebrauch entworfen worden sind. So zum Beispiel können die Lounge, aber auch der Kinderspielraum als Erweiterung des Gemeinderaumes bei Gottesdiensten dienen.

Der Gemeinderaum selbst, das frühere »Schiff«, wird zur Versammlung der Gemeinde nicht nur bei kultischen Feiern, sondern auch bei Gemeinderatssitzungen, Theaterspiel und Tanz benutzt. Er ist nach der normalen Höchstfrequenz eines Sonntagsgottesdienstes (250 Plätze) bemessen. Durch Einbeziehung der angrenzenden Räume kann die doppelte Besucherzahl untergebracht werden.

Das Zentrum ist an manchen Tagen 14 Stunden geöffnet. Es wird während der Woche von etwa 3000 Menschen besucht.

Einfache Holz- und Mauerwerkskonstruktionen bilden den robusten Hintergrund für den ständigen und vielseitigen Gebrauch und den dauerhaften Wetterschutz gegen die Atmosphäre einer Industriestadt.

3

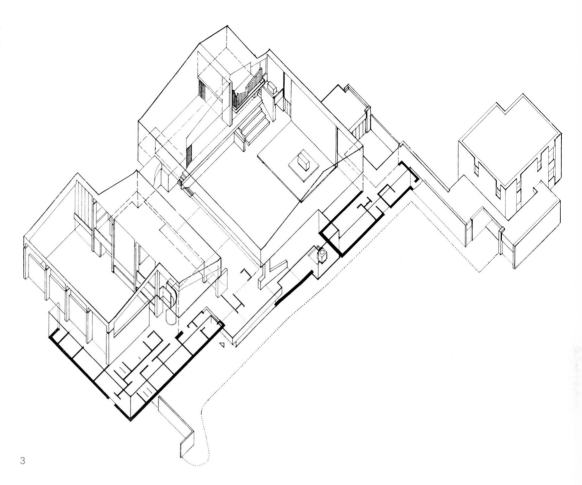

4

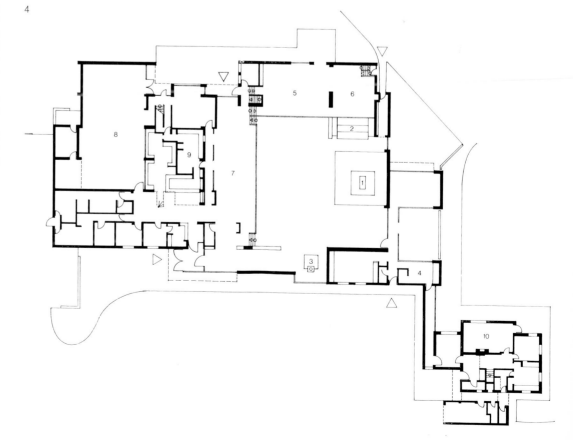

1. Eingangsseite. Die Materialien der schlichten Anlage sind Mauerwerk, Holz und Glas.
2. In nichts unterscheidet sich die Baugruppe von einem außerkirchlichen Gemeindezentrum.
3. Isometrie.
4. Grundriß. Legende: 1 Altar, 2 Sänger, 3 Taufe, 4 Sakristei, 5 Bühne, 6 Abstellraum, 7 Lounge, 8 Mehrzweckhalle, 9 Küche, 10 Wohnungen.

5

6

7

5, 6, 7. Parish activities take place in differently designed and simply constructed premises.
8, 9. The same room used for two different purposes: as a church, and as meeting hall for the Women's Institute. In contrast to the variability of the other premises, the altar zone is permanently marked by communion barriers and a large light-fitting.

5, 6, 7. Die Aktivitäten der Gemeinde finden in differenziert angelegten und einfach gebauten Räumen statt.
8, 9. Der gleiche Raum als Kirche und als Versammlungsort des Frauenvereins. Im Gegensatz zu der Variabilität des übrigen Raumes ist die Altarzone durch Kommunionsschranken und einen großen Beleuchtungskörper als konstant fixiert.

Friends Meeting House in Wanstead, London, 1964–1968
Architect: Norman Frith

Friends Meeting House in Wanstead, London, 1964–1968
Architekt: Norman Frith

In the divine worship of the Quakers ("Society of Friends"), silent contemplation plays a major part. There are no priests and no sacraments. To show Christian love in their daily lives is their principal religious philosophy. Their generous charity after the two World Wars remains unforgotten.

In the more recently built community premises of the Quakers, the seats are orientated towards the centre of the room which remains unemphasised. The plan therefore generally approximates a square or circle.

The specifications for the Wanstead project included: insulation against the traffic noise from the near-by road, inclusion of the garden, provision of a central vestibule, a dwelling for the resident caretaker, and adequate car parking facilities.

The complex consists of a group of pavilions with hexagonal plan. A low-rise vestibule is inserted between the pent-roofed pavilions. Because of the greater number of sides, the hexagon provides a greater variety of views towards the garden and the adjacent woods. Making skilful use of an escarp in the ground, the architect was able to provide a games room below the main hall. The cloakrooms and lavatories are placed on the side facing the road so as to obtain better sound insulation against the traffic noise.

The walls are faced with grey-white clinkers, the single-ply roofs are covered with insulating slabs or plaster. The bright buildings are deliberately contrasted with the woods in the background.

Die Quäker (»Gesellschaft der Freunde«) sind eine Gemeinschaft, deren Gottesdienst vor allem in kontemplativem Schweigen besteht. Sie haben keine Priester und keine Sakramente. Christliche Liebe im täglichen Leben zu üben, ist ihre hauptsächliche Religionsphilosophie. Ihre großzügige Wohltätigkeit nach den beiden Weltkriegen ist unvergessen.

In den neueren Gemeinderäumen der Quäker sind die Sitze auf die – unbetonte – Raummitte orientiert. Die Grundrißformen nähern sich daher meistens dem Quadrat oder dem Kreis an.

Für das Projekt in Wanstead waren gefordert: Isolierung vom Verkehrslärm der nahen Straße, Einbeziehung des Gartens, ein zentrales Foyer, eine Hauswärterwohnung und ausreichende Parkierungsflächen.

1

Es entstand eine Pavillon-Anlage mit hexagonalen Grundrißformen. Ein flaches Foyer ist zwischen die pultdachbedeckten Baukörper geschoben. Die vielen Seiten der Sechsecke gewähren verschiedene Ausblicke in den Garten und auf den anschließenden Wald. Durch einen geschickt genutzten Geländesprung wurde ein unter dem Gemeinderaum liegender Spielraum möglich. Die Naßräume wurden an die Straßenseite gerückt, um als schallisolierendes Element gegen den Verkehrslärm zu dienen.

Die Wände wurden mit grauweißen Klinkern verblendet, die einschaligen Dachdecken mit Isolierplatten verkleidet oder verputzt. Die helle Baumasse ist bewußt in Gegensatz zu dem dahinterliegenden dunklen Wald gesetzt.

1. Entrance side. The pavilions with the assembly hall, emphasised by its greater height.
2. The group of buildings, seen from the adjacent cemetery. The hexagonal pavilions are separated by a terrace.
3, 4. The portable chairs permit different informal groupings. A "sacral character" is nowhere discernible.
5. Plan. Key: 1 worship area, 2 hall, 3 hall, 4 community council, 5 library, 6 dwelling.

1. Eingangsseite. Die Pavillons mit dem betont höher gezogenen Versammlungsraum.
2. Baugruppe vom anschließenden Friedhof aus. Zwischen den sechseckigen Pavillons liegt eine Terrasse.
3, 4. Die lose Bestuhlung ermöglicht verschiedene Arten der Gruppierung. Irgendein »sakraler Charakter« ist nicht erkennbar.
5. Grundriß. Legende: 1 Kultraum, 2 Halle, 3 Saal, 4 Gemeindevorstand, 5 Bibliothek, 6 Wohnung.

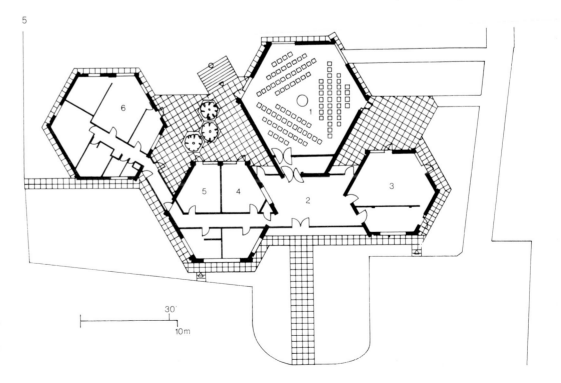

30'

10 m

Synagogue in the Negev Desert, Israel, 1967–1969
Architects: Alfred Neumann, Zvi Hecker

Synagoge in der Wüste Negev, Israel, 1967–1969
Architekten: Alfred Neumann, Zvi Hecker

This plastic building, which belongs to a military camp, stands like a mastaba composed of large, multi-faced stones against the background of a monotonous desert landscape. The space is enclosed by three different three-dimensional concrete units: truncated tetrahedrons, octahedrons and cubo-octahedrons. These units are hollow, with very thin walls. The result is a symmetric, hexagonal room, with entrance, reader's desk and ark placed in the axis, and the pews on either side. The room is like a grotto; the plastic effect is fascinating.
Below the building is a well from which the camp draws its water supply.
This monument, set against the backcloth of the landscape, is one of the most interesting buildings designed by these architects who have a distinct preference for three-dimensional units.

Der plastische Bau, der zu einer Kaserne gehört, steht wie eine Mastaba aus großen vielflächigen Steinen vor der eintönigen Wüstenlandschaft. Der Raum ist aus drei verschiedenen räumlichen Betonelementen gebildet: abgestumpfte Tetraeder, Oktaeder und Kubo-Oktaeder. Diese Formen sind hohl und haben minimal dünne Wandungen. Es entsteht ein symmetrischer sechseckiger Raum, in dessen Achse Eingang, Pult und Schrein angeordnet sind. Seitlich sind die Bänke aufgestellt. Die Raumwirkung erinnert an eine Grotte und fasziniert durch ihre hohlplastische Wirkung.
Unter dem Bau liegt eine Zisterne, von der die Kaserne ihr Wasser bezieht.
Dieses gegen die Landschaft gesetzte Monument ist einer der interessantesten Bauten der vorzugsweise mit Raumelementen arbeitenden Architekten.

1. The strangely alive synagogue building is in strong contrast to a monotonous, lifeless landscape. The polyhedrons are of concrete, partly painted in different colours, partly left unpainted.
2. Architect's sketch.
3. Plan and section. Key: 1 shrine, 2 lectern.
4. Aron ha-kodesch. Polygonal apse with raised platform. Inserted in the Star of David is a hexagonal niche in which the Torah scrolls are kept.
5. A well at the entrance.

1

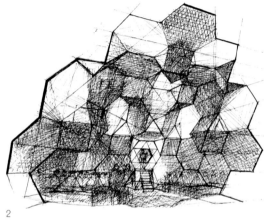

2

1. Die Synagoge bildet den Kontrast eines seltsam lebendigen Gebäudes zu einer monotonen und toten Landschaft. Die Betonpolyeder sind teilweise farbig gestrichen.
2. Ideenskizze des Architekten.
3. Grundriß und Schnitt. Legende: 1 Schrein, 2 Pult.
4. Aron ha-kodesch. Polygonale Apsis mit erhöhter Plattform. In den Davidsstern ist eine sechseckige Nische eingesetzt, in der die Thorarollen aufbewahrt werden.
5. Brunnen am Eingang.

3

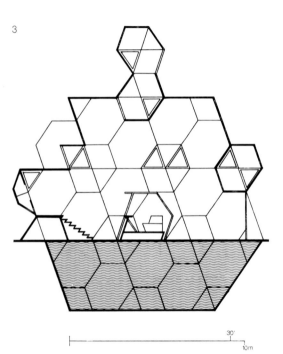

30'
10m

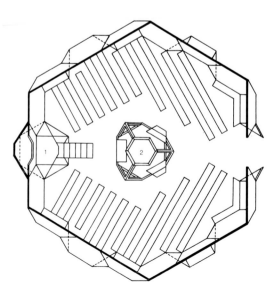

4

5

Heilig-Geist-Kirche, Emmerich, Germany, 1962–1966
Architect: Dieter G. Baumewerd

Heilig-Geist-Kirche, Emmerich, 1962–1966
Architekt: Dieter G. Baumewerd

This church is metaphorically described as "a roof" or "a tree at the wayside". It is indeed comparable to a small woods, consisting of six hexagonal, foliate roofs placed on half-slotted tubular supports. The hexagons are not complete, each of them is lacking one segment. The foliate roofs and their stems are completely integrated. The roofs are of different height, they overlap and rise towards the altar. Between the stems are walls, set off by glass joints. The gaps between the roofs are likewise glazed. The sky is visible from everywhere. One therefore has the impression of a luminous forest with large but thin treetops. The blueness of the sky is taken up by the cloth-covered walls which flank the room like side-scenes in a theatre.

The plan is reminiscent of a clover leaf. The contractions formed by the columns seem to push the altar into the room; at the same time, however, they separate the groups of pews from each other. The result is not so much a community church but rather a nave with aisles. The impression is reinforced by the failure to carry out the original plan of placing chairs in circular rows. The benches placed in parallel rows have no relation to the space.

Another questionable feature is the almost symmetric arrangement of altar and pulpit. For both functions, an almost identical volume of stone has been given an almost identical shape. The metaphor "Table of the Word", invented for this purpose, does not make sense.

The out-size crucifix, weld-assembled from waste metal, serves as an integrating super-symbol of the zone of liturgical activities.

Diese Kirche wird mit der Metapher »ein Dach« oder »ein Baum am Wege« umschrieben. Sie ist in der Tat vergleichbar mit einem kleinen Wald, der aus sechs sechseckigen, blattartigen Dächern auf halbaufgeschlitzten Rohrstützen besteht. Die Sechsecke sind nicht vollständig, es fehlt an jedem ein Segment. Blattdächer und Stiele gehen nahtlos ineinander über. Die Dächer sind verschieden hoch, überlappen sich und steigen zum Altar hin an. Zwischen die Stiele sind durch Glasfugen abgesetzte Wände gestellt. Auch die Schlitze zwischen den Dächern sind verglast. Überall spielt der Himmel hinein. So ist der Raumeindruck der eines hellen Waldes mit großen, lichten Baumkronen. Das Blau des Himmels ist auf die leinenbespannten Wände übertragen – kulissenhaft schieben sie sich um den Raum.

Die Grundrißfigur ist einem Kleeblatt ähnlich. Die starken Einschnürungen, die durch die Stützen gebildet werden, drücken zwar den Altar in den Raum hinein, schnüren aber andererseits die Bankgruppen der Gemeinde voneinander ab. So entsteht eigentlich keine Gemeinschaftskirche, sondern ein Längsraum mit Seitenflügeln. Dazu kommt, daß die ursprünglich geplante Sitzanordnung mit kreisförmig gruppierten Stühlen nicht ausgeführt wurde: Die statt dessen in parallelen Reihen aufgestellten Bänke haben keinen Bezug zum Raum.

Fraglich bleibt auch die – fast – symmetrische Formung von Altar und Kanzel. Für beide Funktionen wird ein fast gleiches Volumen Stein in eine fast gleiche Form gebracht.

Das überdimensionale, aus Metallabfällen zusammengeschweißte Kreuz ist das kompositionelle Superzeichen des liturgischen Aktionsbereiches.

1. Entrance side.
2, 3. Exterior of the church, by day and by night.
4. Plan and section. Key: 1 main altar, 2 secondary altar,
3 choir, 4 baptistry, 5 confessional, 6 chapel, 7 sacristy.

1. Eingangsseite.
2, 3. Kirche von außen bei Nacht und bei Tag.
4. Grundriß und Schnitt. Legende: 1 Hauptaltar, 2 Nebenaltar, 3 Chor, 4 Taufe, 5 Beichte, 6 Kapelle, 7 Sakristei.

4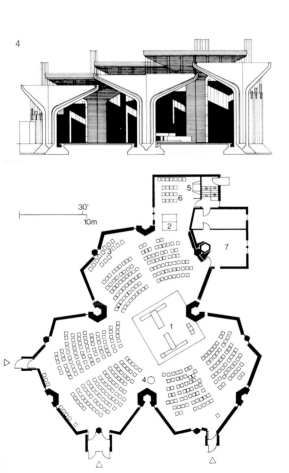

5, 6. Interior. The foliate roofs surround the room like mighty pillars, increasing in height from the entrance towards the altar.

5, 6. Innenraum. Die Blattdächer sind vom Eingang zum Altar hin hochgestaffelt.

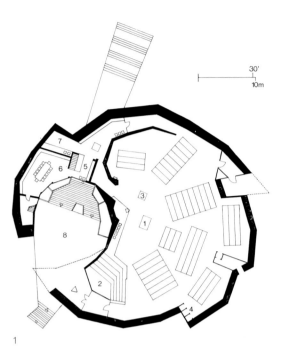

1

The church stands on a hill, facing the old castle of Wildegg. The building emphasises the topography of the ground in the form of a man-made, not particularly high hill top. The nearly circular group contains a small atrium which can be reached both from the car park on the hill and, through a passage below the church, from the valley side.

The column-free room rises centrically towards a convex wall which marks the liturgical centre. The steps and a font with running water are the only permanent installations in the room. The wooden altar and all the other furnishings and seats are portable. Without the seats, the room with the fountain in the centre might give the impression of a large, covered piazza.

Simple wooden chairs are informally gathered around the altar. For private prayer, a slightly segregated weekday chapel has been provided which faces the glass tabernacle. By limiting the materials to brick and wood an intimate atmosphere has been created. The concentrating effect is further enhanced by the lighting. The one large window, placed behind the choir steps, faces the atrium so that there can be no glare. The uniform lighting of the room is due to three skylights in the roof.

The parish premises are on the lower floor; a multi-purpose hall and the sacristy are at the atrium.

With the homogeneous copper cladding applied to the outsides of all the roofs and walls of church and belfry, the whole group becomes a single, plastic unit. Because of its innovational and informative value, it has become a noteworthy and promising example of modern Roman Catholic church architecture.

Die Kirche liegt gegenüber dem alten Schloß von Wildegg auf einem Hügel. Der Bau führt die Topographie des Geländes als künstliche, nicht übermäßig hohe Kuppe weiter. Aus der annähernd kreisförmigen Anlage ist ein kleiner Hof ausgespart. Er dient als Atrium und ist vom bergseitigen Parkplatz und durch eine Unterführung unter der Kirche vom Tal her erreichbar.

Der stützenfreie Raum steigt zentrisch zu einer nach innen gewölbten Wand an. Diese markiert das liturgische Zentrum. Eine Stufe und der Taufbrunnen mit fließendem Wasser sind die einzigen Fixpunkte im Raum. Der hölzerne Altar und alle anderen Einrichtungen und Bestuhlungen sind mobil. Ohne Bestuhlung mag der Raum mit dem Brunnen in der Mitte wie ein großer, überdeckter Platz wirken.

Einfache Holzstühle scharen sich in freier Form um den Altar. Für das private Gebet dient eine leicht abgetrennte Alltagskapelle, die auf den gläsernen Tabernakel ausgerichtet ist. Durch Beschränkung auf die Materialien Backstein und Holz entsteht eine intime Atmosphäre. Der Raum bezieht seine konzentrierende Wirkung auch aus der Beleuchtung. Das einzige große Fenster – hinter den Sängerstufen liegend – ist auf den Hof gerichtet. Blendendes Licht kann hier nicht einfallen. Die gleichmäßige Auslichtung des Raumes erfolgt durch drei ins Dach eingebaute Oberlichter.

Die Gemeinderäume befinden sich im Untergeschoß, ein Mehrzwecksaal und die Sakristei am Atrium.

Durch die homogene Außenverkleidung aller Dächer und Wände von Kirche und Turm mit Kupferblech wird der Bau zu einer plastischen Einheit. Sein Innovations- und Informationswert machen ihn zu einem bemerkenswerten und hoffnungsvollen Beispiel neuen katholischen Kirchenbaues.

1. Plan. Key: 1 altar, 2 choir, 3 baptistry, 4 confessional, 5 sacristy, 6 community area, 7 kitchen, 8 patio.
2. Aerial photograph. The copper sheet cladding, which also covers the walls, contains toplights.

1. Grundriß. Legende: 1 Altar, 2 Chor, 3 Taufe, 4 Beichte, 5 Sakristei, 6 Gemeinderaum, 7 Küche, 8 Hof.
2. Luftaufnahme. In die Kupferblechverkleidung, die auch über die Wände gezogen ist, sind Oberlichter eingelassen.

2

3. Exterior of the church in the area of the confessionals.
4. Courtyard.
5, 6. With the exception of the glass curtain wall at the entrance to the atrium, the walls of the church have no openings. The rising bays of the ceiling emphasise the central zone which can be used for liturgical or other purposes. Chairs and altar are portable.

3. Außenwand der Kirche im Bereich der Beichtstühle.
4. Hof.
5, 6. Die Wände des Kirchenraumes haben – bis auf die Eingangsglaswand zum Innenhof – keine Öffnungen. Die ansteigenden Deckenfelder betonen das liturgisch oder anders genutzte räumliche Zentrum. Mobile Bestuhlung, mobiler Altar.

1

Next to Cologne Cathedral, the pilgrimage church (measuring 50 × 37 metres, with the highest top rising to 34 metres) is the largest church in the Cologne archdiocese. The architect describes pilgrimage as "the expression of a living, continually moving church". The act of worship in a pilgrimage church should be different from that in one's home church. The experience of the pilgrimage should be enhanced not only by the mass but also by common prayer, singing, concerts, dances, play, films and. festivals. For this purpose, the architect provided a chain of piazzas which are separated by steps and finally lead to a large, covered piazza – the church proper. The paving as well as the light fittings of the path leading to the church are continued into the church proper. Logically, the end of the path is marked by the altar – reviving an old idea conceived by Rudolf Schwarz who was related to the Böhm family.

This covered piazza has become an enormous sculptural monument, a strange variant of a cathedral. The large space, the ring of chapels surrounding it, and the galleries are covered by asymmetric, irregularly shaped roofs. This variegated interior helps to provide the variegated experience of the pilgrimage celebration. The lighting scheme and the dimensions of the room bear witness to the mystical interpretation of the task which is further emphasised by the coloured windows designed by the architect himself.

The galleries have genuine communication functions: From the road in the west, an entrance leads to the first gallery. The second gallery, too, is to be connected by a bridge with the planned belfry and will provide a link with the district around the hospital.

In this group, there is a convincing harmony between interior and exterior. Despite its large size, the church is in harmony with its environment – the irregular roof is casually related to the roofs of the adjacent houses – in a rustic manner which, perhaps for this very reason, here provides a convincing solution.

Reinforced concrete is the only building material used. All the concrete faces are sand-blasted.

Die Wallfahrtskirche ist die nach dem Kölner Dom größte Kirche der Erzdiözese Köln (50 × 37 m, höchste Faltwerkspitze 34 m hoch). Der Architekt erklärt Wallfahrt als »Ausdruck der lebendigen, stets in Bewegung befindlichen Kirche«. Anders als am gewohnten Ort soll man den Gottesdienst in der Wallfahrtskirche erleben. Nicht nur die Messe, sondern auch gemeinsames Gebet, Gesang, Konzert, Tanz, Spiel, Film und Feste sollen das Erlebnis der Wallfahrt verstärken. Der Architekt entwickelte hierfür eine Folge von Plätzen, die mit Stufen gegeneinander abgesetzt sind, und als letzten hiervon einen großen, überdeckten Platz, die Kirche. Folgerichtig werden das Pflaster und auch die Beleuchtungskörper des Weges in die Kirche hineingezogen. Folgerichtig steht am Ende des Weges der Altar – ein alter Gedanke von dem mit der Familie Böhm verbundenen Rudolf Schwarz wird hier wieder aufgenommen.

Aus diesem überdeckten Platz ist ein gewaltiges plastisches Monument, ein verfremdeter Dom geworden. Asymmetrische Faltwerke überdecken den großen

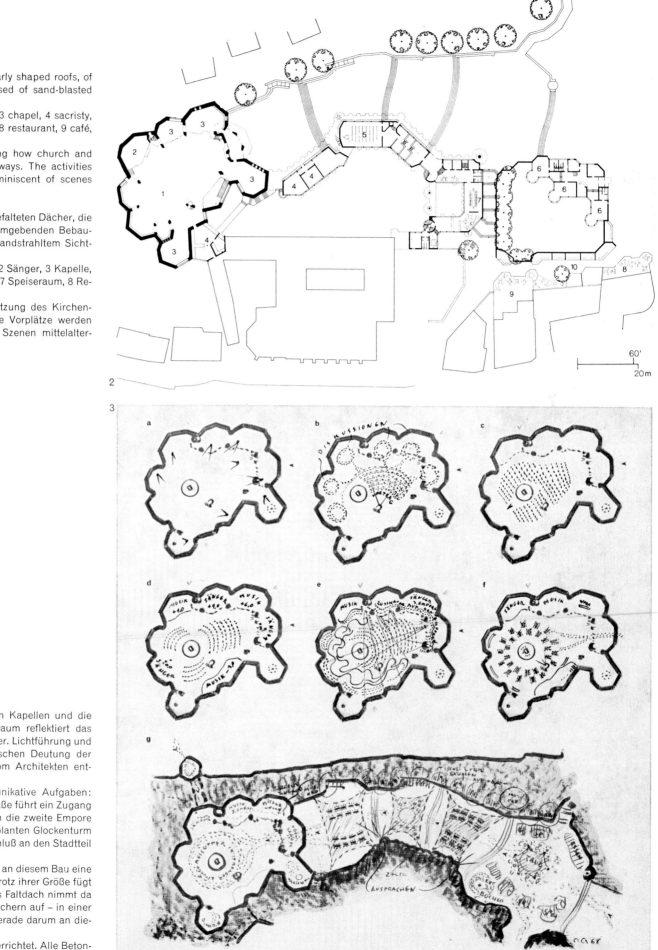

1. The walls, as well as the irregularly shaped roofs, of the pilgrimage church are composed of sand-blasted exposed concrete.

2. Plan. Key: 1 altar zone, 2 choir, 3 chapel, 4 sacristy, 5 hall, 6 group room, 7 dining hall, 8 restaurant, 9 café, 10 shops.

3. The architect's sketches showing how church and piazzas can be used in different ways. The activities suggested for the piazzas are reminiscent of scenes from medieval church festivals.

1. Sowohl die Wände als auch die gefalteten Dächer, die da und dort Beziehungen zu der umgebenden Bebauung aufnehmen, bestehen aus gesandstrahltem Sichtbeton.

2. Grundriß. Legende: 1 Altarzone, 2 Sänger, 3 Kapelle, 4 Sakristei, 5 Saal, 6 Gruppenraum, 7 Speiseraum, 8 Restaurant, 9 Café, 10 Läden.

3. Skizzen des Architekten zur Nutzung des Kirchenraumes und der Vorplätze. Für die Vorplätze werden Aktivitäten vorgeschlagen, die an Szenen mittelalterlicher Kirchenfeste erinnern.

Raum, den Kranz der umgebenden Kapellen und die Emporen. Dieser vielfältige Innenraum reflektiert das vielfältige Erlebnis der Wallfahrtsfeier. Lichtführung und Raummaße zeugen von der mystischen Deutung der Aufgabe, dazu tragen auch die vom Architekten entworfenen Farbfenster bei.

Die Emporen haben echte kommunikative Aufgaben: Von der westlich angrenzenden Straße führt ein Zugang zum ersten Emporengeschoß. Auch die zweite Empore soll durch eine Brücke mit dem geplanten Glockenturm verbunden werden und damit Anschluß an den Stadtteil am Krankenhaus schaffen.

Zwischen innen und außen herrscht an diesem Bau eine überzeugende Übereinstimmung. Trotz ihrer Größe fügt die Kirche sich in den Ort ein – das Faltdach nimmt da und dort Beziehung zu den Hausdächern auf – in einer dörflichen Manier, aber vielleicht gerade darum an diesem Ort überzeugend.

Der Bau wurde ganz in Stahlbeton errichtet. Alle Betonflächen wurden gesandstrahlt.

4. View from the upper street toward the entrance of the church.
5. Galleries. Even in the interior, the exposed concrete has been sand-blasted. Sound-absorbing boxes are inserted in the walls in order to improve the acoustics. The heating system consists of a combination of underfloor heating and convectors built into the balustrades of the gallery.
6. A view from the entrance gallery towards the altar. Portable chairs, decoratively paterned paving.

4. Blick von der oberen Straße auf die Eingangsseite der Kirche.
5. Emporen. Auch der Sichtbeton im Innern ist gesandstrahlt. Zur Verbesserung der Akustik sind in die Wände Schallschluck-Kästen einbetoniert. Kombinierte Luft-, Fußboden- und Konvektorenheizung.
6. Blick von der Eingangsempore zum Altar. Lose Bestuhlung auf einem dekorativ verlegten Pflaster.

**St. Martin, Benediktinerkollegium, Sarnen,
Switzerland, 1963–1966**
Architects: J. Naef, E. and G. Studer

**St. Martin, Benediktinerkollegium, Sarnen, Schweiz,
1963–1966**
Architekten: J. Naef, E. und G. Studer

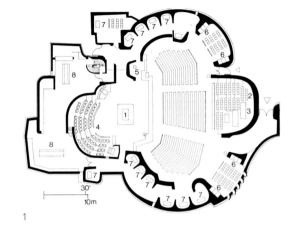

1

The church is used for individual and joint acts of worship of the monks of the College and their students. The central space is developed around the altar and consists of the monks' choir, the space for the congregation and the choristers' gallery. This central space is flanked by two chains of chapels for individual worship and is associated with two conches containing the confessionals. At the monks' choir are the niche for the abbot's throne and the seats of the priests.

In contrast to baroque churches which show a symmetric and therefore constrained rhythm, the different parts of this church inter-penetrate informally. Conches and niches which project into or out of the space to extend it, represent the principle governing the composition of this church. In keeping with this principle, the roof consists of domes, representing vertical niches. Daylight enters through skylights of plain glass. Sky and clouds become part of the scenery and are reflected along the walls which taper upwards.

The elevations of this building hardly lend themselves to orthogonal representation. The most important task which the architects set themselves was to harmonise the shape of the space with its plastic design. The motif in the design of the church is the gathering of the congregation around the liturgical centre.

For the construction of the domes, it was initially intended to use concrete shells; investigations showed, however, that the difficulties of producing asymmetric concrete shells appeared to be insuperable. It was therefore decided to use a timber structure with wooden rafters, covered by wooden panels lined with plastics. The inner shell was formed by expanded metal, and plastered.

Die Kirche dient Mönchen des Kollegiums und ihren Schülern zu individuellen und gemeinschaftlichen Gottesdiensten. Ihr Hauptraum entfaltet sich um den Altar herum. Er besteht aus dem Mönchschor und dem Gemeinderaum mit Sängerempore. Um diesen Gemeinderaum sind die beiden Kapellenketten für die Einzelzelebrationen gelegt, ihm direkt zugeordnet zwei Konchen mit den Beichtstühlen. Am Mönchschor liegt die Nische für Abtthron und Priestersitze.

Die Durchdringung der Raumteile geschieht in freiem Rhythmus – im Unterschied zu den Kirchen des Barock, die einen symmetrischen, also gebundenen Raumrhythmus aufweisen. Halbräume und Nischen, die in den Raum vorstoßen, beziehungsweise ihn erweitern, sind das Kompositionsprinzip dieser Kirche. Logischerweise erfolgt der Abschluß in der dritten Dimension mit Kuppeln, also vertikalen Nischen. Licht wird durch ungefärbtes Glas von oben eingeholt. Himmel und Wolken werden mit einbezogen und von den nach oben sich verjüngenden Wänden reflektiert.

Die Aufrisse dieses Baues sind durch orthogonale Projektionen kaum mehr darzustellen. Wichtig war den Architekten vor allem die Übereinstimmung von Raumform und plastischer Gestalt. Der Leitgedanke der Kirche ist die Scharung um den kultischen Mittelpunkt.

Für die Konstruktion der Kuppeln wurden zunächst Untersuchungen mit Betonschalen angestellt – die Schwierigkeiten, asymmetrische Betonschalen herzustellen, schienen jedoch unüberwindlich zu sein. Es wurde daher eine Holzkonstruktion mit Holzsparren errichtet, die oberseits verschalt und mit Kunststoff belegt wurde. Die innere Schale wurde aus Streckmetall vorgeformt und vergipst.

2

1. Plan. Key: 1 altar, 2 choir, 3 organ, 4 monks' choir, 5 baptistry, 6 confessional, 7 chapel, 8 sacristy.
2. The church is not related to the existing buildings of the College and is clearly set apart.
3, 4. The curved walls are covered with rough white plaster and the domes with pale-grey foil.

1. Grundriß. Legende: 1 Altar, 2 Sänger, 3 Orgel, 4 Mönchschor, 5 Taufe, 6 Beichte, 7 Kapelle, 8 Sakristei.
2. Die Kirche ist von den Kollegiengebäuden deutlich abgesetzt, und auch formal nimmt sie keine Beziehung zu ihnen auf.
3, 4. Die gekurvten Wände sind mit rauhem weißen Putz und die Kuppeln mit hellgrauer Folie überzogen.

5, 6. Interior. The rough white plaster reflects the light and so stresses the modelling of the walls.

5, 6. Innenraum. Der weiße Rauhputz reflektiert das Licht in reicher Nuancierung und betont so die Modellierung der Wände.

Heilig-Kreuz-Kirche, Chur, Switzerland, 1964–1969
Architect: Walter Förderer

Heilig-Kreuz-Kirche, Chur, Schweiz, 1964–1969
Architekt: Walter Förderer

1

A parish centre of monolithic appearance has here been placed in contrast to a highly plastic and fanciful church interior. Whilst the plan, concentrated on the altar, is relatively simple, the elevations show a great variety of super-imposed steps, walls, slabs, niches, galleries, pillars, openings and windows. Altar, ambo, sedilia, tabernacle and even the crucifix have become sculptural elements of a large, three-dimensional negative plastic which, through material and form, suggests heaviness and invariability. It is open to doubt whether, among this multiplicity of shapes and this accumulation of sensual features, the faithful is able to achieve that measure of concentration for which he goes to church.
Förderer is one of the architects who initiated the discussion of the new "multi-purpose" church. His theories go as far as to suggest acts of worship in any premises – apartment houses, railway stations, etc. The Church of the Holy Ghost is far removed from these theories but is of special interest as an architectural monument.

Ein monolithisch wirkendes Gemeindezentrum ist zu einem plastisch sehr reichen und phantasievollen Kircheninnenraum in Kontrast gesetzt. Mit einer relativ einfachen Grundrißform auf den Altar konzentriert, erweisen sich die Aufrisse als eine Vielfalt von übereinandergeschichteten Stufen, Wänden, Platten, Nischen, Galerien, Pfeilern, Löchern und Fenstern. Altar, Ambo, Sedilien, Tabernakel, ja selbst das Kreuz sind zu plastischen Elementen der großen räumlichen Negativplastik geworden, die durch Material und Form Schwere und Invariabilität impliziert. Es bleibt offen, ob der Gläubige in dieser Formenvielfalt, in dieser Häufung sensualistischer Reize zu der Konzentration kommen kann, derentwegen er in die Kirche geht.
Förderer ist einer der Architekten, die die Diskussion um die neue »Mehrzweck«-Kirche in Gang gebracht haben. Seine Theorien gehen so weit, Gottesdienst in beliebigen Räumen, in Wohnblocks, Bahnhöfen und so weiter, vorzuschlagen. Die Heilig-Kreuz-Kirche ist weit entfernt von diesen Theorien, aber als Architekturmonument von besonderem Interesse.

1. From the outside, this group of buildings makes a rather inhospitable impression. The Christian symbol shows an unconventional interpretation.

1. Die Anlage zeigt von außen einen eher abweisenden Charakter. Individuelle Ausformung des christlichen Symbols.

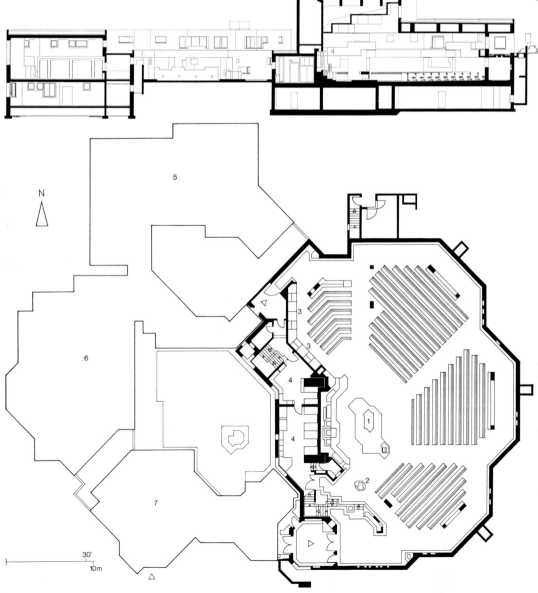

2. A view from the rectory garden.
3. Plan and section. Key: 1 altar, 2 baptistry, 3 confessional, 4 sacristy, 5 rectory, 6 parish house, 7 youth rooms.
4. Detail of the inner patio.
5. Covered passage leading to the main portal.
6, 7. Interior. Altar, cross and pews are of wood.

2. Ansicht vom Pfarrgarten her.
3. Grundriß und Schnitt. Legende: 1 Altar, 2 Taufe, 3 Beichte, 4 Sakristei, 5 Pfarrhaus, 6 Gemeindehaus, 7 Jugendräume.
4. Innenhof.
5. Überdeckter Gang zum Hauptportal.
6, 7. Innenraum der Kirche. Die Altarinsel, das Kreuz und die Bänke bestehen aus Holz.

4

5

6

7

This group of buildings consists of an old church with baroque spire, the new church, and the new rectory. Main access to church and rectory is from a large piazza placed high above street level. The old church, which now serves as a mortuary chapel, stands another few steps higher. Its spire dominates the entire group.

Church and rectory have certain formal similarities: In each case, an octagon rises above a composition of bodies which are either rectangular or chamfered at 45°. Translucid polyester units forming plastic components integrated with the building, cylindrical stairwell towers and creneltype openings reinforce the massive character of the architecture which is reminiscent of the old fortified castles and frontier defences in this area.

The real innovation is the interior of the church; its main features are stratification and super-position. Slabs of different thickness, separated by the polyester units serving as windows, rest on short, three-armed supports. The steps of the walls lead from the irregular space of the lower zone through the altar zone to the becalmed octagon of the upper space. This play with the third dimension is logically matched by the semi-circular lay-out around the altar and is further supported by the noticeable downwards slope of the floor towards the altar.

The liturgical implements are of stainless steel, the font of mauve plexiglass, the seats of polyester.

Die Baugruppe besteht aus der alten Kirche mit einem barocken Kirchturm, der neuen Kirche und dem neuen Pfarrheim. An einem hoch über der Straße angelegten großen Festplatz befinden sich die Hauptzugänge von Kirche und Pfarrheim. Die alte Kirche, die heute als Totenkapelle dient, liegt noch einige Stufen höher. Ihr Turm beherrscht die ganze Anlage.

Kirche und Pfarrheim sind sich formal ähnlich: Ein Acht-eck steigt jeweils aus einem Agglomerat von rechtwink-ligen und unter 45 Grad abgeschrägten Baukörpern heraus. Durchscheinende Polyesterkörper, die als pla-stische Elemente in den Kirchenkörper integriert sind, zylindrische Treppentürme und schießschartenartige Öffnungen verstärken den massigen Charakter der Ar-chitektur. Es werden Assoziationen an alte Wehrburgen und Grenzbefestigungen dieser Landschaft geweckt.

Die eigentliche Erfindung ist der Kirchenraum; er ist mit Schichtung und Türmung charakterisierbar. Verschie-den dicke Platten, zwischen die die Polyesterkörper als Lichtquellen eingeschoben sind, werden von kurzen, dreiarmigen Stützen getragen. Die Treppung läßt den in der unteren Zone unregelmäßigen Raum über der Altar-zone in das beruhigte Achteck hochsteigen. Dieses Spiel in der dritten Dimension entspricht logisch dem halbkreisförmig um den Altar geordneten Grundriß – der Boden, der zum Altar spürbar abfällt, unterstützt diesen Raumbezug.

Die Kultgeräte sind aus nichtrostendem Stahl, die Tauf-schale aus violettem Plexiglas, die Bestuhlung aus Poly-ester.

4

6

7

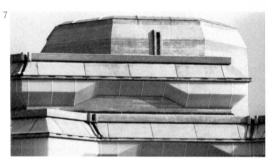

5

1. The aerial photograph shows the grouping of the old and new buildings around the piazza. Lower right the main road, top right the church, bottom left the rectory.
2. From the road, a broad flight of stairs leads to the upper piazza. On the right the church, on the left the rectory.
3. Southwest side of the church with entrance to the weekday chapel below. Beneath the octagonal main tower is the altar zone of the upper church.
4. Top view of the roof. The lower roof, here lying in the shade, is covered with gravel and is accessible from the circular stairwell towers.
5. A view of the church from the rectory roof.
6, 7. The interior is lit by transparent polyester light fittings.

1. Die Luftaufnahme zeigt die Gruppierung der alten und neuen Bauten um den Kirchplatz. Unten rechts die Hauptstraße, rechts oben die Kirche, links unten das Pfarrheim.
2. Von der Straße führt eine große Treppenanlage zum Kirchplatz hinauf. Rechts die Kirche, links das Pfarrheim.
3. Südwestseite der Kirche mit Eingang zu der unten liegenden Werktagskapelle. Unter dem achteckigen Hauptturm befindet sich der Altar der Oberkirche.
4. Dachaufsicht. Das im Schatten liegende untere Dach ist mit Platten belegt und wird von den runden Treppentürmen erschlossen.
5. Blick auf die Kirche vom Dach des Pfarrheims.
6, 7. Der Kirchenraum wird durch transparente Polyesterelemente belichtet.

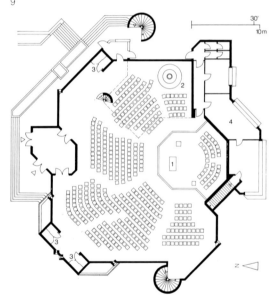

9

8. Interior. Pews covered with beige-coloured synthetic material.
9. Plan. Key: 1 altar, 2 baptistry, 3 confessional.
10. View into the roof area of the church. The staggered roof slabs rest on three-armed supports.
11–14. All the liturgical implements are composed of quadrantal units.

11

12

13

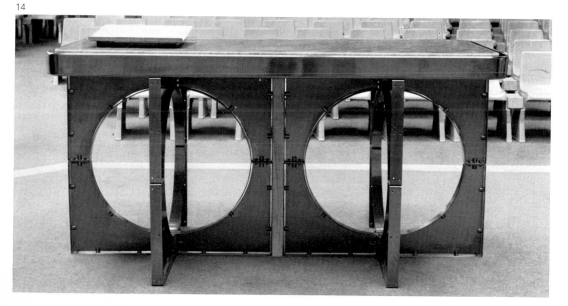

14

8. Innenraum. Reihenbestuhlung aus beigefarbenem Kunststoff.

9. Grundriß. Legende: 1 Altar, 2 Taufe, 3 Beichte, 4 Sakristei.

10. Blick in den Dachraum der Kirche. Dreiarmige Stützen tragen die gestaffelten Dachplatten.

11-14. Die Gestelle aller liturgischen Geräte sind aus Viertelkreiselementen zusammengesetzt.

Index

Photo Credits / Fotonachweis